Quotes and Testin

The Strategic Mind is unique in its class ; essential reading for strategy courses at und level. Managers employed in any organisat. ...y ... of sector will also gain an invaluable insight into strategy from this book. A highly original perspective is offered using organisational stories to evidence that the pathway to success necessitates deeply thought-through processes and a holistic approach.

Sue Davis
Deputy Dean, University of Gloucestershire Business School

The limitations of our current blinkered approach to strategic thinking are painfully clear as we struggle to cope with increasingly catastrophic events such as environmental and climatic disasters, global conflicts, and financial systems verging on collapse. A holistic view with an integrative approach to strategic thinking is needed. In this book, Bob puts forward an approach to strategy that integrates seven key disciplines. He uses an eclectic and fascinating mix of case histories and vignettes drawn from well-known companies such as Google and eBay, small businesses such as Fish Records, and not-for-profit organisations such as Care for the Family, to illustrate and bring the key themes to life. He includes insights derived from past events, such as the impact of the volcanic eruption in Iceland in 1783 on the French revolution, and relates some modern day stories of individuals with innovative approaches to personal and work life change. This blend of perspectives provides a refreshing, often moving, and much needed new look at strategy in practice.

Bob's main premise is that strategic thinking needs to be undertaken at a deeper and more profound level, with the emphasis on coping with uncertainty, acknowledging the interconnectivity of the world around us and acting responsibly. This book, which offers an important contribution to the field of strategic thinking, provides a guide for organisations, senior managers and individuals facing major change in an uncertain world.

Jeff Watkins
Director iRES International research and educational services
formerly Director of Postgraduate Management Programmes,
University of Bristol

This book distils the strategic essence from an astonishingly wide range of business and other stories. Identifying some of the common threads in some of the last 30 years' great success stories is a wonderful way to show the reader how to reach real strategic insight.

Simon Burke
Chairman, Superquinn supermarkets and Majestic Wine plc,
formerly Chairman of Hamleys and Chief Executive of
Virgin Entertainment Group

Excellent – very readable and offers many insightful perspectives on people and situations directly relevant to the world today.

Simon Wright
CEO, Virgin Entertainment Group International

Bob is a gifted writer, teacher and story teller. This book is an inspiration to all of us wanting to explore our own strategy for a more meaningful life. It is full of insight and wisdom; written by a man who truly cares about the world we live in and will leave behind for the next generation. I am proud to have been his student, sometimes his mentor and always his friend.

John Tucker
Founder and Director, The International Centre for Families in Business

An essential book for the 21st-century strategic leader, Bob Gorzynski offers up new thoughts about how to lead a business with heart and simplicity. He challenges many of the traditional paradigms with his 7 disciplines and 3 illusions. If you are looking for a new framework to help you make difficult choices in your organisation with clarity and reality, then this book is the one for you!

June Burrough
Founder and Centre Director, Pierian Centre, Bristol

This thought-provoking book overflows with real-world examples and finely-honed anecdotes. Dip into it at random right now and I defy you not to uncover at least one powerful new insight about something that you presently take for granted, something that may blinker your management vision and handicap your strategic thinking.

David Lloyd
Award-winning chartered accountant
and author of 'Teach Yourself Small Business Accounting'

Yes, *The Strategic Mind* is about Strategy and it's also about Leadership, but it is about a lot more than that. In these tumultuous times of change and complexity this book acts as a guide to those who want to approach strategy, leadership and change in an informed, intelligent way. Filled with anecdotes, vignettes and case studies drawn from the worlds of business, music and the perennial wisdom Bob Gorzynski charts a path through this complex maze and establishes a number of clear and succinct ideas and propositions which act as compass and route map.

Topical, relevant and enduring *The Strategic Mind* puts heart and soul into the concept of Strategic Leadership and fleshes it out with a rich story-telling.

Being a Strategic Leader is no easy feat; this book will be a very valuable companion on the journey.

Mike Green
Author of many business books,
including 'Making Sense of Change Management'
and 'Making Sense of Leadership'

I do not read much really as I prefer to think of myself a bit of a "doer" or facilitator. So when Bob asked me if I would read his manuscript I was secretly filled with a dread that I might not even finish it let alone make any sensible comments. However, I accepted the challenge and have been amazed at not only completing the task but becoming fascinated with the concepts and ideas contained in the book; moreover, how they both challenged and stirred up my own aspirations and ideals too. I have always struggled with how to interpret some of the things going on in my head but with having read this book I feel I now have some of the tools required to get them sorted. Bob has produced an extraordinary piece of work that will delight, inform and inspire us all.

Now here's an idea... buy two copies and send one to a government minister as a present. Bob will thank you for it, and, if the ministers in question become inspired as well as I have, then the world will thank you for it too.

Bob Berry
Musician

THE STRATEGIC MIND

The Journey to Leadership Through Strategic Thinking

Bob Gorzynski

2000

For a complete list of Management Books 2000 titles
visit our website on http://www.mb2000.com

First published in 2009 by Management Books 2000 Ltd
Forge House, Limes Road
Kemble, Cirencester
Gloucestershire, GL7 6AD, UK
Tel: 0044 (0) 1285 771441
Fax: 0044 (0) 1285 771055
Email: info@mb2000.com
Web: www.mb2000.com

British Library Cataloguing in Publication Data is available

ISBN 9781852526078

To *Broken-Wing*, who couldn't fly
but reached the top of the tree anyway.

ACKNOWLEDGEMENTS

Every book is the culmination of many things and reflects the influence of a great number of people. I can only hope to name the most obvious here but I am deeply indebted to all those that I have had the privilege to work with over the years and to the path builders, those courageous souls who have had the strength of conviction to depart from the norm and take the road less travelled. These are the true strategic leaders and they are laying a pathway for the rest of us to follow. A few are mentioned explicitly in this book, most are not. To all we owe a deep debt of gratitude. Thank you! You are helping to turn this world around.

I could not have completed this project without the support and assistance of many people. First and foremost to my wife, Tracy, and my two teenage boys, Scott and Jamie, for your constant support and encouragement and for putting up with me, particularly during the most intense writing phase. A very big 'thank you' also to those who provided me with invaluable help in putting together the case studies and stories that form the backbone of this book including Toni Brodie, June Burrough, Paul Burrowbridge, Tim Butler, Steve Clode, Patrick Hazlewood, Lennie Hookings, Neil Pearson, Sheron Rice, Jacqui Taylor, John Tucker and Simon Wright. Equally important is my debt to all those who gave me support along the way including Simon Burke, Peter and Jill Chandler, Sue Davis, Yvonne Ellis, Jon Finch, Andrew and Sue Gorzynski, Mike Green, John Middleton, Mark Oxton, Bill Salo and Dave Snowden. You have given me not only the inspiration to write the book but also the space to do it! Not least my deep appreciation to Nick Dale-Harris and the team at Management Books 2000 for putting everything together!

Finally, a very special thanks to two people who have a made a very big difference indeed. Firstly, to Rob Parsons for being my informal mentor as a writer all these years. You have no idea how important your role has been! Secondly, to Simon Taylor, who helped me shape the very core of this book and went well beyond the call of duty. Your contribution was invaluable.

CONTENTS

FOREWORD

It was an honour to be asked to write this foreword. I first met Bob in the context of a mutual client, namely the Virgin group and then discovered that he lived in the same village and that our sons were contemporaries (and friends) in Primary School. Through many a conversation over the best part of a decade I have learnt that Bob is that rare being, a thinker who understands the ethical and personal issues that surround the strategic function. In his introduction he talks of the need to situate strategic decisions in the relationships and connections that make up our world. This wider context means that we can no longer make self-centred decisions, as individuals or organisations, based on a limited awareness of our interconnections and wider dependencies.

Ironically I find myself writing this in San Jose California, the capital of that iconic centre of our technology oriented world: Silicon Valley. At the same time the financial world faces up to the consequences of a reward mechanism based on greed. Derivatives after all essentially involve gambling on a down turn in the fortunes of an organisation, with the traders able to drive that price down through strategic selling. More money is made by gambling on movements of money than in producing food or reducing the ecological footprint of our species on our only home. The news on CNN is of repossessions and redundancies. Hurricane Ike last week prevented my spending some days in Houston at a conference on the future of the oil and gas industry. The adjustment to flights meant that I didn't spend the weekend with friends in Austin, which I turn meant I was not there when the father of one of those friends died. Small events interact with major ones, neither fully independent of the other; we live in a world of fearful possibilities, at all points in a range between the extremes of hope and despair; for the organisation, society and the individual. Climate change, economic forces and the day to day tragedy and farce of human life interweave into an uncertain, complex melee of possibilities that require new thinking and direction.

The Strategic Mind is an important contribution to how we think about strategy. Bob uses case studies to illustrate his seven disciplines of strategic thinking, and provides different routes by which this book can be read. This foreword is probably best read after you have at least skimmed the introduction and first chapter. My task is not to summarise the book itself, or attempt to replicate its skilful use of cases. Instead I want to provide a theoretical discourse which will underpin some of the practical advice of the book itself. I will apply that understanding to Bob's seven disciplines.

Chefs or recipe book users?

Strategy as a subset of management science inherits the linear and normative model of causality that pervades that discipline along with its pervasive confusion of correlation and causation. This should be familiar to any critical reader of management literature. The most common practice is for the academic or consultant to study a range of organisations that are perceived to have some form of desirable quality such as *profit*, consistent revenue growth, superior customer care or the like. Various *properties* of those organisations are identified and attempts are made to correlate properties with qualities. Any correlation is then translated into a recipe and propagated as a new method or approach to organisational success.

Now this is a logical error as well as a dangerous conceit. The fact that the CEO's of a group of profitable companies all play golf at least once a year does not mean that that if your CEO takes up golf you will be successful. Of course I can learn from what successful companies do, but no major strategic innovation has ever been achieved by copying industrial best practice. Rather it is achieved by rethinking or re-imagining the field of operation. To do that we need to think like a chef, utilising the principles of cookery rather than a novice user of recipe books, slavishly following a set of instructions with little adaptive capacity.

The issue is well summarised in a delightful metaphor from Christensen & Raynor (2003)[1] as follows:

> **Imagine going to your Doctor because you're not feeling well. Before you've had a chance to describe your symptoms, the doctor writes out a prescription and says "take two of these three times a day, and call me in a week."**
>
> **"But – I haven't told you what's wrong," you say. "How do I know this will help me?"**
>
> **"Why wouldn't it" says the doctor. "It worked for the last two patients."**

---

[1] Christensen, C & Raynor, M, 'Why Hard-Nosed Executives Should Care About Management Theory', *Harvard Business Review* September 2003 pp 67-74.

No competent doctors would ever practice medicine like this, nor would any sane patient accept it if they did. Yet professors and consultants routinely prescribe such generic advice, and managers routinely accept such therapy, in the naïve belief that if a particular course of action helped other companies to succeed, it ought to help theirs, too.

We need to recognise that each organisation is the product of an evolutionary history, and when we engage in strategy we do so as a part of a flow of events. As we prepare a strategic intervention we stand at a unique nexus in time in which the evolutionary possibilities can be influenced (often by small events) but cannot be fully controlled or predicted.

Fads and fantasies

The confusion of correlation with causation is one characteristic of management science and practice, but it is not the only one. Over the past decades a series of waves have swept organisational science. They can be roughly grouped as:

- Extensions or development of a functional view of the organisation. This, the historical legacy of Taylor and scientific management separates different aspects of the organisation such as manufacturing and sales. We can see multiple initiatives here such as Total Quality Management, scientific forecasting, Just in Time and the like.

- The process revolution, looking at product life cycle rather than functions; moving from vertical to horizontal, characterised by Business Process Re-engineering and more recently Six Sigma and Lean approaches

- Technology driven, collaborative systems that can be functional or process based such as knowledge management and the learning organisation.

Now all of these movements have been characterised by a prior consultancy exercise based on the definition of an ideal future state, mostly based on best practice cases, and followed by technology driven roll outs of new practice with associated cultural change programmes and training. The approach is an engineering one based on seeing design and implementation as a controllable and linear process. There is also a tendency to universalism, the attempt to create a single approach or way of doing things. Each of these movements has tended to come in waves; a few early adopters create the case studies which are then commoditised by consultants into recipes.

Now there is nothing wrong *per se* with a fad. Humans need novelty, and a process of change and renewal can be healthy. However the disruption of practices that have evolved over time to handle difficult or intractable problems is an issue. In practice, while most of these fads have brought benefits it has been at a cost, also the ideal or fantasy state is never obtained leaving space for the next movement. Like many other managers who lived through the process I got increasingly frustrated with the underlying assumption that there is a right answer that can be determined in advance. Start up companies just go out and make things happen. Yes, they have a vision, but it is more of an abstract goal than the precise targets and analysis of a three or five year plan. As I lived this experience, and studied it, it became increasingly apparent that what was a fault was the underlying assumption of linear causality, and with it the assumption that a right answer awaiting proper data capture and analysis; management and organisational theory was (and in the main still is) stuck in a 19th Century paradigm of science.

By great good fortune, at this time I was working for IBM in a body called the Institute for Knowledge Management. That organisation provided the space, and the experimental subjects to attempt to take a new look at old problems, to seek new wineskins for old wine (Matthew 9:17). A small group of us determined to forget (or rather unlearn) our MBAs and go back to the natural sciences to see if there was a new way of moving forward. As a result of that work and a chance encounter or two we obtained US Government funding to research new approaches to asymmetric threat both before and after the tragic events of 9/11. The overall approach that emerged from that experience is known as naturalising sense-making. Sense-making here is defined as *How do I make sense of the world so that I can act in it?* and *naturalising* references the base in the natural sciences (a key contrast with Weick and others). One of those sciences, namely complex adaptive systems theory, proved critical to understanding the deficiencies of traditional thinking. Sometimes called the *science of uncertainty* it deals with the non-linear, connected and holistic world which is subject of this book. Critically an understanding of complexity also allows us to recognise the value, within boundaries, of existing management practice. To understand how this is done, we need to look at the different type of systems that exist in nature and some of the implications for strategy.

The nature of systems

My use of *system* in this section does not refer to information technology, but to the whole system with which an organisation interacts. I also need to explain my use of the word agent. By this I mean *anything which acts*. This can be an individual, but it can also be a collective identity or an idea or myth (I eschew the concept of memes as the metaphor with genes is faulty). So with that explanation out of the way we can look at different types of system. Most management theory is familiar with two:

- **Ordered systems**, in which there are repeating relationships between cause and effect which can be discovered by empirical observation, analysis and other investigatory techniques. Once those relationships are discovered we can use our understanding of them to predict the future behaviour of the system and to manipulate it towards a desired end state. In science we see this capability in the laws of motion and thermodynamics, experimentally derived with predictive capability. Critically in an ordered system, the nature of the system constrains agent behaviour to enable that predictability.

- **Chaotic systems** in which the agents are unconstrained, and present in large numbers. For this reason we can gain insight into the operation of such systems by the application of statistics, probability distributions and such like. The number and the independence of the agents allow large number mathematics to come into play. In recent times we have seen some popularisation of this with varying degrees of success and intellectual integrity in phrases such as *crowd-sourcing* and the *wisdom of crowds* (Surowiecki 2004).[2]

During the 20th Century natural science (in the main from chemistry and biology) became aware of a third type of system namely a **Complex Adaptive System**. Here the system lightly, but not fully constrains agent

---

[2] Surowiecki, J. 'The Wisdom of Crowds: Why the Many Are Smarter Than the Few and How Collective Wisdom Shapes *Business*, Economies, Societies and Nations', Little, Brown 2004.

behaviour and in turn the agents through their interactions constantly modify the nature of the system. The technical word for this is co-evolution. In essence each agent in a co-evolutionary relationship exerts selective pressures on the other, within an environment which itself creates pressures, thereby affecting each others' and the system's evolution. The net result is a system which operates in far from equilibrium conditions with some important characteristics for strategy.

- High susceptibility to small changes in starting conditions the consequences of which can magnify quickly and in unexpected ways. This makes it inherently unpredictable (more so than a chaotic system). It also means that any attempt to diagnose the nature of a system in effect creates a fluctuation in the system itself with the consequence that any diagnostic is by definition an intervention; and every intervention should therefore be designed as a diagnostic.

- There is a constant danger of observers using retrospective coherence (more colloquially hindsight) to assume linear causality which is not present. There are many examples of this in human systems. For example, post the tragic events of 9/11 it became clear that we should have paid attention to people being trained to fly aircraft but not to take off and land. At the time however it was simply one data item in many million. All commissions of inquiry, whether royal or congressional all identify a cause of failure after the event, that is fixed, but then the system fails in a different way. Hindsight does not necessarily lead to foresight.

- Complex systems constantly adapt to local interactions. In a human system the influence of family, work colleagues, etc., have a disproportionate effect. Think of the effort parents take to prevent their children falling into *the wrong company* and you will see how this operates. The nature of interactions can produce radical and unexpected change. Those changes can be catastrophic failures, but they can also be an unexpected stabilization of a belief system.

- Change in complex systems can be sudden and catastrophic in nature with very little prior notice. One example of this is the way in which dominant narratives can emerge and then rapidly change. A strong brand can be destroyed by a minor incident, or a politicians reputation switch overnight on the basis of a single poor decision, or just because the press have got nothing better to pay attention to. Once a negative story starts to spread it can create a pattern which rapidly dominates the landscape.

- Complex systems are non-aggregative in nature, and therefore non-reductionist. The whole is never the sum of its parts; it may be more, it may also be less! Accordingly problems of strategy relating to complex systems need to take a holistic perspective. It's not possible to break the problem up into smaller chunks and deal with them separately.

- With co-evolution comes the associated phenomenon of irreversibility; in a complex system we can only move forwards from the present, we cannot reset and start again. One of the best studied is the point at which a civilian population despair of civil redress and give passive support to terrorism. The tipping point once past makes recovery costly and time-consuming; up to the tipping point reversal is easier, but the need may not be self-evident.

Now the astute reader will by now have recognised that an understanding of complex adaptive systems theory gives a scientific base to what we know as common sense. In our day to day interactions with friends and children we manage for the emergence of beneficial coherence. We respond to weak signals and amplify or dampen our response based on a vague idea of the overall objective we want to achieve. To put it very simply; you don't organise a party for a bunch of children through learning objectives, mission statements, milestone targets and after action reviews. Instead you create some simple enforceable boundaries and take a safe-fail experimental approach to directing play. We need to learn to live in a state of requisite ambiguity in our strategic lives at work, as we do without issue or conscious thought at home and with friends.

Traditional planning has focused on planning based on a series of steps towards a predefined future. This requires investment and time and it is difficult to cope with unexpected deviations. An understanding of the different types of systems involves a recognition that this *fail-safe* approach to planning only applies to the ordered aspects of our existence. Where we are dealing with complex systems we need instead to progress based on close monitoring of a series of parallel *safe-fail* experiments; exploring evolutionary possibilities. This shift from a *fail-safe* design approach, to one of *safe-fail* experimentation is critical to a complex systems understanding of strategy. It's also an insight that can lead to greater resilience and robustness in strategic decision making. Each experiment needs to have specific strategies for monitoring for both good and harm, and for amplification or damping as appropriate. This is a much faster way of resolving conflict and is likely to identify possibilities in that evolutionary future which could not have been anticipated. Critically it is also all that can be done to handle the future if the system is complex. A huge amount of expensive and talented resource is wasted in organisations to create complicated and detailed plans when in reality we know the future will change. It's not just a waste of effort; it also blinds us to the unexpected, often until it is too late.

Of course this does not reduce the need for planning, but it radically changes its object and focus. In essence instead of trying to achieve an idealistically defined future state, we create a series of safe-fail experiments and then manage the emergence of beneficial (to us) coherence within boundaries. We need to put considerable effort into understanding what boundaries we can create and maintain, as well as into experimental design. We need to place similar levels of effort to traditional process, but we need to direct it so that it has purpose relevant to the nature of the system. Neither should we abandon traditional techniques, many of the situations we face are ordered or chaotic and existing tools can be applied. The key idea here is something I call *bounded diversity*; different methods and tools work in different contexts and fail outside of that context. Process based methods (which have dominated management theory for several decades) work well for ordered systems; they fail spectacularly when the system is complex. A recent illustration of this is 3M abandoning Six Sigma for their R&D divisions, while maintaining it for manufacturing.

A complex perspective on the seven disciplines

The seven disciplines outlined by Bob are part of an integrated approach to strategic thinking that have an intuitive understanding of complexity theory. I now want to relate that theory in turn to each discipline to augment Bob's ideas.

Know your own story

Narrative is fundamental to human intelligence. Indeed several authors use the phrase **homo narrans** rather than **homo sapiens**, and in marked contrast to **homo economicus**; we are the story-telling apes. Our evolutionary position is in a major part due to our ability to communicate knowledge and learning through story, a uniquely human property. Narrative defines most of our interactions and forms the weft and the weave of social interaction. In human complex systems most interaction between agents is narrative in nature. In a virtual world this is increasingly the case with the fragmented patterns of social computing and the internet starting to mimic some of the forms of the oral tradition that dominates our evolutionary history. It therefore follows that narrative intelligence, both self awareness and the ability to listen to the underlying patterns of incoming narrative is a strategic skill of considerable importance. It can also give us insight into decision processes. Shared stories are the filters through which groups sieve data and make decisions, so understanding those stories is one of the exciting new methods of research that are emerging.

Think small

The essence of complex systems is that small changes to the system can produce major system level effects. This can be good, a small idea or innovation producing a massive impact. It can also be dangerous in that an apparently stable situation can suddenly get out of hand, such as the sudden loss of confidence in financial markets to take a current example. So small safe-fail experiments represent a less risky strategy that traditional planning. However the volume of experiments is also important, in a safe-fail environment you need failure! Here we also enter to one of the key emerging fields in strategic thinking, namely the use of distributed cognition. This involves allowing the market itself to make many small decisions. A good example is micro-lending, where villages who form a lending group and guarantee each other's debts receive loans without traditional credit scoring (centralised cognition). In the case of the Grameen Bank in Bangladesh the performance of this distributed system has outperformed western banks.

Act slowly

Any complex system is a form of ecology, so the best metaphors come from nature. Think of tending a garden. You plan over varying time frames; you accept the possibility of major changes in weather. Judicious pruning and fertilizing produce better effects than more drastic interventions. I remember when I was young, learning this lesson attempting to catch a blenny (a form of small fish) in the rock pools of Porth Colmon on the Llŷn Peninsula in Wales. My sister would sit patiently with her net in a pool making sure her shadow did not fall on the pool. I would charge in with net waving, splashing through multiple pools to little effect. Needless to say my sister was the more successful. It's a metaphor that many a newly appointed executive should pay attention. Acting more deliberately and consciously (i.e. taking the time to become more aware of connectivity, monitoring safe-fail experiments can help prevent unanticipated consequences – a real disease of our current world. At the very least it can mitigate negative impact and increase resilience thus aiding recovery.

Serve Others

There is a long standing debate in political science between atomistic and communitarian (not to be confused with communism) understanding of society. Simply put the atomistic approach assumes that society is an aggregation of individual interests, while communitarian assumes that individuals gain meaning through participation in community. Like all dichotomies the distinction is useful but not absolute. However it is true to say that western approaches to strategy are atomistic in nature. This includes using the individual as a metaphor for the organisation. The Eastern tradition with its focus on context rather than object tends to communitarianism. Experiments in cognitive science, for example, have shown that American students given three objects will focus on the most prominent, while Chinese students will focus on the connections between them. In a world where resource is unconstrained an atomistic approach can provide exploitative (not intended negatively) advantage, but in a connected worked in which resource is constrained its limitations are increasingly apparent. It follows that awareness of connections and the obligations of those connections is of increasing importance. Complex systems theory makes us aware that immediate agent interaction has a greater effect than overall system awareness. To translate, a single bad experience with an organisation or with my immediate manager will have a disproportionate affect my actions. Consistent integrity is key to being able to act without past negative patterns overwhelming agent response. The gifting impulse is also a part of our evolutionary inheritance and reciprocation in times of crisis is the great leveller.

Reflect

The more self aware an agent, the more able it is to act to influence the behaviour of other agents, and to avoid being trapped into a pattern of behaviour based on the foolishness of crowds, i.e. herd behaviour in the worse sense of the world. Let me return to my example of managing a children's party. The wise parent is not engaged with every child seeking to ensure through tight shorter term targets their conformity with predetermined behaviour. Instead they think through multiple scenarios in determining the boundary conditions for the party, they make sure a diversity of opportunities are available which are likely to lead to beneficial self-organisation. Finally in the party itself they stand aside to effectively monitor the whole. In a complex system any engagement can produce unexpected results and reflection is therefore key. Remember however that reflection is not the same as retreat; reflection can take place in praxis, in interaction with the world.

Be simple

Complex systems create emergent results of staggering sophistication. Birds flocking behaviour can be simulated by three simple rules: *Follow the next bird, match speed, avoid collision.* The air conditioning and architecture of a termites nest is a result of genetically encoded rules responding to chemical triggers. Simple rules lead to outcomes the nature of which cannot be anticipated in advance. The leader who has a few clearly understood values and applies those consistently and simply is more likely to succeed than a leader who creates complicated constructs and attempts to micromanage. Remember as well that there is a big distinction between being simple and being simplistic. The desire to use so-called *best practice* from your industry sector, or simply call in consultants to do your decision making can appear attractive, but it is simplistic and dangerous. Great leaders and great strategies are insightful, simple to understand and novel in execution. If you can only cope with the familiar then they may appear strange or unnecessarily academic. Anti-intellectualism and a fear of concepts are endemic in many organisations, which paradoxically condemns them to being simplistic in their actions. There is, to use a cliché, nothing so practical as a good concept and investment in learning can produce a delightful simplicity.

Dream

Humans have an ability to transcend their environment and create their own realities. They can engineer their physical and social environments rather than just respond to them. This is a responsibility as well as a capability. If we don't dream of futures that enable ethical systems then we will never get them. Innovation is the result of mavericks or accidents not planning, and mavericks have what I call *awkward passion*, it disturbs people. Too many people try to make things familiar and ordinary; they do not attempt to transform the limits of the present to seek new possibilities. It's too easy to destroy a dream and loose its value in the process. The Sufi masters understand this. In Sufi tradition wisdom is communicated through story and one of the great story traditions is that of the Mullah Nasrudin, the wise fool in western literature. Mullah Nasrudin stories are used to convey learning from stupidity and there is one I always used to quote to Vice Presidents who wanted to make my dreams into something more familiar. I will use that to close this Foreword, and leave its lesson for your reflection.

Nasrudin found a weary falcon sitting one day on his windowsill.
He had never seen a bird like this before.
"You poor thing," he said, "how ever were you to allowed to get into this state?"
He clipped the falcon's talons and cut its beak straight, and trimmed its feathers.
"Now you look more like a bird," said Nasrudin.

As you read this book, please don't turn Bob's falcons into pigeons.

Dave Snowden,
Founder and Chief Scientific Officer, Cognitive Edge,
formerly a Director in the IBM Institute for Knowledge Management

---

Footnote

I have provided a brief explanation of complexity theory here. More extensive material can be found in the following publications: on **strategy**, Kurtz, C & Snowden, D, 'The New Dynamics of Strategy: sense-making in a complex-complicated world' in IBM Systems Journal Volume 42 Number 3 pp 462-483, 2003; on **leadership**, Snowden, D & Boone, M, 'A Leader's Guide to Decision Making' Harvard Business Review, November 2007; on **networks**, Kurtz, C & Snowden, D, 'Brambles in a Thicket' in Gibbert, Michel, Durand & Thomas 'Strategic Networks: Learning to Compete', Blackwell 2008.

INTRODUCTION

'Go where there is no path, and leave a trail.'

Ralph Waldo Emerson

The world as we understand it is dying. It is not necessarily evident as we go about our day-to-day business but we have reached a crucible in human history. As with all severe trials or tests, it is a point of enormous opportunity as well as significant challenge and it will affect each one of us, both in our personal and working lives. What is at stake is the future of our planet and our race and the conditions that we bequeath to our children and their children. What is being asked of us is whether we can accept responsibility for our actions, to recognise the broader relationships and connections that make up our world and to think and act accordingly. Some challenges, such as climatic change, global inequality and environmental degradation, are self-evident and we are beginning to understand and acknowledge the very serious impact they may have on us. Others, as we shall see, are far subtler but their impact is likely to be more devastating still. This book is written with the intent of providing a pathway for change using the stories of organisations and individuals who are not only at the leading edge of new thinking but are acting accordingly and in doing so are defining the legacy that we will leave to our children.

The scale of the challenge

The world is used to natural disasters but what made the devastation wrought by Hurricane Katrina in New Orleans in September 2005 so symbolic was that this was in the heart of the United States where the most powerful and prosperous nation on earth could do very little to affect the terrible outcome. What is unusual for the United States, of course, is commonplace for other nations who often bear the full brunt of issues such as global poverty, environmental and climatic change. The most important lesson to be learned from the tragedy of New Orleans is not that specific mistakes were made from which we can learn or even the acknowledgement that there are inherent limitations to the idea that we can control natural forces in an area with such a delicate and complex ecosystem. Ultimately, the only learning that may give some sense of meaning to those who suffered in the disaster is the knowledge that it dispels the myth that a similar thing could not happen to you and I, whether we live in London, Hong Kong or Cairo, and that all of us must make a permanent change in the way we think and act to bring ourselves into sustainable relationship with the world in which we live. Albert Einstein summarised our dilemma very well in his statement:

'The significant problems we face cannot be solved at the same level of thinking we were at when we created them.'

The challenge to our current thinking is not only on the global and planetary scale of 'big' issues. It also lies at the very heart of the decision making process in our commercial and public institutions. The issues that face us can no longer be resolved by simply 'doing more of the same only better'. Markets and electorates alike are very hard on such linear thinking. At best such gains are likely to be short term. A commercial organisation playing with the price mechanism in a distinctive manner may gain a short term competitive advantage only to see it rapidly eroded away as competitors replicate the parts of the strategy that work (while ignoring or re-engineering those parts that don't!). A political party may gain a temporary lead in poll ratings by advocating policies that tap into the public mood on an issue only to see the lead crumble when the hard reality of dealing with the trade-offs which underlie the policy become all too readily apparent in implementation. The call that we face is to think more strategically, to develop a way of looking at the world and the issues and challenges that it throws at us from a deeper perspective that recognises the complex interrelationships that exist within it. That is what this book is all about. And when we look at our challenges, issues and practical problems in this light we uncover something that may surprise us for there, hiding in the shadows, are often the biggest opportunities.

This need for a step-change in the way we think and act is not merely of academic interest, a vague woolly feel-good concept that can while away the time during the 'graveyard session' immediately after lunch at a business seminar. Our best leaders across all fields – private and public, entrepreneurial and corporate, social and commercial – are already laying the tracks. There are very good indications of what this new thinking means in the practical everyday world and we will look at many examples from all walks of life throughout this book. So, for our starting point let's keep things simple. For the moment we will not worry about coming to a precise definition of strategic thinking. Instead, we will look at its application in the real world and observe what happens when leaders do genuinely think differently, that is to begin to think more strategically. Then, when we are convinced that the end point is indeed worthwhile we can give serious attention to understanding the process and developing our capabilities. After all, we are not going to shoot for the moon if we are not convinced that it is even there!

Developing strategic leadership

Occasionally, when I am working with a group of executives or students one of them will announce loudly that they are a 'strategic thinker'. I always find this vaguely disconcerting as the best thinkers I know are rather humble about their abilities and it puzzles me why some people seem to like to set themselves up for a fall! However, by far the most common reaction to the topic of strategic thinking is interest coupled with either vague apprehension or scepticism. 'I am not really sure I can do this' is one reaction, while the other is 'interesting theory but show me how it works in practice'. As a result, I have structured this book extensively around case studies, especially when discussing the core disciplines of strategic thinking. The aim is to demonstrate that not only do we need to think at a deeper level but that many of our most successful organisations are already actively doing so. These are the strategic leaders who are laying the pathway for us to follow. By using supplementary case studies and stories of much smaller organisations in both commercial and not-for-profit sectors my objective is also to show that the ability to think more strategically is certainly not skewed towards large organisations. In fact, if anything, the reverse is almost certainly true; much of the truly innovative thinking is coming from outside the corporate and institutional mainstream, as, indeed, it always has done.

There are a good many definitions of strategic leadership but mine is a very simple one, it is the point where knowledge translates into action in pursuit of a vision or a dream. As such it is not necessarily defined by role or position (not all leaders are those at the top of organisations) or by value judgement (leaders can act in positive or negative ways). A higher order definition of strategic leadership may be the point where *wisdom* translates into action or non-action. The word 'wisdom' as we shall see in chapter one, is derived from the same root as the word 'vision' and implies something more than knowledge alone; it is seeing our body of knowledge in the context of the whole and that provides us with a clue about the nature of strategic thinking. It is holistic. Moreover, a vision, no matter how compelling, needs to be founded on a clear view of reality based on experience and intuition. This is deeply paradoxical. We cannot move to a better place if we do not acknowledge our roots in our current situation and see its nature clearly; the more profound this understanding, the greater our capacity for change will be. Many great leaders, including Nelson Mandela and Mahatma Gandhi, spent considerable amounts of time incapacitated, which allowed them to contemplate the nature of their reality in great depth, albeit in enforced circumstances. This was not 'wasted' time or a period of 'lost opportunities'. It was immensely important in enabling them to bring about the profound changes that they did. For the moment, however, let's explore the definition of strategic leadership further by looking at some practical examples. Can you answer the following questions?

- How is it that Apple does virtually no market research before launching a new product, such as the iPhone, when the success or failure of new products is core to the company's profitability and market capitalisation?

- What lies at the heart of Google's success?

- What makes Starbucks unique?

- What is the glue that holds Virgin together?

- Toyota was once famously described as the 'machine that changed the world'. Why is it that it remains the company in the automotive industry that is most likely to do so again?

- What makes Amazon's business model much more than an online superstore?

- What is a social entrepreneur and why is the emergence of social entrepreneurs so important in our world today?

- Garth Brooks is one of the most successful recording artists in history and yet was rejected by all the major labels when he was first seeking a recording contract. He has gone on to sell some 120 million albums before he retired in 2002. What did the record executives overlook?

In truth, there are no simple answers to these questions but there are simple *insights* into the answers! Insights often guide us into deeper thinking, a process that will inevitably yield some surprising conclusions. We will explore each of the questions above in the case studies throughout the book, but you may wish to take a peek at the suggested 'answers' in Appendix A and see how you fared. These contain some common elements, which give us further clues into the nature of strategic thinking and strategic leadership. The individuals and the leaders of the organisations involved are self-willed, often 'mavericks', who do things in their own way. This uniqueness translates into the ability to make a big difference (another potential definition of strategic leadership!). Our task in this book is to find out how this process works. You may find that you disagree with some of the suggested 'answers' and, given their brevity, this is not only unsurprising but also very healthy. The process of questioning and evaluating the underlying assumptions behind the 'factual' information presented to us is a critical part of the process of learning to think strategically. It leads us to dig deeper into our understanding of a situation, issue or event, which inevitably yields a wealth of valuable knowledge and insight into how best to move forward. It also allows us to challenge received 'wisdom' and the accepted ways of doing things. This becomes an essential part of the process of developing new and innovative approaches to resolving the many issues and challenges that face us.

Approach to strategic thinking

When I presented the original concept of this book to a friend he snorted at my suggestion that it would represent a 'new' approach to strategic thinking. 'Nothing is really new in management,' he corrected me, 'what comes around comes around, all that really changes is the packaging.' To a certain extent my friend is right and my terminology was not particularly helpful. Much of the underlying philosophy and concepts upon which this book is based are timeless. There is certainly nothing 'new' about them from that perspective and I believe that is a very good thing. It merely means that they have been tried and tested and that they work. Indeed, I have attempted to make the structure of the book as straightforward as possible because we can *all* learn to think at a deeper level without resorting to complex theories or abstract, esoteric practices. As a result, we will be using a simple framework of seven key disciplines for developing our ability to think strategically and looking at organisations and individuals which exemplify these principles in real life.

The key to strategic thinking is to be able to see a bigger picture, to distinguish the wood from the trees, and the framework below allows us to clearly identify the key practices that will enhance our ability to do so. This is important because there is a world of difference between understanding something at an intellectual level and integrating it into our day to day activities as a practical discipline. The purpose of this book is just that; to help us think more strategically in every aspect of our lives. That is what is called for by scale and size of the challenges that confront us. Nothing less will do. We will be unpacking the concept of strategic thinking in more detail in chapter one and considering how it relates to other areas such as creativity and intuition but for the moment let's concentrate on establishing the core framework for the book.

The seven disciplines

At the core of this book lie seven key disciplines that form the basis for developing our ability to think at a deeper and more profound level. At first sight some may appear counter intuitive ('act slowly'), while others will be more familiar ('dream'). We will begin by looking at each discipline separately, relating it to organisations that are regarded as strategic leaders in their fields and exploring its practical application. Naturally, in practice, the seven disciplines overlap and form an integrated whole so we will be pulling everything together into a holistic framework in chapter nine. For the moment, we will limit ourselves to a brief preview of the main principles.

Know your own story

The foundation for success for both individuals and organisations alike is to know who we are and what we stand for, both in terms of where we come from (our background, family and history) and where we are going (our purpose and vision). Authenticity and originality are intimately connected with success. We will be looking at this principle in chapter two using the stories of Sir Richard Branson and Virgin, Google, Bono and the Pierian Centre in Bristol as some of the case examples.

Think small

We understand intuitively that vision is critical to strategic leadership.

What we often tend to overlook is that so is attention to detail. Successful organisations tend to obsess over the 'small' stuff because they appreciate how important detail is in the successful execution of strategy. They don't forget that 'big' things are always built from small beginnings using an iterative step by step process. Moreover, what may appear on the surface to be an insignificant detail often turns out to be far more important than it seems! Entrepreneurs willingly embrace this paradox. They have a strong sense of vision combined with a tendency to 'meddle' with day to day operations. They know intuitively that the 'small' things need to be right to make the 'big' vision possible. At a practical level, some of the largest and most successful organisations today are also built on an almost obsessive attention to detail. We will be exploring this principle in chapter three through a variety of case studies including Amazon, Wikipedia, Fish Records and the Prince's Trust.

Act slowly

Things that are built on solid foundations tend to last. The ability to be flexible and adaptable (and make decisions quickly when necessary) comes, paradoxically, from the time spent knowing who we are and what we stand for. It is interesting to reflect upon the fact that the seeds of the largest plants and trees spend their early life entirely underground in the darkness simply getting ready for the right time and conditions to shoot for the sun. We will be looking at a number of organisations in chapter four to illustrate this principle including Honda, Toyota, The National Trust and the Wildlife Trusts in the United Kingdom.

Serve others

No one and no thing exists in isolation; we are all in relationship with everything else. Serving others moves us from a position of pushing our 'stuff' out towards others to aligning ourselves to meeting the needs of the greater whole, thus acknowledging the web of life and tapping into the synchronicity that lies within. This fundamental principle lies at the heart of holistic thinking; if we cannot see ourselves in relationship but fall prey to the 'illusion of independence' we will always be limited to a partial understanding of the whole. We will be exploring this principle in chapter five using a broad range of case studies including Starbucks, Care for the Family, Cafédirect and a village primary school.

Reflect

Reflection is the lynch pin of strategic thinking. We cannot access a deeper part of ourselves and the inherent wisdom contained therein unless we put some time aside to do so, time spent away from the constant demands of our hectic day-to-day schedules. This time can be spent in a formal practice such as meditation or yoga but it can equally be centred on walking, exercise, sport or being in nature. It is not so much *what* we do as becoming conscious of the importance of slowing down, observing and reflecting before acting. Reflection is the foundation of strategic thinking and it is the most difficult discipline in the book to put into practice. As a result, we will be looking extensively at BP in chapter six and examining how John Browne, its former CEO, built an enduring legacy at the company, leaving BP as a highly successful commercial organisation and a strategic leader in green energy.

Be simple

Simplicity plays a critical, and largely unrecognised, role in defining strategic and competitive advantage. The ability to focus on our task in hand is one of the key determinants of successfully meeting our key goals and objectives. It allows us to direct our energy in a purposeful manner avoiding fragmentation and distraction. Simplicity in life allows us to reduce the baggage that we carry around with us and makes us far more flexible and adaptable in our personal and working lives. It works even better within organisations where 'complexity creep' can reduce innovation, creativity and sometimes even the will to live of the people who work there! We will be seeing that 'less is more' through the examples of eBay, Pret A Manger, Innocent Drinks and Waitrose in chapter seven.

Dream

There is nothing as powerful as a dream. We instinctively recognise the truth in this statement but the process by which our dreams become a reality is far less obvious. Some dreams come from a positive vision of a better place or a sense of opportunity of what *could* be. Many, however, reflect some area of our lives where we have either experienced pain or where things simply aren't working as well as we would like. Dreams often lurk in the shadows, occasionally arising directly from the most painful experiences of our lives. It is our desire to mitigate this pain for ourselves and for others that often drives us to change the circumstances that led to it. The process of revealing and energising these dreams – at the simplest level a better way of doing things then we have experienced – provides the commitment and passion to make them a reality. We often look at people who are regarded as great leaders and comment that they have made the impossible happen. So can we all! We will be exploring the power of dreams in chapter eight through the stories of Apple, the International Centre for Families in Business, Tilley Endurables and Garth Brooks.

The disciplines as an integrated whole

Although we look at each of the key disciplines of strategic thinking separately in this book they are, of course, all part of an overall framework to help us think more holistically. At the foundation of this holistic approach lies the importance of reflection, which is also an integral element of each of the separate disciplines. In chapter nine we will pull together the separate principles into a whole using the story of Whole Foods Market to guide us. We will then have the chance to examine the overall framework and consider some of the important tools and techniques that can help us improve our strategic thinking skills.

The power of working and thinking together

Learning to think strategically is not a solitary pursuit. The act of sharing our insights with our colleagues and friends brings another deeper dimension to the process. We often find ourselves in the frustrating position of *almost* knowing something. It's as if we are two-thirds of the way there but we just can't put those final parts of the jigsaw together. Then a work colleague or friend mentions something (perhaps not even directly relevant to the issue at hand) and we know we finally have it. The feeling when this happens is almost always the same, '*how* did I manage to miss this?' There is great synergy in working together with others. We can do this through formalised processes such as workshops, techniques such as story-telling and scenario analysis or numerous other routine work-based practices. Alternatively we can do it informally by simply 'hanging around' and spending time together. It is easy to dismiss the profundity of this process because it is so normal. Strange as it may seem, I find that the 'simple' act of bringing people together around an agenda of walking in nature followed by some form of structured debate can yield astounding insights and unblock all manner of seemingly intractable problems. This process combines the power of creating a reflective space, in a particularly positive environment, with the synergistic effects of working in groups.

The task before us

'Every intelligent person in the world knew that disaster was impending but knew no way to avoid it.'
H G Wells, a quote placed at the entrance of In Flanders Fields Museum in Iepes (Ypres), Belgium

The first impression that you have of Ieper, a small medieval market town close to the French-Belgium border, is of the spacious Grote Markt (Market Square), teaming with cafes and the busy life of a small town. The enormous Lakenhalle (Cloth Hall) was begun in the year 1200 and took over 100 years to complete and is truly vast, an amazing feat of construction even today. Behind that lies the magnificent Cathedral, both buildings providing potent symbols to the illustrious heritage and wealth of the town's past. A quiet medieval town and a perfect place for lunch you might think. In fact, lunch aside, nothing could be further from the truth.

Ieper has had a turbulent history. With France to the South and the Low Countries to the North, the town was from its early days a tempting prize and military strong point. However, nothing could prepare Ieper for what happened during the First World War. The town was completely destroyed and half a million people perished on the Ieper Salient, the front that curved round the town. There are no words that can really describe the madness that happened. However, we can experience some of the horror through the stories of the people who lived through that period by visiting the In Flanders Fields Museum. The museum tells the stories of ordinary soldiers and the people of the region with the hope of creating an emotional experience that creates a deeper understanding for the visitor, one that 'kindles a flame' that will burn long after the return trip home. Although labelled 'the war to end all wars' the 'Great War' did nothing of the kind. At the end of the museum there is an exhibit that records all the subsequent wars that have happened and this is a salutary reminder of how little has changed since the end of the conflagration that engulfed Ieper. It is estimated that 100 million people have died in the various wars of the 20th century alone. The museum continues to play its part, tending the flames of recognition and understanding in order to create meaning from the suffering of the past. As Chairman, Frans Lignel, so eloquently puts it in the introduction to the museum's guide book:

'The City of Ieper hopes that this museum will contribute to the worldwide pursuit of peace and tolerance. Ieper has chosen to focus on the little people in the Great War. We do so for the sake of our children and for all the generations to come.'

The reason why I am discussing the experiences of Ieper in the First World War here is to remind us that, whilst our economic and social systems have served us well in certain areas (particularly in terms of increased standards of living in the developed world) in other areas (the environment, poverty, warfare and the distribution of global wealth) the limitations to our thinking are becoming abundantly clear, particularly in the area of environmental and climatic change, warfare and terrorism and our increased susceptibility to potential global epidemics such as avian flu. In each case, if we view a problem in isolation, we *may* be able to minimise its potential impact and take some form of appropriate action but our effectiveness will be limited by our knowledge of how our actions affect the system as a whole. Moreover, put together, these challenges are symptomatic of the increasing fragility of our social-economic system. Although this system that has brought us tremendous benefits, we need to recognise that our actions in one area have caused repercussions in others. At first the effects may be small (for example, a small rise in the concentration of wealth or minor increases in carbon dioxide emissions) and their impact will be subtle. However, as we now know with climate change, small changes to a complex system can result in dramatic consequences over time. Our task today is to adopt a more holistic way of thinking, to join up the dots between the issues and challenges facing us and to act accordingly. Simply doing more of the same only better is no longer an option. That inability to learn from experience and to change accordingly is precisely why so many people have died in 20th century wars despite the horrific experiences of the First World War.

Anyone who has some familiarity with the body of knowledge that is coming out of the 'new' sciences will know that natural and ecological systems are complex and that we can learn a great deal by looking at anomalies (events that run counter to expected patterns and behaviours) which often allow us to identify emergent phenomenon and potential changes to the system as a whole. This means appreciating the significance of small, and sometimes imperceptible, changes, something that runs counter to our tendency to equate significance with size. Living in the South West of England I'm aware that I enjoy a mild temperate climate largely as a result of the beneficial impact of the Gulf Stream and it is wise to take any changes to its flow, no matter how small, very seriously. For Northern Europe, climate change may bring the delights of a milder Mediterranean climate and an abundance of olives and citrus fruit or it may mean something far more severe. We do not know whether current changes to the Gulf Stream will reach a trigger point but when I point out to my colleagues that Madrid is on the same latitude as Toronto and that London is almost equivalent with the Southern shores of the Hudson Bay it normally generates an interesting response! One thing that is certain is that for the world as a whole, climate change threatens to be potentially devastating, particularly in the some of the poorest regions on earth. When you are at the margins of life even the smallest incremental change for the worst can be the difference between life and death.

The true extent of the challenge cannot be seen, however, by looking simply at the 'big issues' covered so extensively by the media. New thinking requires us to see the connections between the parts, to see how all things are related to the whole. Knowing, for example, that studies have shown that many insects in the United Kingdom are showing alarming declines in abundance and diversity, we can immediately recognise the significance for the food chain as a whole and for human beings as part of the web of life. We can begin to join the dots in our thinking on what this might mean about the way we live within our world and what actions we may need to take in order to bring us back into sustainable relationship. Insects may be small (and attract much less sympathy than larger animals similarly threatened by environmental change) but even a small decline in invertebrates is highly significant as insects are at the heart of many of our ecosystems.

Laurence Packer, a biology professor in the Faculty of Science & Engineering at York University in Toronto has been raising awareness of the potential consequences of declining bee populations long before the news broke in 2006 that half the honeybees had mysteriously disappeared in the U.S. and Europe. 'When you lose bees, you lose flowers and all the things that feed upon those flowers,' he says. 'Bees are the agricultural equivalent of canaries in a coal mine and their death signifies a much larger problem.' Indeed, bees pollinate a third of the world's food crops and 95 per cent of its flowers. We are only just beginning to understand what this might mean for us and Laurence Packer is doing his bit to make us more aware of the vital role they play in providing us with our fruit, berries, vegetables and nuts. 'I want people to watch bees the way they watch birds,' he continues before adding wisely, 'People don't love things unless they know about them.' [3]

In common with many other global issues, it is recognising the level of interconnectivity that is important as a starting point to generate new approaches and potential solutions. What is true for environmental and climate systems is also true for cultural, social and economic systems. We need to think at a deeper and more holistic level so that we can tackle global issues from a profound understanding of the whole and an acceptance of our responsibility to it. The consequences of a failure not to do this are likely to be devastating. Václav Havel, who was then President of Czechoslovakia, talked of nothing less than a need for a shift in human consciousness when he addressed a joint session of the US Congress as long ago as February 1991:

'Without a revolution in the sphere of human consciousness, nothing will change for the better ... and the catastrophe towards which this world is headed – the ecological, social, demographic or general breakdown of civilisation – will be unavoidable.'

Václav Havel

Strategic thinking as the key to opportunity

'Progress has not followed a straight ascending line, but a spiral with rhythms of progress and retrogression, of evolution and dissolution.'

Johann W von Goethe

We are taking a practical approach in this book by illustrating each of the key disciplines of strategic thinking through organisations and individuals that are strategic leaders in their fields. By using stories we not only get a deep appreciation and insight into the complex and paradoxical world of strategic thinking but also inspirational examples of successful practical application by some of the most dynamic and interesting organisations around today. The individual disciplines reflect time honoured wisdom that often predates our modern industrial world and each can make a significant difference when practised on its own. However, it is together, as part of a process, that the seven disciplines really come into their own by enabling us to develop a more holistic perspective on the challenges, problems and

---

[3] Laurence Packer, Professor of Biology at York University in Toronto, reported in YorkU magazine in February 2008 in the article 'Green Gallery'. See also www.biol.yorku.ca/grad/faculty/laurencedp.htm

issues that confront us. It is this that allows us to generate additional insights and highlights innovative solutions that are not immediately apparent at a superficial level. As important, we find that by taking a more reflective approach and entering the 'shadow' of the challenges that face us we often discover the greatest opportunities to move forward.

This talk of finding opportunity in the shadows of challenge may sound too philosophical for some but our most visionary business leaders already use this process with very effective commercial results. When Steve Jobs announced Apple's new iPhone in January 2007 he talked enthusiastically about the fact that 'everybody hates their phone ... and that's not a good thing'[4] because this was a key opportunity to Apple with its strong product development culture. In the eyes of Apple, so good with consumer functionality and sleek design, exiting phones do lots of things – calling, web browsing, music playback, photos, video and even satellite navigation – but they do it badly by forcing the consumer to press all sorts of tiny buttons and navigate through a diverse range of different interfaces. Instead of marvelling at how dexterous teenagers can become why not redesign the phone so that those of us who are now in a more mature phase of our lives can also use it in comfort? Steve Jobs was able to see opportunities in the challenges faced by the mobile phone operators and use these to Apple's advantage. In fact, he is particularly good at challenging imbedded assumptions and overturning them. Instead of asking 'why?' he 'simply' asks 'why not'? This process of asking 'simple' questions is a decidedly rare quality as we will discover when we look at simplicity in chapter seven.

Apple's dominance of the digital music market is another striking example of its ability to challenge and override taken-for-granted assumptions, this time within the music industry. When the music majors faltered over the digitalisation of music, Apple took advantage of the vacuum created and jumped in. Within months it had sold more digital downloads than the entire music industry had managed up to that point and it now has over 80% of the market with its iconic digital music offer (the combination of iTunes and the iPod). Indeed, it is largely this success that has transformed Apple into one of the most creative and admired companies of the 21st century. And this process continues. Steve Job's call to the music industry in the spring of 2007 to abandon the technology that guards music downloads against theft (the so-called 'digital rights management' restrictions) resulted partly from adversity, in this case

---

[4] Time Magazine, 'The Apple of Your Ear', January 22nd 2007

related to Apple itself. The company was faced with pressure from European regulators who regarded its refusal to license its own rights protection system, 'FairPlay', as monopolistic behaviour. This placed Apple in a 'catch 22' position as the use of protective technology was also a prerequisite demanded by the music companies in exchange for the rights to sell music by their artists. Indeed, selling secure music was traditionally a mantra for the big labels. This is a classic 'no-win' dilemma, the sort of intractable problem that cannot be solved easily by linear thinking. However, by turning the issue on its head and suggesting that such protection should be scrapped, Apple put itself in the happy position of being seen not as the defender of content control (which is highly unpopular with many consumers) but, as the Economist put it, 'as a consumer champion who helped bring it down.'[5] This has served only to highlight Apple's commanding lead in digital music and further reinforce its powerful brand image.

In reality, opportunity is very often the flipside of the problem or the challenge that confronts us. This is much easier to talk about in the abstract then to see in our own lives because it inevitably involves challenging the habitual response patterns that we have adopted. How much easier it is to observe a 'master' at work, such as Steve Jobs or Sir Richard Branson, than attempt to confront our own habitual way of thinking, especially when times are difficult and the temptation is simply to do more of what has worked well for us in the past. Unfortunately, that is often the equivalent of a person stuck in a hole continuing to dig! To think strategically, we need to reframe the problem, look at it from a different angle, and that can take us into some very challenging territory, either because we don't really want to go there or because the organisations for which we work have effectively defined these areas as 'out of bounds'. Naturally, we will be fearful of 'getting it wrong' because we no longer have an established record of past experience and success to guide us. However, if we look closely at a 'master' at work, we quickly see that they too sometimes 'get it wrong'. It is not whether we are immediately successful that matters but rather how open we remain to the possibilities and opportunities before us and how quickly we can recognise the need to amend our action or even to change direction if necessary. Strategic leaders are capable of simultaneously changing tack and remaining steadfast to their overriding vision. Achieving our goals and making a real difference is not a linear process. We combine cumulative insights,

---

[5] The Economist, 'Music wants to be free', February 10th 2007

knowledge and experience that we gain on the way. And it is worth remembering that the pathway is not always a straight one!

Strategic thinking as a practical discipline

There is a common flaw in business books that choose to eulogise organisations as exemplary in some fashion or other. Shortly after they are published, some of the organisations discussed inevitably fall from grace and we are left wondering whether the advice given really can be put to any practical or useful purpose. Indeed, many of the organisations discussed in this book have been through challenging circumstances and some have been in the news recently as much for their perceived failings as their successes. Starbucks (discussed in chapter 5), for example, saw its share price fall by over 40% in 2007 and reported its first ever year-on-year decline in customer visits in America in the final quarter of that year. Meanwhile, Meg Whitman, CEO of eBay (discussed in chapter 7) announced that she would step down in 2008 as a result of unhappiness with some of the decisions taken during her tenure as CEO, including the high price paid by eBay for Skype, a provider of internet-based telephony services. Yet both these organisations remain very good examples of strategic thinking so how do we 'square' this apparent 'circle'? We do it by being honest and acknowledging that thinking strategically is an ongoing process and that good decisions do not guarantee success for evermore. The world is a rapidly changing place and even good organisations get things wrong some of the time. It is the way that they deal with these 'failings' that truly distinguish them.

I remember looking at my core presentation on strategic thinking at the beginning of 2008 and thinking that rather too many of the organisations that I use to illustrate strategic leadership were going through challenging times and were not necessarily the conspicuous successes that they had once been. My first thought, to my shame, was that I might need to do a little 'case study re-engineering', a euphemism here for changing some of the organisations! However, time pressure, followed by some late intellectual honesty, stopped me from making the changes. I am very happy that it did because what I have since found is that the ambiguities raised by the case studies have been met with a much greater degree of audience engagement and participation. Because the sessions are rooted in the messy business of real life groups have responded by quickly connecting with the key issues raised about the nature of strategic thinking and its relationship with organisational success. As a result, not only has the level of debate dramatically improved but the degree of learning has also increased immeasurably, for my benefit as well as the audience!

Strategic leadership

Strategic leadership is a complex area and this book takes a broad outlook that embraces both the 'positive' and 'negative' aspects of what it means to be a strategic leader. All the leaders discussed in the book, regardless of the size of organisation, have clearly made a big difference. Yet working for men and women such as these can be hugely demanding; expectations can be very high indeed. Leaders can be highly obsessive and many are workaholics by any conventional standards. However, the fact that strategic leaders make us feel uncomfortable at times or have flaws, just like the rest of us, does not diminish the importance of their legacy as leaders! Similarly, one of the key characteristics of the organisations that they lead is that they often embrace paradox. Starbucks, for example, is both very community-oriented and commercially astute. Sir Richard Branson, as we shall see, is both opportunistic, with an unfailing entrepreneurial ability to see opportunities, and also genuinely concerned with making the world a better place. One of the critical elements of thinking strategically is for us to become more comfortable with paradox and acknowledge that self conflicting elements can hold true at the same time. Leaders who make a real change in the world are energetic, self determined and often obsessive. As a result, they can be tough people to work with and work for. But that is why they are able to make such a dramatic difference!

If becoming a strategic leader is difficult, being in a position of leadership can be equally challenging. In May 2007, John Browne, CEO of BP, resigned from his position after losing a four-month legal battle to keep his personal life private. He is an exceptionally talented and committed strategic leader. Under his tenure at BP he steered the company into an industry leadership position as well as building the foundation of a highly successful commercial organisation. This, in its own right, would be an exceptional contribution. However, his advocacy role in recognizing the seriousness of environmental and climatic change and his willingness to put the resources of BP behind this position may well prove his most enduring legacy. In the long term, it is in this sense that he will be remembered. In the short term, however, there is little doubt about the very significant cost that he has paid for being in the public domain. The story of BP under the leadership of John Browne provides a classic example of strategic thinking in a large organisation. It also demonstrates very well the difficulties of building and maintaining strategic leadership and the personal costs that sometimes result of being in the public spotlight. This is the practical world within which we live and it would be nonsense not to consider it in a book such as this.

The oil and gas industry is truly global, intensely competitive and at the forefront of environmental and climatic change. It is also very sensitive politically; especially as fears of energy depletion and lack of self-sufficiency ('energy security') become more prominent. BP has had its fair share of well publicised problems including a fatal Texas City refinery explosion in 2005, which killed 15 employees and injured many more, and the necessity to shut down its key Alaskan fields as a result of oil spillages. This is not an easy business environment! Yet, despite these problems, BP is clearly a strategic leader in its field and has achieved a remarkable transformation by thinking distinctively and holistically, while at the same time delivering the bottom line results demanded by the markets. Although traditional energy sources (oil and gas) still account for most of BP's business it has moved concertedly towards renewable energy sources, setting the pace for its competitors. This process has been led and championed by John Browne and involved a major re-branding in 2000 when the new 'Helios' logo (named after the sun god of ancient Greece) depicted, amongst other things, BP's move towards a diversified energy company with a green mission (reinforced by changing the meaning of the initials 'BP' to 'Beyond Petroleum').

Yet even before this John Browne was a man on a mission. As early as 1997 he drew attention to the threat of climate change and the need to take responsibility for that change. It is this sense of broader purpose that lies at the heart of BP's business transformation, something that John Browne stressed throughout his tenure as Group CEO of BP:

'And then one further change, which to me is the most important of all. A change of behaviour … based on a rethinking of purpose … That means delivering results, and doing our business exceptionally well day by day … but it also means aligning our activity with the world's needs … leading change and being a force for progress in everything we do.' [6]

---

[6] Remarks made by John Browne at Morehouse College in the United States on September 29th 2000 sourced from BP.

If you work for a large organisation or institution will know only too well how difficult it is to make deep changes and how long it takes to make such a significant transformation as BP has embarked upon. You will also know how much of a balancing act is required to ensure that the performance metrics on which the company is continuously judged are maintained at the same time. Such a top line strategy needs to be supported by constant attention to operational matters and also to be intensely practical. If it is not, it simply will not work. In addition, oil is a business where critical mass matters big time (both in terms of overall size and proven energy reserves) so BP's strategy will be heavily influenced in this area too. At the point of BP's re-branding in 2000 (which was widely disparaged by many of the market analysts at the time) it was not clear that following a diversified energy strategy was the most appropriate way forward in the industry. Indeed, BP continues to be compared in terms of its performance relative to the other oil majors who have not adopted such a diversified approach to energy supply. The markets are not in the business of being kind to underperformers! That so much *has* been achieved over the past 12 years is a major achievement for John Browne and something that we will discuss further in chapter six when we look at the power of reflection.

The three illusions

The purpose of this book is to help you develop the ability to think more holistically by taking a 'step by step' approach backed with extensive case study material showing the practical application of new thinking by individuals and organisations today. As we have seen, the ability to think strategically, to see the wood from the trees, is directly relevant to all the issues and challenges that we face in our lives, however large or small, so it can be applied both in our home and working lives. We will be adopting an incremental approach to developing our strategic thinking abilities, looking at each one of the seven core disciplines separately before bringing them together as part of an overall framework for change in chapter nine. It is useful at this stage, however, to point out some of the key challenges that we will face when we try to broaden and deepen the way we think. I have labelled them the 'three illusions' and they all relate to deeply ingrained patterns in our way of thinking. They are:

1. **The illusion of independence** – the idea that we, as human beings, are independent from the world around us, that the observer and the

observed are separate. We need to recognise that we are all deeply connected within the web of life and that our notion of separateness is an illusion – the observer and the observed are in relationship!

2. **The illusion of size** – the idea that big is important and success can be measured in terms of size. This idea permeates all aspects of contemporary society, not only in terms of individual and organisational achievement but also in our ideas of economic growth and general well being. In fact, there is little correlation between what is truly important and size, as we shall see.

3. **The illusion of control** – the idea that we can control the environment around us, based partly on the first illusion of independence. In reality, our relationship with the world around us is far more complex than we currently acknowledge and we need to recognise the natural limitations in our ability to control it and attune ourselves to the wealth of opportunity that flows from learning to live in relationship with it rather than in opposition to it.

Naturally, changing our way of thinking is not going to happen overnight or simply because we read a book, even this book! However, once you begin the process you will never want to go back!

Getting the best from this book

In order to make this book simple to navigate I have adopted a relatively standard format for each of the chapters outlining the core disciplines of strategic thinking. They all interweave theory with practical application and usually include the following:

- A discussion on the meaning of the core concept underlying the discipline, often using supporting examples from organisations.

- The primary story, a leading organisation that exemplifies the concept and is a strategic leader in its field.

- Further supporting case studies and stories that expand and support the understanding of the discipline and place it within a broader context (for example, within smaller organisations, not-for-profit organisations or with individuals).

- A section called 'ideas into action', which discusses the practical application of the discipline and related issues in the wider world, particularly where the discipline can add understanding to key global issues and challenges that face us today.

- A discussion of the personal implications and benefits of adopting the discipline.

As a result, it is quite possible to read the book in any order that you like, except perhaps for this chapter and the two concluding chapters (framework for change and the way forward) which assume some knowledge of the preceding chapters. My intention is that the book is a useful tool for the application of ideas as well as for providing a framework for change and my hope is that the ideas and further references provide a pathway for further study and application. The next chapter, foundations of strategic thinking, is the most conceptual in the book and looks at what it means to think strategically and how this relates to other areas such as creativity and intuition. If you are practical by nature and are keen to get to the core disciplines and case studies please feel free to go directly to chapter two, which is the first of the core disciplines, 'know your own story'.

PART 1

STRATEGIC THINKING

1

FOUNDATIONS FOR STRATEGIC THINKING

'Thinking strategically starts with reflection on the deepest nature on an undertaking and on the central challenges that it poses.'

Peter Senge [7]

Strategic thinking in action

When Jesse Helms, the former Senator from North Carolina, was first told in 2000 that Bono, lead singer for rock band U2, wanted to meet with him in order to talk about boosting U.S. aid to Africa, he admits that he did not know who Bono was and had to ask his Senate staff. Bono wanted to discuss the scope of the tragedy in Africa, especially the pain that it is bringing to infants, children and their families with the aim of enlisting his support. In the event, Jesse Helms not only promised to do all that he could to help but followed through with action, working with Senator Bill Frist in creating and passing a bill to commit $200 million to fight aids in Africa. How did Bono create such an immediate and positive impression? The answer lies in two things. Firstly, he was living his truth and communicating about something on which he cared deeply. Secondly, he was exceptionally well informed and prepared. This mixture of vision and practical action is very powerful. Mr Helms put it this way in an interview with Time Magazine in May 2006:

> I had met enough people to quickly figure out who is genuine and who there for show. I knew as soon as I met Bono that he was

---

[7] Peter Senge, Director for the Centre of Organisational Learning at MIT's Sloan School of Management, 'The Fifth Discipline', Century Business, 1990.

genuine. He had his facts in hand and didn't have any agenda other than doing all he could to help people in desperate need.

The foundations for thinking strategically are based on two key elements, the capability to think outside the box and to envisage a different way of doing things and the practical capacity to do something about it. Strategic thinking needs to be both conceptual and practical because without both these aspects even the very best ideas, dreams and visions will not be translated into significant changes in the real world.

Raffi Cavoukian, who is better known to millions simply as Raffi, is a Canadian children's singer-songwriter who has sold over 14 million records in North America and has been described by the Washington Post as 'the most popular children's entertainer in the Western World'.[8] His story shows both the visionary and practical elements of strategic thinking clearly at work. Now involved in global advocacy for the rights of children worldwide and founder of 'Child Honouring' (which seeks to profoundly change our society by placing the recognition and honouring of our children at its centre) Raffi's career as a children's 'troubadour' began modestly. From the very beginning, however, he was passionate about treating each child with the respect and dignity that they deserve. This deep respect that lies at the core of his music was accompanied by a refusal to dilute any of the artistic and production standards associated with his music for children. In the early 1970's, when albums for children were low budget affairs, this child-centred approach was nothing less than revolutionary. In doing so Raffi laid a pathway for the other children's artists who were able to follow him and so left a truly lasting legacy.

There is no doubt about the visionary aspect to Raffi's work; he is very much a dream builder who is actively making this world a better place. There is, however, also a very significant practical element to Raffi's story, as anyone who has ever tried to build a career as a recording artist will know, especially in a niche market like children's music! Indeed, an important part of Raffi's legacy is his very significant contribution to creating an acceptance that a defined market niche for children's music exists, something that was not taken for granted in the early stages of his career and is still periodically questioned by the music industry. This would have involved plenty of hard legwork, from playing elementary schools in the early days to forming and running his record label, Troubadour Records, which was an essential prerequisite to stay the course within the

---

[8] Source: Raffi's website, www.raffinews.com.

vicissitudes of the music industry. It was this combination of the visionary and the practical that has enabled Raffi to become an international spokesperson for children today and it happened step by step with, I am willing to bet, a lot of challenges and frustrations along the way! And that is, no doubt, quite an understatement!

Approaches to strategic thinking

There are two dimensions to approaching a definition of strategic thinking. One is to observe it in action, either in others or in ourselves and to identify the key elements that were necessary to enable the changes to take place. By looking at the achievements of Bono and Raffi, for example, we can see certain common threads that underlie each of their stories including the passion, commitment and persistence that both men share on their life journeys. This approach enables us to keep our feet firmly on the ground and allows us to learn by example. It is very much a key part of the exploration of the core disciplines in the following chapters of the book.

The other dimension is to look more deeply at the conceptual process of thinking itself and use the knowledge gained to adapt our way of thinking, in effect to 'train' ourselves to think differently. There is no value judgement attached to this process, it's certainly not a question of learning to think 'better' or trying to 'improve' the output of our thinking. We are simply learning to open a space to access both a broader and deeper perspective and to allow more insights to come to the surface. We will be using both these approaches throughout this book but let's look first at a simple yet powerful example of strategic thinking in practice.

Learning from friends

There is a wonderful example of strategic thinking in the comedy series, *Friends*, when Chandler and Joey's friendship is put at risk when they fall out over a girl. Joey is mortified that Chandler has kissed his ex-girlfriend without approaching him first and demands that Chandler spends time in a large coffin-like box in recompense. At first, Chandler cannot help but play the fool and ignores Joey's insistence that he remains silent. Eventually he falls into line and it is at this point that the girl in question enters the room and wants to speak to Chandler. She cannot live with the fact that the boys' friendship is being torn apart over her and has decided that she must end her relationship with him despite the fact that it could have been something very special. Throughout her speech Chandler says nothing, only poking his finger through the air hole in the box to wave goodbye to her as she leaves the room. Of course, Joey relents at this point shouting 'open the box, open the box' and Chandler is able to pursue her to tell her that they now have Joey's blessing on their relationship.[9]

Why does this represent such a good example of strategic thinking? It is because Chandler finds himself in the position of having to reflect deeply before acting. In doing this he has:

- Contemplated on what his friendship with Joey really means to him, which interestingly he does in silence (away from the everyday distractions of life).

- Reconnected with who he is and what is important to him (his 'story'). To do this he has had to put defensive mechanisms on one side (he is no longer allowed to play the fool, one of his key outward personas) and go into a deeper place within him.

- Evaluated the painful trade-off between his friendship for Joey and his natural desire for the girl. At the end of the day, he can choose one but not both. All important decisions in life involve some form of trade-off, although we often seek to avoid this by attempting to have the best of both worlds!

The outcome of this process is that Joey's anger melts away. 'You have done some *real* good thinking in there' he says and the situation changes. An opportunity for Chandler to keep both his close friendship with Joey *and* his new relationship with the girl arises because he has proven his friendship through his actions. However, this has *only* arisen because of the nature of his actions arising from the reflective process itself. There is the final irony of the fact that he has thought 'outside the box' by being put inside a box!

This story allows us to put our finger on one of the critical factors underlying our ability to think more deeply, putting aside the space for reflection before acting. Within this space we can slow down, observe the situation carefully and choose to act in a way that is not habitual. As we shall see this process is used extensively by organisations such as BP,

---

[9] Friends, 'The One with Chandler in a Box', the Complete Fourth Series, Warner Bros Television.

where it is explicitly recognised as part of the internal leadership model. Paradoxically, the process of slowing down before acting allows us to respond *more* quickly in many circumstances because we have taken the time upfront to really think things through. The key is in becoming conscious of our habitual response mechanisms so that we open up the possibility of new thinking and new potential outcomes. We move from an automatic response to a fully conscious one. Becoming aware of deeply engrained ways of thinking and challenging the assumptions that underlie these patterns is one of the most powerful ways of developing the ability to think more deeply and more effectively.

Defining strategic thinking

There are many aspects to strategic thinking but all relate in some form or other to the ability to see the whole and extract significant patterns from it. I have summarised some of the more common definitions of strategic thinking in the box below along with key aspects of the thinking process that are often termed 'strategic':

Common elements of strategic thinking

- Seeing the 'big picture' or 'seeing the wood from the trees'.
- Thinking 'outside the box'.
- Pulling together the threads into some meaningful whole.
- Thinking holistically or creatively.
- A deeper level of thinking connected with establishing purpose, priorities, underlying values and meaning.
- Working effectively (doing the right things) as well as efficiently (doing the thing itself well).
- Creating synergy where the whole is more than the sum of the parts.
- Being able to take a perspective on things, seeing them within an overall context.
- Looking at the finer detail within a problem, issue or situation
- Seeing in 'shades of grey' rather than 'black and white'.
- Surfacing and working with deeper assumptions, which are often hidden or unconscious (sometimes referred to in organisational theory as 'paradigms').
- The ability to synthesise a range of information, events and experiences and draw meaning and patterns from this synthesis that

---

may not be apparent from viewing each item in isolation.

- The ability to cope with paradox, the simultaneous existence of events or information that appears to be mutually exclusive.
- Acknowledging intuition ('gut feel' or hunches) within the decision making process
- Part of a process that is inherently interactive and dynamic rather than sequential and discrete.
- Understanding the interdependence and connectivity between different parts of a system.
- A mixture of both 'left brain' analytical thinking and 'right brain' creative insight, sometimes described as 'part science, part art'.

At first sight this can seem a bit daunting! However, if we look closely at the key elements above we can see a number of common threads that run through them. These include the following four primary themes:

- Challenging deeper assumptions and beliefs that may be unconscious or hidden.

- Seeing the whole picture rather than simply the parts, including a sense of the connectivity and relatedness of all things.

- Determining patterns within the whole including emerging trends that will shape the future.

- Acknowledging that we have access to deeper parts of ourselves that have wisdom of their own (which we sometimes simply call intuition).

If we bring these core elements together we can develop a definition of strategic thinking as 'a discipline that uses our full capabilities to look at the whole, recognising the interconnectivity and relationship between the parts (including ourselves) and sensing the shifting patterns that lie within'. Since this is a bit of a mouthful we can abbreviate this further to something that is more succinct and has greater impact. Our definition becomes *'strategic thinking is an intuitive ability to see the whole'*. This emphasises a number of important things. Firstly, strategic thinking is *not* solely an analytical 'left brain' process. In its own right, a traditional analytical approach is entirely valid and provides not only intellectual rigour in terms of useful management methodologies but also valuable insight into the resolution of issues and problems at hand. However, strategic thinking is actually much more than this because it is concerned with understanding the whole rather than merely the parts. When we start to look holistically at something we begin to use our creative 'right brain' facilities and it is this combination of both left and right brain capabilities that makes strategic thinking so powerful.

The synergy between left and right brain thinking becomes more obvious when we look at the language that we often adopt to describe strategic or creative thinking, namely that it is a perceptive quality, most often described in terms of seeing. We call a desirable future a 'vision' and somebody with the ability to see the future is 'clairvoyant' (clear sighted). A vision is often described as a 'picture of the future'. We talk about receiving a 'flash of insight' when something becomes clear, or alternatively, being 'blindsided' when something happens that we did not foresee. Indeed, the word 'wise' also comes from a related root and refers to the depth and breadth of our inner vision, of the knowing that transcends the surface level of the mind, dominated as it is by the ego. To possess wisdom is thus the ability to think and act using both inner knowledge and outward experience, a combination of insight and practical common sense. This dovetails nicely into our discussion of the key elements of strategic thinking above.

This may sound a little too philosophical for some of us so it is worth remembering that strategic thinking is also a practical skill that can be nurtured and developed. We do not need to be highly philosophical to become a good strategic thinker, only to recognise how to access the key qualities. In fact, this is a core ability that lies within all of us that we can develop simply through awareness and practice. Whilst it is true that some of us may be more adept at this process by nature it is certainly *not* something inherited as a gift only by the lucky few! Not only is it a core human ability that we all possess but when combined with the capacity to act (something else that can be improved through practice) it becomes very powerful indeed. It is nothing less than our birthright.

Strategic thinking, creativity and intuition

'Every child is an artist. The problem is how to remain an artist once he grows up.'

Pablo Picasso

I am sure that many people will tell me that there are significant differences between what I call strategic thinking, creativity and intuition.

Certainly, the focus of attention and applications may differ. However, all three essentially come from the same source and I believe that it is more useful to think in terms of their common characteristics than the different nuances that may exist between different applications. This enables us to take the large body of work that has been developed on accessing our creativity and use it directly to help us in our task of learning to think more strategically. Indeed, many of the exercises that are designed to help us develop our creativity or overcome a creative block are ideal for nurturing our ability to think strategically. Take something as simple as walking. When I am writing I sometimes hit a creative block and it is often counter-productive for me to remain at my PC hoping that inspiration will leap from the screen. I know from experience that an hour spent walking in the woods close to my house is much more likely to free the creative flow. Spending time in nature, whether in the woods or walking across the hills that surround our village, works equally well for me whether it is in terms of writing, creative problem resolution or formulating new approaches in my professional work. In fact, it works in terms of any creative endeavour. Both strategic thinking and creativity relate to the ability to draw from a deeper well, which is encapsulated in J S Bach's advice to his pupil, Johann Ziegler, that a musician should express the emotion of music in performance, that he should not just play the notes!

Naturally, we are all different and some approaches will prove more fruitful for us than others. The critical element is not what specific form we use to allow us to be more creative but simply the fact that we have opened up a space to tap into that greater wisdom that lies within each of us and the spontaneous insight that it can bring. For some it will be playing golf, for others daily meditation, yoga or simply a regular exercise routine. The key point is that the same process works equally well for developing strategic insight as it does for thinking creatively. Both come from the same inner source. But here comes the rub, while we are prepared to accept that walking, physical exercise or being in nature nurtures our creativity capacity we don't see it aligned with our working practices or decision making processes. Just imagine telling your boss tomorrow morning that you are taking two hours off to walk in the woods in order to deepen your thinking around an issue. The response may be that you ought to seriously consider taking your innovative approach to another organisation. We are locked in organisational practices that encourage shallow thinking, fire fighting and a reactive 'me-too' approach rather than genuine innovation. In return for our efforts we inherit overly busy working lives (going through the same loop again and again), a great deal of stress and even poor health. For many, the bitterest pill is the gradual erosion of any sense of meaning and purpose from work. And it doesn't have to be this way!

A different approach is right under our noses. I spend part of my professional life working with entrepreneurs and the owner/managers of small businesses. All would readily admit that 'intuition' plays a major role in how they make decisions even though defining what intuition actually is proves surprisingly difficult. In discussion, an owner/manager will often refer to 'gut feel' or 'following my hunches' or sometimes, simply just 'knowing' from experience or instinct. In reality, the source for this intuition is exactly the same as for creativity and strategic thinking. However, in the entrepreneurial context, we see this capability expressed in a very practical action-oriented way. It always amuses me when, despite big efforts to introduce professional management practices and processes in the business, an entrepreneur overrides the information and advice in front of them because their instinct points in a different direction. I know of a very successful entrepreneur who directly went against the wishes of his entire senior team and made a major commitment for the organisation that they only read about later on in the newspapers! From a business perspective, however, that decision proved to be particularly successful and none of the senior team would have denied that it was the right one in hindsight. We might call this practical gut feel 'instinct', 'intuition', business 'savvy', a finely tuned sense of opportunity or countless other things. However, the bottom line is that intuition also draws from the same inner well as creativity and entrepreneurs provide a working model of how to integrate a strategic thinking approach into the decision making process. We spend an inordinate amount of time teaching smaller businesses to be more 'professional' but it's about time that we realised that the knowledge transfer goes both ways. Larger organisations have a lot to learn from what is, in reality, one of the most dynamic sectors of economic activity.

Developing a foundation based on humility

> **'The sobering truth is that our theories, models, and conventional wisdom combined appear no better at predicting an organisation's ability to sustain itself than if we were to rely on random chance.'**
>
> *Richard Pascale* [10]

---

[10] Richard Pascale, 'Managing on the Edge: How Successful Companies Use Conflict to Stay Ahead', Penguin, 1990.

'How should companies set about developing the insights that will give them exciting yet practical strategies? The answer is, we don't know.'

Andrew Campbell and Marcus Alexander, Ashridge Strategic Management Centre [11]

It is quite natural if you feel slightly uneasy or sceptical about the strategic thinking process that I have described. It does, after all, rely on an approach that is not completely understood or subject to reductive analysis. For the moment, I ask only that you keep a relatively open mind and reflect on the case studies and stories that support each core discipline that we discuss. It is also worth remembering that creative people of all kinds, whether they are artists, musicians, painters or landscape gardeners, learn to work with their creative muse without necessarily fully understanding it. In fact, it should be very liberating to realise that we can all learn to think more strategically without ever needing to comprehend the process! The singer, Neil Sedaka, for example, apparently never felt fully confident of his ability to write another hit song despite an enviable record of penning classic songs over several decades. The songs came to him as part of a creative process over which he was he had little direct control. Julia Cameron, in her excellent series of books, *The Artist's Way,* [12] sites many similar examples from artists throughout history, with many attributing their abilities directly to a divine process:

'Straightaway the ideas flow in upon me, directly from God.'

Johannes Brahms

'The music of this opera [Madame Butterfly] was dictated to me by God; I was merely instrumental in putting it on paper and communicating it to the public.'

Giacomo Puccini

'I, myself, do nothing. The Holy Spirit accomplishes all through me.'

William Blake

---

[11] Andrew Campbell & Marcus Alexander, 'What's Wrong with Strategy?', Harvard Business Review, November/December 1997

[12] Julia Cameron with Mark Bryan, 'The Artist's Way, A Spiritual Path to Higher Creativity', Tarcher Putnam, 1992.

We do not necessarily have to accept that creativity is a divine process to acknowledge that it comes from a deeper source and is not ruled by the linear thinking patterns most represented in traditional business and management literature. As we saw earlier, business decision making in entrepreneurial and smaller businesses incorporates a strong intuitive element, which derives from the same deeper source. In fact, below the surface level, most organisational decision making includes a surprisingly high intuitive factor, sometimes expressed as learning from experience, but which often simply represents the managers' gut feel about what the best decision may be given past history, a view of the future and the nature of relationships around the decision making area. This is partly, of course, because managers have to make decisions on the basis of limited information and need to 'best-guess' how their actions will affect the system as a whole. Yet, this intuitive element is rarely fully acknowledged. It normally exists in the shadows submerged beneath the logical analytical decision making framework imposed from above. One effect of this is that we have to be relatively senior in an organisation, or be in a designated 'creative' zone (for example, movie animators or designers in the automotive industry) to be allowed to think creatively! And, as we see only too often, creativity in these areas often dries up too with disastrous effects for the organisations concerned.

I recently attended a meeting at my son's high school on the International Baccalaureate (the 'IB'), the two year course that is taken by 16 year old students all over the world who are preparing to go to University. The official mission statement of the IB talks of developing inquiring, knowledgeable and caring young people to help to create a better and more peaceful world through intercultural understanding and respect, all of which is, of course, very commendable. However, what struck me most forcibly during the evening presentations was one of the core purpose statements about the IB; that it helps students 'act responsibly in an interconnected but increasingly uncertain world'.[13] The emphasis on coping with uncertainty, acknowledging both the interconnectivity of the world around us and the importance of acting responsibly is very much what strategic thinking is about. It is very heartening to see this message being put so succinctly to our young people and very encouraging to see their response. If you ever want to see how many restrictions you put around your thinking spend some time talking to young people. If you are anything like me you will be amazed and

---

[13] International Baccalaureate World School presentation, February 12th 2007

humbled.

One of the most powerful ways of developing an ability to see the bigger picture is to give up the illusion that we control the environment around us in a superficial sense and develop a sense of humility about what we can and cannot do, based on our deeper relationship with the world. I am not recommending an attitude of self-defeatism or an excuse to put aside all your dreams about changing your organisation or the world for the better. I am simply making the point that we need to be 'in right relationship' before we can make truly lasting changes. We may go more slowly initially, but we will not have to go through the continual cycle of moving ahead quickly and then crashing back to earth and being forced to begin all over again. Humility allows us to build our foundations securely because we make no false assumptions on what they may have to withstand.

As with any creative process, strategic thinking travels at its own pace refusing to accept the linear time demands of our society. At first, this may appear frustrating. Indeed, given the practical realities of the time-bound world within which we live, it can sometimes drive us to distraction when the insight that we *know* is there simply won't come on demand. However, adapting to working with a much more organic creative process in terms of the way we think is not as difficult as it seems, partly because there is enormous value in learning to do so. We begin by accepting that our decisions will not always be optimal, that sometimes we will fall short of our expectations. This process is very familiar to anyone who is involved in any creative endeavour, who is required to operate within both the commercial and creative worlds. Janis Ian, one of the most respected American singer-songwriters of our generation, neatly summarised this point in a comment made during an interview given to the BBC several years ago:

> **You know, to be a writer, it's to be any kind of artist, and be dedicated to it. It's to have a monkey on your back, and that monkey sits there and if you've finished the best song you've ever written, a couple of mornings later, you're sitting there going either, 'I'll never write anything that good again or you're going, 'Why don't I write this well all the time?' It's always this [way]. That's why we're our harshest critics. It doesn't matter how much anybody else likes a song or a show or a record. It's wonderful if they like it but if it's inferior I know it and it bothers me.**[14]

---

[14] Janis Ian, BBC Radio 2 interview for 'Janis Ian at 50', 2001. See also www.janisian.com

The most important point here is that we are learning to use a process which is new to most of us and has its own natural flow, which is quite at odds with the kind of linear analytical approach which we are used to working with. While we may fall short of our expectations on occasions, this deeper thinking will allow us to develop a much richer perspective over the long term, which not only allows us to see the big picture but to shape and influence it accordingly. By giving up the illusion of control in the short term we enable ourselves to truly shape our destiny over the long term.

A changing world

The analytically-based management decision making process worked well for most of the period after the Second World War because the world was relatively stable and the pace of change moderate. In this environment modelling the system (through budgeting and planning systems for example) and making decisions on the basis of these models increased certainty and made perfect sense. In fact, technology has enabled us to vastly improve our modelling capabilities with consequent increases in organisational efficiency. However, this has come at a cost; it has fostered the illusion that we have far more control over our world than we actually do. It has encouraged us to make decisions that do not take into account the full extent of the consequences of our actions on the world around us (because these are too complex to model easily or invisible to us!); carbon dioxide emissions, pollution and environmental degradation being only three of the more obvious examples.

A quick look at the limitations of mathematical modelling in the financial sector and the impact that this has had on the turmoil in the financial markets in 2007 and 2008 demonstrates only too clearly the practical consequences of an over-reliance on traditional modelling techniques. Roman Frydman, Professor of Economics at New York University talks about forecasters needing to be entrepreneurs rather than scientists. A good forecaster, he says, 'uses quantitative methods, but he also studies history, and relies on intuition and judgement. He is not a scientist.'[15] This again places considerable emphasis on those intuitive processes that allow us to see the relationship of disparate parts within the context of the whole.

---

[15] Source: The Economist, 'Economics Focus, A New Fashion in Modelling', November 24th 2007. See also www.econ.nyu.edu/user/frydmanr

Many of the problems and issues that we are experiencing today are the direct result of the failure to account for what economists call 'externalities', things that happen as a result of our actions for which we do not bear the cost as individuals or organisations. For a while, this cost is born by 'society as a whole' (including, of course, those who had no part in causing the issue) and we do not feel much pain personally. Instead, in a similar way to insurance, the consequences of our actions are shared amongst the many, which dilutes the motivation for us to change our actions. Unfortunately, however, consequences do not simply go away. We are now sufficiently far along this path that the *cumulative* effect of our failure to take responsibility for the whole *is* now beginning to have a direct effect on us as individuals. Whether it is life threatening issues such as crop failure, desertification or lack of water or relatively minor inconveniences such as higher insurance costs, additional waste disposal charges or simply coping with the amount of litter on our city streets, we are all being affected in one way or another in our daily lives. Simply put, our level of thinking is no longer serving us.

At the same time, the world itself has also changed, with the pace of change increasing and the business environment becoming more complex and chaotic. This undermines our traditional way of doing things still further. We have reached a critical point where we need to build new approaches that not only bring a deeper level of understanding of the whole and a more strategic approach to our day-to-day thinking but also manifest in our actions. For those of us our live in the 'developed' world we need to acknowledge that we will be asking other nations and peoples to bear the costs of helping us resolve the issues that we have created, for which they have had no direct responsibility. We would also be advised to take a long hard look at the legacy that we have bequeathed to our children and future generations and to learn a lesson in humility because ultimately they will be required to clean up our mess.

The importance of relationship

Rob Parsons is Executive Director of Care for the Family, a national UK-based charity that is dedicated to promoting family life and helping those hurting because of family breakdown. He stresses the importance of vulnerability within the organisation, the ability to 'get alongside' those who come for comfort, help or advice rather than coming from a position of providing answers. Care for the Family works with that principle in a very practical sense to do the very best that it can for those who come to it. It recognises that people who are hurting don't necessarily need answers, more often than not they simply need somebody willing to listen to them. It is very hard, if not impossible, to genuinely listen to what somebody has to say if we believe that we are in an 'expert' position dispensing advice from above. To get alongside somebody is to be with them without judgement, a place where healing becomes possible. It is humbling in this context to remember the old saying that we can only really help somebody else if we have been 'broken' in the same place!

This same principle very much applies to developing our capacity to think strategically. The biggest obstacle we face is a belief that we are 'above' the situation we are observing, that in some way or other (whether in role, status or intellectual capacity) we are superior to it. As soon as we take on the role of expert we isolate ourselves and limit the insight that flows from acknowledging our relationship with those around us. We have effectively removed ourselves from the 'system' that we are observing and placed ourselves in the position of independent observer. This effectively denies our relationship to the whole and the wisdom that flows from this relationship, the very thing that enables us to see the big picture from the myriad of little things that are evident on the surface. Sir Kenneth Cork, one the most famous insolvency practitioners in the City of London in the 1970's, is a very good example of a gifted strategic thinker in this regard. Sir Kenneth had a wonderful knack of getting alongside all kinds of people who worked at a troubled company, no matter what their official position, rank or status. By doing so, by chatting, for example, with the elevator attendant, he was able to build a picture of what was really happening at the company and what had gone wrong. I doubt that Sir Kenneth would have called himself a strategic thinker, more likely he would have called it common sense. But it is a form of common sense from which we can all learn a great deal.

What we can achieve

Whilst developing our capability for strategic thinking can certainly be frustrating it is immensely rewarding and powerful. In the year 2000, after his defeat in the US presidential election, Al Gore chose to focus on the issue of climate change, a topic which he had felt passionately about from college days. He began simply, by adapting a slideshow that he had compiled several years before into a multimedia presentation on global warming, which he presented across the US and then around the world. As it happens, the presentation in New York City in 2004 was attended by producers Laurie David and Lawrence Bender, who left sufficiently inspired that they met with director, David Guggenheim and talked about the possibility of making a documentary movie out of the show. Initially somewhat sceptical, David Guggenheim attended a presentation and came away inspired not only by the importance of the issues but also determined to do something about it. As he recalls, 'I had no idea how you'd make a film out of it, but I wanted to try.'[16] The resulting movie, *An Inconvenient Truth*, premiered in 2006 and has become one of the most influential documentaries of all time. It is the fourth-highest grossing documentary in the United States to date and the accompanying book, also called *An Inconvenient Truth*, went to the top of the New York Time bestseller list. By May 2007 the movie had grossed $50 million globally and sold more than 1.5 million copies in DVD form.[17] However, its commercial success is not the reason why the movie will be remembered. It has proved to be hugely influential in the debate on climate change and a wake-up call for us to act on the serious challenges that it presents; in short, to begin to take responsibility for our actions in this area.

Al Gore's actions took passion, courage and commitment. It was not obvious in 2000 that he would be taken seriously, in fact quite the opposite might have reasonably have been expected. He started simply, taking and modifying existing work built on the solid foundation of a lifetime passion for respecting the environment. As early as 1989 he began writing *Earth in the Balance*, a book on environmental conservation, which became the first book by a sitting Senator to make the New York Times bestseller list since John F. Kennedy's *Profiles in Courage*. It is very interesting to note that what spurred him into action at this particular point was a very serious automobile accident that nearly killed his six-year-old son, Albert, whilst he was leaving the Baltimore Orioles opening game. At one point he faced the very real prospect that his son may not pull through. He chose to stay near to his son during the lengthy healing and recovery process instead of laying

---

[16] Source: WorldChanging.com, phone interview of David Guggenheim by Alex Steffen, Executive Editor, WorldChanging.com, May 4th 2006. WorldChanging.com works from a simple premise: that the tools, models and ideas for building a better future lie all around us. That plenty of people are working on tools for change, but the fields in which they work remain unconnected. That the motive, means and opportunity for profound positive change are already present. That another world is not just possible, it's here. We only need to put the pieces together (www.worldchanging.com – 'our manifesto').

[17] Source: Time Magazine, 'The Last Temptation of Al Gore', May 28th 2007.

the foundation for a presidential primary campaign and took this opportunity to begin to write the book. At this time, Al Gore could have had no idea of where it might lead and just how important his contribution would be. He knew it mattered deeply and, perhaps, he had a sense that his destiny was wrapped around this issue. As a parent he had faced something which every parent hopes never to face and he had emerged from this crisis with a deep sense of purpose. His story is still in play but already he has helped to bring about a profound change in understanding on what is undoubtedly one of the most important issues that mankind faces today.

The story of Al Gore's work on climate change illustrates a number of the important elements of strategic thinking discussed earlier in this chapter. Firstly, he developed his work incrementally, beginning initially with very simple steps based around amending existing climate presentation material. Secondly, there was a high level of synchronicity; meaningful events that, when taken together, significantly affected the course of his journey, but which were not related together in some simple causal fashion. These were hardly small matters! They included the way in which the future producers and director of the movie came on board and the loss of the presidential election in 2000. And, thirdly he was building on strong foundations, a passion for the subject area built over a lifetime. This allowed him to be both a genuine visionary and make things happen. Simply put, this is something that matters a lot to Al Gore. It may seem on the surface that success came quickly but this far from the truth. As he puts it, 'I feel like a country singer who spends 30 years on the road to become an overnight sensation'.[18] In reality, the pathway was over a much longer time frame, marked at times with pain and trauma. However, it is because of this that Al Gore has emerged as a world leader today, not in a narrow political sense, but in the true sense of the word, as a man who has already profoundly helped to take the world into a more informed place. And he makes it clear that his journey is not yet done despite winning the Nobel Peace prize in 2007. 'It's hard to celebrate recognition of an effort that has thus far failed,' he says, 'but I do genuinely believe that the political system is not linear. When it reaches a tipping point fashioned by a critical mass of opinion, the slow pace of change we're used to will no longer be the norm. I see lots of signs every day that we're moving closer and closer to that tipping point.'[19]

---

[18] Source: Time Magazine, 'The Last Temptation of Al Gore', May 28th 2007.
[19] Source: Time Magazine, 'The Gore Interview', January 7th 2008.

Strategic thinking in action

We can all think strategically, indeed, it is our birthright. How to develop that capacity is, of course, what the rest of this book is about. However, it is worth establishing some realistic expectations at the beginning of the process. I am very careful not to call myself a 'strategic thinker', not least because I am afraid of being put on the spot to provide instantaneous solutions to problems and issues and failing miserably! Somehow, it's not very satisfying to be explaining that strategic thinking is a process around gaining insight when an answer is clearly expected in the moment! It worth remembering that strategic thinking is the antithesis of strategic consulting; it is not based on an 'expert' model but on acknowledging our relationship with the whole. If it were an expertise, we would all be very limited in our development potential since we cannot, by definition, be experts across the board.

Once we are freed of the need to be experts the world opens up, not least because we are free to make mistakes. In fact, the ability to acknowledge and learn from our mistakes is a key part of the process of strategic thinking. How can we broaden and deepen our perception if we insist on always being right! My family and friends can be very quick to point out where I have got something wrong and rightly so. I am lucky that I have strong intuitive skills that enable me to 'join up the dots' and see the big picture but I can also be spectacularly wrong in terms of the timing. I am not somebody who should ever give investment advice. So, even within the frame of strategic thinking there are some things that we will be better at and some that will be more challenging for us. Recognising our limitations is advisable, which is why I go to *other* people to sort out my investments. The wonderful thing is that none of this impairs our ability to develop and improve our thinking skills and put them to very practical use in our personal and working lives. All that is required, in fact, is an open mind.

PART 2

THE SEVEN DISCIPLINES

2

KNOW YOUR OWN STORY

'To me, business isn't about wearing suits or pleasing stockholders. It's about being true to yourself, your ideas and focussing on the essentials.'

Sir Richard Branson [20]

'To thine own self be true and it must follow, as the night the day, thou can'st not then be false to any man.' [21]

Polonius in *Hamlet* (Shakespeare)

Authenticity and success

When I am running a workshop on leadership I often play a tape comprising extracts from the speeches of famous people and ask delegates to identify them. The list includes such obvious leaders as John F. Kennedy, Winston Churchill and Martin Luther King but also less obvious ones such as Woody Allen, James Stewart and Bing Crosby, individuals who have exerted a significant influence throughout their lives. I do this partly to begin a debate about what constitutes leadership but I also have another point to make. Every person is instantly recognizable and the group quickly finds that we share a common view of each one, whether we like the particular individual or not. In reality, we do not really 'know' these people (many of whom were very private people behind their public personas) but we do connect with their story. There is a tremendous power in achieving this clarity and it provides the foundation for effective strategic leadership for those who achieve it. This is true both for those traditionally viewed as leaders such as Winston Churchill and Margaret Thatcher but also for those

---

[20] Sir Richard Branson quoted in an advert for Virgin Atlantic, 2007
[21] William Shakespeare, Hamlet, Act I, Sc.3

who may be seen as leaders due to the influence that they exert during their lives rather than the position they attain or role they play. If Churchill evokes images of steadfastness, compassion and resilience in the face of adversity, Woody Allen has laid a pathway for a whole generation of actors and writers with his brilliant stand up comedy routine and his introspective movie style which contains great tenderness for his characters, however zany or cerebral the plot! In short, most successful people are indefatigably themselves, warts and all; they know and communicate their own story.

In reality, we spend our lifetime discovering who we really are. Some of us are born with a very strong sense of our identity, for others it takes longer, forged through work experience, parenthood, adversity, bereavement or any number of other life events. Our story incorporates both where we have come from (our family, background and history) and what we are passionate about (our beliefs, values, interests, gifts and talents). This combination of our roots and what we truly care about becomes the essence of who we are, expressed through what we are seeking to do in this world. When we have an inner clarity about our story *and* our words and actions are aligned we are able to communicate this to others and influence them. As we saw in the last chapter this is precisely what rock star, Bono, did when he went to Senator Jesse Helms to enlist his support on alleviating the tragic consequences of aids in Africa. Like Bono, we begin draw like-minded people to us; in other words we become a leader. In doing so, we have also fulfilled our two criteria for strategic leadership, clear vision and the capacity to act.

The importance of knowing who we are is best seen from example. If we look at any area of endeavour we see examples of strategic leaders who have this sense of focus and clarity around their story and have forged highly successful and influential lives around it. Let us take at three examples from very different areas.

Google

Google owes its current status as one of the world's leading organisations to its phenomenally successful internet search engine. The company's initial breakthrough was derived from the realization that there was an implicit mathematical order within the seemingly chaotic environment of the internet. Using this insight, through a process of counting, weighing and calculating the structures of the linkages between web pages, Google's founders, Sergey Brin and Larry Page, developed a search engine that was far more effective than its rivals. Google cemented its leadership position by supplementing its superior search algorithms with advertising algorithms that enabled it to make money from the searches that it attracted. Even today, these mathematical strengths lie at the very core of the company and are directly linked with its founders. Both come from mathematical families. Sergey Brin's father was a professor of statistics and probability and his mother worked at NASA, the parents of Larry Page were both computer-science teachers. A love of, and fascination for, mathematics is embedded throughout the organisation. Google uses mathematical puns and riddles in all sorts of places, from puzzles on billboards alongside the highway to attract staff to using mathematically significant numbers in its stock market listings. Mathematics lies at the very heart of the organisation and gives it a clear and unique story. The challenge for Google as it expands into other broader territory (for example, with its acquisition of YouTube in October 2006) is to maintain this clarity and focus. For the moment, however, the deification of mathematics has given it a unique ability to innovate and lead its sector, and provides that special and very distinctive 'googley' culture.[22]

Paddy Moloney and the Chieftains

Leading Irish traditional group, the Chieftains, recorded their first album in 1962 and have since gone on to win six Grammy Awards (and be nominated another eighteen times) an Oscar, an Emmy and a Genie. Arguably, the most influential traditional Irish band in history, leader Paddy Moloney has been at the helm throughout with both an unwavering commitment and passion for the music and the energy to take it across the world to a much broader listener base then anyone would have thought possible in the early days. Paddy Moloney lives and breathes that passion into the music, providing the focal point for other members of the band (who are very talented in their own right) and for the veritable 'who's who' of other musicians and artists who have worked with the group over the years, making it the most popular traditional Irish/Celtic group of our day. It is always tempting to look back in hindsight and attempt to 'explain' this kind of success but this misses the point; it was anything but obvious in the 1960's in a world dominated by rock and pop music. It was the Chieftains who carried the torch, influencing and inspiring countless other bands and

---

[22] For a further discussion on the distinctive 'googley' culture go to the company's corporate information page on www.google.com/corporate/culture.html

singers along the way, bringing their story of traditional Irish music onto a truly global stage.[23]

The Pierian Centre

The Pierian Centre is a management and personal development centre located in a beautiful Georgian square in the City of Bristol in the South West of England.[24] At the heart of the Centre is a simple premise, to look after each and every person who comes through the door. There is also, however, a broader social purpose, to support and sustain the local community (which was one of the most deprived in the city), to build bridges between communities at a wider level and to make the world a better place. The Centre meets both its commercial and social enterprise objectives by offering not only a unique meeting place for businesses with exceptional customer service but also a venue to host a very diverse range of social and community activities that are aimed at supporting, sustaining and healing people and communities. It is both an Art Gallery and a music venue for world music; it supports refugees through Celebrating Sanctuary Week and runs a philosophical debating society. It is even used as a unique venue for weddings at weekends! Such a broad canvas of events shouldn't really work but it does so for two reasons. Firstly, there is an exceptional attention to detail and every person who passes through the Centre is made to feel very special. Secondly, the Centre reflects the passion and drive of its Director, June Burrough, who founded it in June 2002, using her life savings and the proceeds of the sale of her apartment to do so.

June Burrough is a classic example of a social entrepreneur combining the drive, energy and talent of an entrepreneur with an unshakeable passion for justice. She possesses both vision and an enviable ability to act; periodically steering the business along a financial knife-edge, mustering support and resources where necessary, driving the business forward by motivating staff, community and clients alike and always willing to support and act on behalf of the underdog. As a result, she often achieves what appears to be 'the impossible', although, if we look closer, we see the now familiar combination of the visionary ability to see a bigger picture and a strong capacity for action. This is not easy and very few of us have the steely determination, passion and energy to do it. There is also a cost to be paid and it comes from being with the business 24/7. What makes it

---

[23] See also the Chieftains official web site on www.thechieftains.com
[24] See the Pierian Centre's web site at www.pierian-centre.com for more details.

possible, however, is the unshakeable knowledge that June has of who she is and what she is all about. She is a wonderful example of both a social entrepreneur and somebody who knows her own story.

The crucible of leadership

'It seems counterintuitive to suggest that wholehearted acceptance of one's own individual nature is a more profound form of personal growth than change. But most of the people we most admire reached their level of achievement not by changing into somebody else but by embracing their natures fully and using their personalities as instruments of self-expression.' [25]

Nicholas Lore

Embracing our natures fully, as Nicholas Lore suggests in his book, *The Pathfinder*, is the stuff of a lifetime; it isn't easy and it doesn't come quickly. There is a great danger with over simplification in this area. We look at a successful person, notice that they are forceful and determined and get things done and conclude that this is what we should emulate and so make a half-hearted attempt to model these characteristics at a surface level. You know the kind of thing that seminars and self-help books so often peddle – ten easy steps to success, minimum fuss and no pain! The problem is that no matter how wonderful the model, framework or process these are not necessarily *our* characteristics! In fact, not only does the journey to self-knowledge generally happen over a long period of time but it is also often characterized by pain and trauma. It is not accidental that so many of our entrepreneurs are outsiders, fuelled with a determination to succeed on their own terms. As we will see with the story of Sir Richard Branson below, entrepreneurs often fail at school, their talents and gifts unrecognized until much later, and then only on their own terms. The bottom line is that if we are comfortable and successful in the system, that is where we tend to stay; we play by the rules and don't rock the boat!

Rick Jarow, author of *'Creating the Work you Love'* and currently Assistant Professor at Vassar College in Poughkeepsie, New York, teaches about living from the most authentic part of ourselves and learning to express our values and talents through work. When somebody approaches

---

[25] Nicholas Lore, 'The Pathfinder, How to Choose or Change Your Career for a Lifetime of Satisfaction and Success', published by Fireside, Simon & Schuster, 1998

him and explains that they have difficulty in getting a project going or moving towards an aspiration and then asks 'When will I make it happen?' his reply is both simple and brief: 'When you get angry enough.'[26] Simple it may be but it is both powerful and insightful. The fact is that we can't expect to make something happen unless there is some real 'fire in our belly', unless what we're aiming for really means something to us (or there is simply no alternative!). All of us like to daydream occasionally, after all it is nice to imagine what might be possible, but only some of us act upon this and make our daydream into a dream and then into a reality. Those that do generally have one universal characteristic, they share a passion for what they do; it matters a great deal to them.

Warren Bennis and Robert Thomas interviewed more than 40 leaders in business and the public sector and found that all of them, whether old or young, had been through some form of intense or traumatic experience that had transformed them and contributed directly to their leadership abilities. The authors published their results in the Harvard Business Review in September 2002 and called these shaping experiences 'crucibles', after the vessels that medieval alchemists used in their attempts to turn base metals into gold. These crucibles were often seen as trials or tests and took many forms but all required the individuals to question who they were, what they stood for and what was important to them. Some were life threatening events while others much less dramatic, sometimes simply episodes of self-doubt. What they had in common, however, was that they enabled the leaders questioned to create a narrative around the episode and extract meaning from it. In short, they constructed a story of how they were challenged, how they met this challenge and became better leaders. [27]

It is worth pointing out at this point that we are talking about knowing our own story and learning to communicate it effectively in order to make us better leaders, but this does not imply that we become perfect people! In fact, we will probably continue to struggle with the very same life issues that we did before; we remain reassuringly normal! However, one

---

[26] Rick Jarow, 'Creating the Work You Love: Courage, Commitment, and Career – The Complete Anti-Career Book' published by Inner Traditions, 1995 and 'The Ultimate Anti-Career Guide: The Inner Path to Finding Your Work in the World', CD/tape box sets, published by Sounds True 1998/2000. See also Rick Jarow's web site at www.anticareer.com

[27] Warren Bennis and Robert Thomas, 'Crucibles of Leadership', Harvard Business Review, September 2002. For further details see Harvard Business Review online at www.hbsp.harvard.edu/hbsp/hbo/articles/article.jsp?ml_action=get-article&pageNumber=1&articleID=1717

fundamental thing *has* changed in the process; we now have a choice of how to use our growing leadership abilities, for better or for worse. Being a strategic leader does not necessarily make us easy to live with or work for either. Indeed, the reverse may be true since powerful people with a sense of certainty about their mission and objectives in life can be very demanding on others. This is, after all, a big part of how significant changes are achieved. It takes this kind of energy and willpower to move through the many obstacles that need to be surmounted before something actually happens. Steve Jobs is one of the most iconic leaders of our age and Apple has achieved an amazing renaissance under his leadership. He can also be very introspective but it would be a mistake to think that he runs Apple on the basis of consensual decision-making. Make no mistake; it is Steve Job's show, as Time Magazine neatly summed up:

> **'Ironically Job's personal style could not be more at odds with the brand he has created. If the motto for Apple's consumers is 'think different,' the motto for Apple employees is 'think like Steve'. [28]**

Take a little time

We all get a little impatient when somebody says 'it's going to take time'. Our whole society is predicated on almost instantaneous gratification. 'Here' and 'now' are very important words in our language! So, talking about knowing ourselves over a lifetime is going to evoke some resistance. Of course, we can act at the same time, after all part of our growth will come through learning from our mistakes. However, it is also worth remembering that we do not have the complete picture of our lives at any point of time. Rick Jarow tells the story of Henry David Thoreau in his book, *'Creating the Work you Love'*. Thoreau's father was a pencil maker and he initially followed his father into the same business. In fact, he was so successful that when he exhibited his finished work in Boston his pencils were judged to be as good as those made in London, which at that time made the best pencils in the world. However, instead of patting himself on the back and continuing with his career as pencil maker, he stopped and resumed his walks in the woods and with his lifelong fascination with nature. At first his contemporaries were mystified but he would not be turned and 'evolved a lifestyle that allowed him to deeply experience the

---

[28] Time Magazine, 'The Apple of Your Ear', January 22nd 2007

natural world and its wisdom.' [29] From our perspective today, however, his lasting influence is clear and it has nothing to do with pencils! His book, Walden, published in 1854, is very relevant to the environmental issues that confront our world today and his work has directly influenced both Mahatma Gandhi and Martin Luther King. In his Nobel Lecture in December 1964 Martin Luther King put it this way:

> **Our problem today is that we have allowed the internal to become lost in the external ... So much of modern life can be summarized in the arresting dictum of the poet Thoreau: 'Improved means to an unimproved end.' [30]**

Being practical

Not all of us are introspective by nature. Some of us prefer learning by doing. All this talk of 'finding oneself' may seem very arduous, if not just plain navel gazing. There is also the matter of timing, we cannot expect defining moments to turn up on cue just as we arrive at some critical junction and wonder whether we really should be moving forward or changing direction! Epiphanies, by their nature, are rare. On a practical level we may find it more rewarding to use down to earth strategies that can help us develop our sense of personal story over time in practical steps. For example, Herminia Ibarra, who is Professor of Organisational Behaviour at INSEAD, suggests nine strategies that can make a difference over time, varying from simply acting our way into a new thinking to using a strategy of 'small wins', in which incremental gains enable us to make more profound changes in bite sized chunks. [31] She also recommends seizing opportunities that arise, using extracurricular activities to explore and develop new interests and working with people who represent what we would like to be. These are all common sense but good common sense, it turns out, can often change something nebulous into something achievable. The bottom line is that knowing our story does not have to be all about introspection. Indeed, there are a host of small practical steps

---

[29] Rick Jarow, 'Creating the Work You Love: Courage, Commitment, and Career – The Complete Anti-Career Book' published by Inner Traditions, 1995
[30] Martin Luther King, Acceptance Speech for the Nobel Peace Prize on December 11th 1964. The full text and a sound recording is available on the Nobel Peace Prize web site (nobelprize.org) at nobelprize.org/nobel_prizes/peace/laureates/1964/king-lecture.html
[31] Herminia Ibarra, 'Unconventional Strategies for Reinventing Your Career', published by HBS Press, 2004

that we can take to explore different aspects of ourselves and build on our talents, abilities and interests in ways that are incremental and relatively low risk; everything from running a project at work that requires different skill sets to the ones we normally use to taking a hobby to the next level, perhaps by selling products online. In this way lots of small actions accumulate into big changes.

Virgin

I have only met Sir Richard Branson once and it was not a formal introduction. I was visiting his house in Holland Park to meet with a good friend who was, at that time, CEO of Virgin Entertainment. As it was school vacation time, I had taken my eldest son, Scott, with me, who being no more than six or seven was having a wonderful time taking in everything from the underground trains to the busy streets and eateries. When we entered the building Sir Richard was in the foyer talking to a number of Japanese businessmen and as we passed he swung round and offered his hand to Scott and said something like 'and who are we, then?' Scott is mildly autistic and uncertain around social circumstances at the best of times, so was completely taken aback at this unexpected turn of events and quickly disappeared behind my back, steadfastly refusing to come out. And then it happened. In an attempt to coax him out, I uttered one of the most embarrassing things I think I have ever said: 'You should really shake his hand,' I said, 'he's really very famous, you know.' When we finally made our way to my friend's office, he was not very sympathetic, merely muttering, 'Good God, I hope you didn't tell him who you were coming to see.' In my very brief and rather inauspicious meeting with Sir Richard I was struck by two things. Firstly, he is very open and secondly he very normal, very much himself. What you see is what you get, in the most positive sense.

Although much has been written about Sir Richard I don't think that anyone would argue that he is not entirely his own man. That simple, and rather obvious, statement is absolutely critical to understanding his success but it also makes him rather unusual – in fact, more unusual than most of us would care to admit. Of course, we all achieve a degree of authenticity in some areas of our lives, sometimes through our role at work and often by expressing ourselves outside work through our families, friendships, hobbies or interests. However, few of us can really put our hands on our hearts and say we are simply ourselves across all areas of our lives as Sir Richard plainly is. Few of us, for example, could say, as he has done, 'I don't think of work as work and play as play. It's all living.'[32] He has written his story large, across a wide range of businesses and around the globe. And, with his planned space flight business, Virgin Galactic, we might even be tempted to add, 'beyond the world'. Yes, he is larger than life but there is no mistaking who he is.

Detractors of Virgin sometimes claim that it is little more than a ragbag of diverse businesses that have been put together as a result of Sir Richard's opportunistic and entrepreneurial abilities and that, without him, it is unlikely to continue to exist. Virgin management disagrees and Virgin's web site talks of the businesses being held together by the values of its brand and the attitudes of its people. The Virgin brand stands for value for money, quality, innovation, fun and a sense of competitive challenge. It delivers exceptional products and service to customers, through employee empowerment, customer focus and innovation. That, if you like, is the Virgin promise.[33] The reality is that Virgin has created over 200 companies worldwide, employing over 35,000 people with total revenues in 2002 of over £4 billion ($US7.2 billion). It takes more than one man to do that. While it is true that some businesses (such as Virgin Record and Virgin Airlines) have been spectacularly successful while others (Virgin Cola and Virgin Vodka) have struggled, it makes much more sense to view Virgin as a whole and taken as a whole it has flourished. Of course, Virgin and Sir Richard are inextricably interlinked and it makes little sense to look at each separately, so here I propose to focus on the current achievements of Virgin and how this links directly to Sir Richard's story.

Like all famous men and women, constantly in the media spotlight, Sir Richard attracts more than his fair share of 'hero and villain' mythology. On the one hand, he is the hero, lionized for his entrepreneurial abilities, communication abilities and his vision, all of which have made him one of the most popular business leaders in the world. I sometimes do a leadership exercise where groups prepare a leadership Top 10 and Sir Richard is one of the *very* few business leaders who invariably makes these lists. On the other hand, he attracts more than his fair share of detractors,

---

[32] Source: Fortune Magazine, 'Richard Branson: What a Life', an interview with Betsy Morris on September 22nd 2003, available at www.mutualofamerica.com/articles/Fortune/September03/fortune.asp

[33] Further information on Virgin's brand and values can be found on its web site (www.virgin.com) at www.virgin.com/AboutVirgin/WhatWeAreAbout/WhatWeAreAbout.aspx

many of whom can be very cynical about his motivations and achievements and sometimes seem to begrudge *any* acknowledgement of what he has achieved. We should be careful, however, not to confuse myth with reality. I would argue that Sir Richard's success – and that of Virgin – comes directly out of his unique story, that he is neither hero nor villain, but a very real person with a passion both to challenge himself and to make the world a better place. It's a rare combination as it happens, which is part of the reason why Virgin is different from most business organisations around the world. To understand it we need to look at Sir Richard's early years and, in particular, his dyslexia.

How learning disabilities can forge an empire

I remember the first time that somebody took me aside and gently suggested that my oldest son might be autistic. At the time he was about four years old and completely immersed in his own world, toddling from side to side flapping his hands. I was very defensive and refused to even think about it, after all he had always done this and it would pass like these things do. It didn't of course, and in time both Scott, and my younger son, Jamie, were diagnosed with Asperger's syndrome[34], a mild form of autism. In the early years there was little, if any, awareness within the school system of the practical effect of the learning disability on Scott's performance. We wrote letters and battled the system through the years and gradually things changed and support was put in place. Jamie, on the other hand, being three years younger than Scott, has sailed along in his brother's slipstream, with every provision made for him! We are never completely sure whether this is because of our constant battles or because knowledge of learning disabilities has been transformed within the educational system during this time. No doubt, it is a mixture of both. For us, this has been the defining element of our family life and, despite the frequent tussles with educational establishments over the years, a profound blessing for our family. It has brought us very closely together as a family and it has forced us to challenge many of our most cherished assumptions, about initiative, attainment, intelligence and success. It has been tough at times and we have made very conscious trade-offs in terms of work-life balance so that we can support our boys. It has had a direct effect on our career paths, the friends we have made and every other

---

[34] One of the best sources of information on Asperger's syndrome is the National Autistic Society ('NAS'). A good starting point is its web site at www.nas.org.uk

aspect of lives. It is no small thing.

When Sir Richard Branson was at school there was no such awareness of the profound impact that learning disabilities could have on academic performance. He had dyslexia, a condition that causes difficulty with reading and writing, and his school performance suffered accordingly.[35] At the age of eight he could still not read and at 12 he says he had the worst school report ever, 'I was always bottom of the class and I left school at 15. If you have a problem like dyslexia, I think you try to be better at other things'.[36] Although dyslexia is relatively common (with some 40 million people in the US alone affected to a degree) it doesn't make it any less painful to live with. For Sir Richard, it was not just the feeling of being written off but also the inability of his teachers to detect his true gifts, which include an intuitive sense of people and an ability to connect with them on a personal level. I know this from my own son, who has had to work very hard to keep in the academic mainstream but also has a profound intuitive gift with people, which his teachers sense but find difficult to truly appreciate or put in a wider context. But again this is now. When Sir Richard was at school there would have been little or no such empathy or understanding of his disability. We can get a feeling for what it must have felt like from others who have dyslexia and their comments on their schooling and childhood experience.

Living with Dyslexia

- **Jackie Stewart**, motor racing legend and successful businessman, recalls his school days as the 'most painful and humiliating period of my life' and continues, 'When you are being called thick, dumb and stupid, you end up leaning towards others who are like you, who won't humiliate and abuse you.' It wasn't until he was 42, when one of his sons was diagnosed with dyslexia, that he discovered, 'I wasn't stupid at all. It felt like I had been saved from drowning.'[37]

---

[35] There are many excellent sources on dyslexia. A good starting point is the British Dyslexia Association (www.bdadyslexia.org.uk) or Dyslexia Action (www.dyslexiaaction.org.uk)

[36] Sir Richard Branson, 'When I was 12', CBBC Newsround, updated September 27th 2004, available at http://news.bbc.co.uk/cbbcnews/hi/uk/newsid_3694000/3694488.stm

[37] Excerpt of an article by David Leafe published on the Daily Telegraph web site (www.telegraph.co.uk) reproduced by Bright Solutions for Dyslexia LLC, available at www.dys-add.com/symptoms.html

- **Jack Horner**, one of the best known palaeontologists in the United States (and technical adviser for the Jurassic Park films) wasn't diagnosed until adulthood and 'struggled through school being considered lazy, dumb, and perhaps even retarded' before flunking out of college seven times. 'Most people expected I'd wind up working at a service station, or if I was really lucky, I might get to drive a truck at my father's gravel plant. Nevertheless, I guess I've always found low expectations rather liberating. Disparaging assessments just fired my determination.'[38]

- **Tom Cruise** talks about how his dyslexia led him to be bullied and ridiculed at school. 'My childhood was extremely lonely. I was dyslexic and a lot of kids made fun of me. That experience made me tough inside, because you learn quietly to accept ridicule.'[39]

- **Noel Gallagher**, from the rock band Oasis, speaks of his school days as being 'unbearable' because of his dyslexia and says, 'I have problems with words over six letters long. Someone was having a joke when they made me.'[40]

There are countless other examples of well-known people affected by dyslexia including some of the most creative and talented people in history. The list is far too long to even begin to quote here but includes Albert Einstein, Winston Churchill, Thomas Edison, Walt Disney, Pablo Picasso, Leonardo Da Vinci, Whoopi Goldberg and Agatha Christie. They all report similar experiences, of the stigma of being thought to be stupid, of being ridiculed by their peers (and often by their teachers and parents) and the internal resolve that it inspired. Thomas Edison's teachers thought that he was addled, his father thought him stupid and he almost concluded that he was indeed a dunce. Albert Einstein was considered 'mentally slow, unsociable and adrift forever in his foolish dreams' and even Winston Churchill reported that 'I was, on the whole, considerably discouraged by my school days. It was not pleasant to feel oneself so completely

---

[38] Jack Horner: An Intellectual Autobiography, LD Online, available at www.ldonline.org/firstperson/11333
[39] Source: IMDb (The Internet Movie Database), 'Tom Cruise Speaks Out About Battle With Dyslexia' available at www.imdb.com/name/nm0000129/news
[40] Source: IMDb, (The Internet Movie Database), 'Tom Cruise Speaks Out About Battle With Dyslexia' (http://www.imdb.com/news/ni0051583).

outclassed and left behind at the beginning of the race.' [41] All these successful dyslexics have another thing in common; they learned to overcome or sidestep their barriers in order to accomplish their dreams and desires.

I think many people looking at Virgin or Sir Richard miss the point because they attempt to analyze Virgin through the lens of their own perspective, which tends to be a very traditional one. Virgin does not fit this model, even though it has a highly talented management group running the individual businesses. A good friend of mine once told me never to tell people who have been through serious traumas or difficult life experiences that you understand if you haven't actually been in that place. 'Try just simply being there for them' he advised. Similarly, if we haven't lived with dyslexia let's not pretend to understand how it feels. We can, however, acknowledge its importance and begin to look through that lens. We can notice, for example, that Sir Richard has emerged with an enormous need both to challenge himself and change the world for the better. These two things are inextricably linked and it serves no real purpose to attempt to disaggregate them. To ask whether Sir Richard's pledge of £3 billion ($4.3 billion) in 2006 to fight climate change is charity or investment is again to miss the point. It is both because both aspects are critical to success. The charitable and potential commercial elements are closely interlinked and it is in precisely this manner that Sir Richard has been successful in the past, often achieving things that were thought to be 'impossible' at the time. The gesture is undoubtedly genuine because it is coming from that deeper need to improve the world and make it a better place, which is a core part of his personal story. Of course, Sir Richard is a maverick and will do it in his own way, but perhaps that is just as well given the inability of our politicians to martial the resources and commitment necessary to make real changes.

Mavericks make things happen and they do it from the _totality_ of whom they are. Within all of us there are conflicting elements, things that seem oddly paradoxical or ill at ease together, but that is often where the uniqueness is found. Winston Churchill, like Sir Richard, was also a maverick (after all, he crossed the floor of the House of Commons twice during his political career) but in 1940 he had precisely the characteristics

---

[41] The source of these quotes from Thomas Edison, Winston Churchill and Albert Einstein is an excellent article written by Michael Charles Messineo to commemorate U.K. Dyslexia Awareness Week, November 7th – 13th 2005 and is available in full at http://www.authorsden.com/visit/viewArticle.asp?id=19984

that were required to lead the United Kingdom and the wider world against the tyranny of fascism. This included the strong 'masculine' abilities normally associated with leadership (such as mobilizing the war effort) but also an important 'feminine' aspect born of a deep empathy for others, *both* of which were essential to do the job. Both aspects were intrinsically part of who Churchill was so we wouldn't dream of trying to separate them. Indeed, former Prime Minister, Harold Wilson, writes of Churchill as follows:

> **There was his great quality of humanity. The man who could move armies and navies and embrace the world in one strategic sweep could himself be moved to uncontrollable and unashamed tears at the sight of an old soul's cheerfulness in a shelter, or of a street of devastated houses, at the thought of the human realities which lay behind the war communiqués.**[42]

Persistence

What most characterizes Sir Richard is not creativity, vision or risk taking; it is persistence. I sometimes ask groups to give me just one word that best describes an entrepreneur and it takes some time, and usually a little prodding, before somebody suggests persistence. This is followed quickly by an almost palpable feeling of let down, 'oh, is this it?' 'Isn't there some secret ingredient, you know, one of those kinds that can make us all rich without any risk or effort? But the capacity to continue to try to do something, find new avenues and new approaches, accept failure time and time again and still not give up, this is a very rare quality indeed. And Sir Richard has it in spades. How many times do we do something before giving up? How many times do we allow ourselves to be rejected before concluding that maybe we aren't cut out for this after all? I guarantee that the answer for most of us is 'not many.' It is much easier to quote Henry Ford's dictum, 'failure is simply the opportunity to begin again, this time more intelligently', than to live it! Persistence is that special ability to continue towards our goal despite all signs that it may never happen! It is not born out of an intellectual appreciation, nor is it achieved by benchmarking others. It comes from deep experience, often from living through traumatic experiences where we learn the hard way how not to

---

[42] Harold Wilson, 'A Prime Minister on Prime Ministers', published by Weidenfeld & Nicolson and Michael Joseph, 1977 (copyright by David Paradine Histories).

give up. If we look at Virgin through these eyes, we can see that a conventional analysis of business profitability throughout the group will not provide the key to understanding and neither will noting how many failures have happened along the way. The key lies in understanding that Sir Richard is exactly as he appears to be, neither sinner nor saint, but someone who has forged a hugely successful career out of his early traumatic experience. He is a man who knows his story and lives it.

This is not small stuff. We have a tendency to reverse engineer success and place too much importance on specific events. Knowing, for example, that Virgin Records' first release was Tubular Bells by multi-instrumentalist, Mike Oldfield (which sold two million copies in the UK and 15-17 million copies worldwide) we might be tempted to conclude that Virgin had its fair share of luck in the early days. This may be true (but only if we ignore all the challenges that the business faced at the time!) but it is, of course, *not* the reason for Virgin's early success. Once again, we need to look at Sir Richard's extraordinary persistence and determination to change things for the better and it is these characteristics that created the opportunity in the first place. That is precisely why Virgin signed Mike Oldfield when the album had already been rejected by the major labels at the time. After all, a multi-instrumental concept album by an unknown artist was pushing the boat out quite far even by standards of the early 1970's. I suspect there was also a sense of kinship between Sir Richard and the artist, both men with a sense of being outsiders, which may have initially cemented the relationship. Small things often provide clues and the original album sleeve of Tubular Bells pokes fun at record label conventions by replacing the standard statement on stereo sound with a much more irreverent message, something that would be core to Virgin's culture and brand over the years.

Tubular Bells – Taking a Dig at Record Label Convention [43]

In the early 1970's, stereo albums normally had a message on the cover that the album could also be played on old mono record players, which would normally read something like:

'This stereo record can be played on mono reproducers provided that either a compatible or stereo cartridge wired for mono is fitted. Recent

---

[43] Source: Wikipedia, 'Stereo record joke', from the article on Tubular Bells, available at http://en.wikipedia.org/wiki/Tubular_Bells

equipment may already be fitted with a suitable cartridge. If in doubt, consult your dealer.'

Instead, Tubular Bells had the following text printed on the bottom of the cover:

'This stereo record cannot be played on old tin boxes no matter what they are fitted with. If you are in possession of such equipment please hand into the nearest police station.'

The comment on the sleeve is classic Virgin and part of its maverick nature. But again, it is often mavericks that change the world, people who do things their own way and see it through. It can be tempting to point to fortuitous circumstances, luck or opportunism to explain the success of others. There is a degree of envy in all of us. However, the story of Sir Richard and Virgin reminds us that some of our best leaders create their own luck, and they do it by coming from a position of knowing exactly who they are and what they want. They know their own story.

Story-telling in the wider world

It is not only individuals who can benefit immensely from knowing their own story, living it and communicating it effectively to the outside world. The same is true of organisations, particularly when they want to communicate with the broader world outside the sphere of traditional financial reporting. Naturally, maintaining a clear and coherent story is harder at organisational level because of the size and the complexity of the environment in which they operate. However, the ability of an organisation to tell an interesting, consistent and meaningful story, to construct a sensible narrative around its activities, is becoming much more critical in areas ranging from the ability to raise capital to recruiting the best employees, particularly when there is a need to pitch to a much wider audience, well beyond traditional stakeholders.

Organisations often try to be all things to all people, customer-responsive to those who use their services or buy their products, profitable for stakeholders, responsive to the environment and so on. Look closely, however, at many of our most successful companies and we find a great deal of clarity about what they represent. Apple is about sleek, innovative and empathetic design driven by customer functionality. Starbucks is about providing a space for its communities; a meeting place for customers, a selling space for growers and an enabling space for the communities around it. Google, as we have seen, is about the application of mathematics. Wal-Mart's story of low prices emerged from the desire of its founder to provide good quality, low priced, everyday goods to ordinary folk. In each case, it is easy to summarize precisely what the organisation is about in one sentence and often without reference to the product or service it sells. Look at organisations without this focus and we see another story. Sainsbury's, the third largest supermarket chain in Britain, is ... well what is it exactly? It carries a premium food range compared with some competitors but not compared to others. It has relatively low prices but, again, not as consistently low as either of the two market leaders. Its brand is supported by a strap line that struggles to bring some kind of differentiation to the store. Both 'try something new today' and its predecessor, 'making life taste better' give very little idea of what the company is all about. Overall, there is a strong sense of 'me-too' in both its proposition and aspirations. In short, it has no distinctive story. That matters, because without a sense of identity it is difficult to build strong customer loyalty and when things get difficult financially, as they do for all organisations at some point of time, it is very difficult to weather the storm.

Ideas into action

There is a story in Indian folklore about a lion cub that is orphaned when his parents are killed by hunters. Luckily he is taken in by some kindly sheep and raised as part of the flock. As our lion cub grew he learned to eat grass, bleat and frolic in the meadow with the other sheep, and by the time he was a teenager he was especially keen to behave like all the others so that he could fit in. Then, one day a lion suddenly appeared causing terror in the flock. All the sheep fled, leaving only the lion cub. The lion looked at the cub with both a puzzled and disdainful expression on his face. 'How can you behave like this,' he asked, 'cavorting like a sheep, you are a disgrace to our kind!' 'What do you mean?' replied the lion cub, now all but fully grown. 'Am I not a sheep?' The adult lion took pity on him and showed him his reflection in a pool of water. 'You see now who you are' he said, 'you are born to run, hunt and roar!' A memory stirred for the lion cub and without thinking he opened his great mouth and roared, and when he did so he recognized himself.

We have looked at just how powerful it is when individuals and organisations know their story and communicate it effectively. It is one of the key aspects of strategic thinking because it enables us not only to articulate our vision (what is most important to us) but also gives us the energy and self-assurance to act upon it. Simply put, when something matters to us we put a lot more energy into it. Our sense of power is closely connected to our sense of who we are. We all do this to some extent, particularly in areas where we are confident and passionate. However, we can work with our story over time to improve our self-awareness, clarity of purpose and capacity for action. One way that this brings immediate reward is in increasing our ability to say 'no' to things that are not aligned to our deeper purpose and capabilities, releasing both time and energy for things that really matter to us. But it is more than this; it is coming into realization of just how powerful we really are when we are aligned with our deeper sense of who we are, when we realize that we are not sheep after all but lions!

Practical tools

There are a great many practical tools for improving our self-knowledge. Some are reflective, others more analytical. Some we can do on our own, others are better in groups. Some can be done in isolation; others build together as part of a more structured programme or sequence of activities. What works for you will depend on who you are. If you are reflective by nature you may find a workbook of exercises and reflections insightful. One common exercise that you may come across is the lifeline where you identify the high and low points of your life and then plot them on a chart to see if you can determine the threads and patterns that underlie your experience. If you learn by doing, you may find it easier to take on new tasks and projects, extend your networks or interests or simply give something new a go, learning by what works and what doesn't. If you are like me, you may prefer to walk across the hills with a small notepad and jot down what occurs to you. Nature is a great instructor for me. However, there is no set way to do this, only an intention to become more knowledgeable over time in whatever way suits you best.

There is also great synergy in working with other people. Many of the greatest insights of my life have been brought to my attention by other people and have come literally as bolts from the blue. Many years ago I attended a course on moving your career into a deeper sense of purpose.

In truth, interesting as the course was, I did not find it particularly illuminating. However, towards the end we were asked to do a brief meditation on what mattered most to us in our career and then discuss it in pairs. Having duly finished, and with no dramatic insight to announce, I suggested politely to my partner that perhaps she might like to talk first about her experience. And talk she did. Out popped what seemed like a perfectly manifested career and the more enthusiastically she talked the more my heart sank. Not that I wasn't happy for her at one level but I would have to go next! Finally, the time came and I was fully resolved for defeat. 'So,' she said, 'and how about you.' By now fully demoralized, I remember blurting out something like 'nothing, absolutely nothing ...the only thing I could think about was my kids.' My partner remained quiet and waited expectantly. It was then that the full meaning of my words hit me like a thunderbolt, something so obvious that it had been under my nose all the time, if it were not for the fact that I had been looking entirely in the wrong place.

I would like to tell you that the experience left me elated but shock would be a much better word to describe it, together with a distinct feeling of being rather daft as if I were the only person in the world not to see something so plain. Since that time I have moulded a portfolio career around my family with my wife, Tracy, and I taking turns in acting in the principal care giver role, albeit that she did by far the most challenging period in the early years. I cannot claim that this has happened as a result of a well-considered strategic approach but it has made a very profound difference to my life in all ways.

3

THINK SMALL

'As with sex,
So with lies.
Intention matters
More than size.'

Jane Miles[44]

The illusion of size

Most of us are conditioned to believe that bigger is best. Yet, when the Prince of Wales founded The Prince's Trust in 1976 he took a very different approach. By providing small loans and grants to some of the most disadvantaged youth groups the Trust has been able to make a significant impact on the lives of many thousands of young people each year. In 2004/05 alone it supported nearly 42,000 young people (generally aged between 18 and 30) providing training, personal development, business start-up support and mentoring and advice. It has grown to be the leading youth charity in the United Kingdom and one of the most effective in any field. Its success is partly due to its small scale funding approach, much of which is in the form of low interest loans, which must, of course, be repaid. During 2006 these loans varied from £2,000 to £5,000 with grants available in special circumstances up to a maximum of £1,500.

At the heart of the Trust's work is a dedication to help each individual who applies, not only through funding but also through effective mentoring and support. In this the Trust reflects the Prince of Wales' strong belief in working at an intimate human scale and his passion to make the world a better place by developing deeper and more balanced

---

[44] Jane Miles, 'No Added Sugar, Poems by Jane Miles', published by St Andrew's Press of Wells, 2006 (for availability, please call 01749 672477)

responses to problems. The Prince of Wales comments, 'I have always felt that to have helped just one person to put their life back on track would make it all worthwhile.'[45] If the Prince's Trust runs on a human scale, where the welfare of each person is critically important, there is nothing small about the vision that underlies it.

'This sense of what is sacred has helped to shape my understanding of the mysterious nature of the human soul; of our shared humanity, and of the untapped potential of so many. Perhaps it is this which lies at the heart of the work of my own Trust. Over nearly twenty-five years The Prince's Trust has sought to find ways in which to help young people who are often hopelessly adrift in society and with nowhere to turn; to help rebuild in them that sense of community and common endeavour which I believe are so necessary to enable our society to tackle effectively the wounds of despair and desperation which afflict so many of our fellow human beings.'

The Prince of Wales [46]

The Trust lives and breathes these principles in its work. Support is targeted at those who are most disadvantaged including the unemployed, those underachieving in education, young people leaving care and young offenders and ex-offenders. It now includes those still at school who are at risk of exclusion because of behavioural problems, truancy or other issues. It is also remarkably effective, with nearly 80% of young people supported moving into employment, education or training, which has further significant benefits to families and communities around them. Since 1983 the Trust has helped over half a million young people including 60,000 set up in business. By 2003 the top fifty businesses turned over almost £150 million and employed around 2,300 people. In addition, the Trust currently has a network of over 8,000 voluntary business mentors to enable it to do its support work. There is nothing 'small' about what can be achieved from building a vision step by step, maintaining passion and focus in every small thing that we do. In fact, it is precisely this passion that is invested at the smallest level that allows the vision as a whole to manifest.[47]

One business that owes its existence to the Prince's Trust is Fish

---

[45] The Prince of Wales in an exclusive interview with Radio Times ('A Family Affair'), May 20th -26th 2006

[46] The Prince of Wales quoted by David Lorimer in 'Radical Prince: The Practical Vision of the Prince of Wales', published by Floris Books, 2003

[47] For more information on the Prince's Trust see its web site at www.princes-trust.org.uk

Records, an online specialist supplier of singer-songwriter, folk and acoustic music run by Neil Pearson. In addition to running one of the leading specialist retail sites in the UK, Neil is also actively involved in managing the Shrewsbury folk festival and helping overseas artists, particularly from the United States, distribute their product. All this was made possible by an initial small loan of £1,500 from the Trust, albeit followed through by plenty of entrepreneurial ability and a lot of hard work. Neil's comment on the Trust is simple and telling, 'I wouldn't have set up Fish Records without them.' For his part, Neil now offers support through the Trust to other young people seeking to start a business. [48]

The way in which Neil Pearson has built Fish Records also exemplifies the principle of thinking small. When we first met he was operating from his tiny spare bedroom, at the centre of which was the PC that he used to run his business. His stock of CD's was on shelves all around us, a very limited space indeed that provided a very powerful incentive to keep inventory levels under control! He has developed the business step by step with very high levels of individual customer support, a personal touch (orders currently contain small bags of candies as a thank you) and a huge passion for the music. 'Small' in this context means not over-extending the business in the early years, attention to detail, maintaining focus and allowing important relationships to grow organically. Indeed, developing relationships is a critical determinant of long-term success and results primarily from word of mouth within the industry, itself a by-product of living the values of the business day by day through countless small acts. As Neil says, 'relationships don't just happen, you can't find them ... you can't make them happen ... they come to you.' One particularly important example of this is the relationship that Neil has forged with Bob Harris, one of the leading radio presenters in the UK. This initially came through a customer contact as a result of sourcing an unusual disc and it demonstrates one of the most important rules in 'thinking small.' Never underestimate the significance of any small act; you never quite know the broader picture and where it might lead!

---

[48] I have known Neil Pearson since the early days of setting up Fish Records and he is an exemplary example of how to set up a small business successfully. Full contact details are available on his web site at www.fishrecords.co.uk. The comments in this section came from a conversation with him in early 2007.

The business perspective

Strategic leadership is about vision but it is also about attention to detail, about focusing absolutely on the next customer, next client or the smallest of details on a new product design. This is deeply paradoxical and it is difficult to live but our best organisations do exactly this. Toyota 'reinvented' the global automotive industry through its famed just-in-time production system and it is this 'individualisation' of the production process (the associated empowerment of employees working in this way) that lies at the heart of its strategic leadership of the industry. This perspective is deeply embedded within Toyota and manifests in unexpected ways. A receptivity to small changes – which are often indicative of much larger emergent changes – lie at the heart of why Toyota (along with fellow Japanese company, Honda) has focused much earlier than competitors on growing concerns around environmental sustainability and now has a significant technological lead in the development of the next generation of 'green' cars.

When recognition of the importance of getting 'small' things right is deeply embedded within an organisation's culture, as it is with both Toyota and Honda, it results in the organisation being more adaptive, flexible and innovative. It is, for example, part of the reason why the Honda Accord was so successful in the United States (it was one of the first cars in the US to have a coffee cup holder) and why Toyota is experimenting with systems that disable the engine if the driver is too drunk to drive (an innovation very much in line with current social concerns about drinking and driving, which may well yield the company a competitive advantage). Treating every small action with a high level of attention often lies at the heart of process driven innovation just as attention to small anomalies and unusual feedback often alerts an organisation to deeper and more significant changes that are emerging within its industry or marketplace.

Close attention to detail is also an essential part of the 'grounding process' that enables a long term vision to evolve and manifest itself in reality. It is easy to sit together with friends one evening over a bottle of wine and solve all of the world's problems but it is much more difficult to actually do something the next morning in the cold light of day! As we have seen, strategic leadership requires both vision and the capacity to act and this capacity to act is always expressed in the next small thing that we do. It is the *accumulation* of small acts that makes a 'big thing' possible. Strategic leaders have the capacity to engage fully at both levels simultaneously, holding a vision while energising each individual small act;

in other words, they think big and they act small at the very same time.

Changing the world one step at a time

It is by acknowledging the importance of simultaneously thinking big and acting small that we give real power to our desires to change the world. An overarching vision behind what we do is critical because it provides the motivating force for us to make significant changes by weaving a powerful story that gives meaning to our individual actions. However, we also need to see ourselves successfully achieving small practical steps along the way if our direction is to be affirmed; it is this 'success on the ground' that keeps the vision alive. As human beings, we need a sense of firm practical progress, tangible results that we can achieve in the short term to motivate us on our journey. We need to be able to connect the dots between the grand design and what we are working on at this very moment. If we cannot relate our day to day tasks, no matter how humble they may appear to be, to this bigger picture, it will simply cease to have meaning for us. If we look closely at our most successful organisations, whether in the commercial, public or not-for-profit sectors we find this connection in the level of attention to the small things. It is there in the greeting by the barista in one of Starbucks coffee shops as it is with a teacher sitting with a child with learning disabilities taking another approach to explain something during the break time. Starbucks excels one coffee at a time just as a high performing school excels one student at a time. Strategic thinkers are there in the moment, fully attentive to what is before them irrespective of the size of that matter. One cup of coffee is not more important than another and one child is certainly not more valued than another. Strategic leaders look to the future but live in the moment.

Small acts of kindness

Don't say 'it's only a drop in the ocean.' The whole ocean is made up of drops.

Mother Teresa

There is a universal principle that reinforces the power of small acts. When we come from a place where we are fully realising our individual identity we come into contact with part of ourselves that transcends the ego and links us directly to the wider world. It is that part of ourselves where we share our common humanity and are linked with everyone and everything else. This is why the most specific acts are often also the most universal (sometimes known as the 'law of specificity'). Think of how we might connect with one of Beethoven's piano sonatas, a song by a singer-songwriter of a broken love affair, a picture by Turner or a 'simple' story told by a child about what they did over the previous weekend. On the other hand, the more generic the subject matter, the less we connect. We might care very much about the fate of whales but a two hour PowerPoint presentation providing statistics on illegal whaling is very unlikely to draw an emotional connection.

Yet one seven tonne northern bottle-nosed whale that swum upstream in the River Thames in January 2006 certainly did. For a short time Britain was galvanised by the fate of one single five metre bottle-nosed whale. This specific event connected at a universal level in way that discussion of the 'big whaling issues' never could. As one observer commented, 'I thought I should go and see it but I then got in a taxi and was heading somewhere else … I then thought, you just live your life … you've got to come and see that whale.'[49] It is for the same reason that practicing 'small acts of kindness' has the capacity to change the world, it is not the size of the act that matters but the intention and when that intention is aligned to a deeper level of authenticity it is very powerful indeed. Multi-million selling acoustic jazz artist, Norah Jones, used a similar theme to this with great effect when advertising her first album, with copy that read 'sometimes, in a room full of shouting a whisper is the loudest voice.'[50] Strategic thinkers never underestimate the great power that lies in the specific, regardless of the apparent size of the act.

Amazon

Amazon is more than simply a successful online retailer. Along with eBay it has become one of the most iconic organisations of the internet generation, trail blazing a path that has not only brought online retailing into the consumer mainstream but has also proved its financial viability. It is easy to forget that financial analysts waited with baited breath after the 'dot-com' bubble burst so see whether Amazon could turn a profit. In the

---

[49] Source: BBC News online. The full story is available at
http://news.bbc.co.uk/1/hi/england/london/4631396.stm
[50] Source: Billboard Magazine advertisement promoting, 'Come Away With Me', Norah Jones, 2001, available on Parlophone (Capitol Records)

fourth quarter of 2002 it finally did so, generating a meagre profit of $5 million, small but symbolically important. With sales of some $14.9 billion in 2007 (and a trading profit of some $476 million) it is now a global internet powerhouse with some 17,000 employees. No one could accuse Amazon of being small; either in size or ambition. However, the underlying reasons for success lie as much in the attention given to each small aspect of the business as in the overarching vision. Both aspects come directly from the strategic leadership of Jeff Bezos, its founder and current CEO, and are inseparable in practice. From the very beginning Bezos saw Amazon as 'the world's most customer-centric company' and he has continually emphasised six core values to achieve this goal; customer-obsession, ownership, bias for action, frugality, high hiring bar and innovation. Both goal and values emphasise a responsive listening culture which places individual customers at the heart of the business model.

Jeff Bezos founded Amazon in 1994 as an online bookseller, which provided customers with a single place on the internet to search available stock and order books directly. The company grew very quickly and soon broadened its original aim of becoming 'Earth's biggest bookstore' to becoming 'Earth's biggest anything store' by diversifying into a broad range of products including music, videos, toys, electronic goods and clothing. What did *not* change, however, was its culture or ethos, which remained obsessed with serving customers and gaining market share even at the expense of short term profits. Amazon did this not only by keeping prices very low but also by building distributed intelligence networks that now lie at the heart of its business model. In order to provide intelligent choice for customers across the huge range of products and continue to keep prices competitive it has built sophisticated market trading and customer feedback systems that have revolutionised the retailing function well beyond the company itself. Many aspects of this development have been genuinely innovative (such as the application of 'one click' ordering), while the company has also shown a great capacity to learn from and absorb successful aspects of other businesses (the most conspicuous example being the adoption of aspects of the auction-based trading model of eBay).

Amazon is attracted to distributed intelligence systems because it comes from such a strong customer perspective. Centralised knowledge-based systems are expensive to develop and can quickly become inflexible, with the danger of reducing rather than increasing customer choice. In a traditional retailing model, for example, limited shelf space (the physical equivalent to inflexible data systems) has meant that media sellers have been very discriminating about what they release and promote, generally using intensive marketing on a very limited number of popular titles. This 'big hit' approach is less relevant to Amazon, which sells approximately one third of its book sales *outside* the top 130,000 titles (the capacity of the largest physical bookstore). As a result, Amazon has developed a plethora of ways to promote a much broader range of titles including customer reviews, recommendations (using collaborative filtering to analyse past purchases), linkages between purchase patterns ('customers who bought this item also bought'), easy search facilities and the ability to access further information on an existing or related artist or author's work quickly and easily. The result is to make obscure items profitable by aggregating demand and exploiting what economists call 'long tail economics', which in simple terms means encouraging a customer to explore the history of an artist, author or movie producer and purchase previous works (or those of similar artists). Much of the information that customers rely upon is in the form of other customer reviews, resulting in a very positive customer loop with high levels of trust and brand loyalty. Amazon's total business may be large but each customer transaction becomes the focal point of intelligence for the system as a whole.

The effect of this approach is dramatic for two reasons. Firstly, it significantly changes the core retail model. Instead of Amazon having to try to second guess what customers want it can concentrate on making the broadest range of product available for *customers* to decide what they want. Secondly, it provides an incentive to ensure that there are good navigation trails for customers to use so that they can move easily and knowledgeably through the huge amounts of information. Chris Anderson, who is editor-in-chief of Wired, a technology magazine, summarises this process by concluding, 'you need not just variety, but information about variety … a long tail without good filtering is just noise.'[51] Because this 'filtering' information often derives from third parties it keeps the business system firmly customer focused and decentralised. And Amazon continues to innovate in this area. In 2005 it began to add 'wiki' features (the use of an open source model to update information) to its product database, allowing any customer who had purchased at least one item from the company to edit a section of each product page. It has since extended this in other areas, launching a collaborative wiki for user-generated content in early 2007 related to the products that a customer likes the most.

---

[51] Source: The Economist, 'Economics Focus, Profiting from Obscurity', May 7th 2005. This article references 'The Long Tail', an article by Chris Anderson, editor-in-chief of Wired, published in 2004, available at www.wired.com/wired/archive/12.10/tail.html

3. Think Small

'Retail is detail' is a time honoured adage of the retail industry and simply means that successful retail requires constant attention to all the 'small' aspects of the business that together make the retail proposition. The emphasis is on optimising each single element of the retail proposition in day to day operations regardless of size, whether it is the quality of individual customer service, queue waiting times, shelf stocking disciplines, the friendliness of returns staff, the authenticity of a 'greeter's' smile or toilet cleanliness. Amazon, like all good retailers is exceptionally aware of the importance of detail, using technology and customer feedback to build exceptional online customer service. In many ways, it has defined the retail experience online and has become the benchmark for other online retailers to follow. In particular, the decision by Amazon to allow third parties to compete with it, selling through its own product pages, was an extraordinary move at the time, one that was controversial even within the company. Ultimately, it has provided customers with greater choice and better value, made Amazon as a whole more competitive and intensified the underlying strengths that the company enjoys through its infrastructure and systems. It has also further decentralised the customer facing operations, now often in the hands of third parties, bringing in their detailed product knowledge and experience into the system. It further emphasises the 'collegiate structure' of the organisation, where individual customers and traders all make a vital contribution to the knowledge of the organisation as a whole and help police standards through the feedback process. This produces a self reinforcing virtuous cycle, where long term success is predicated on a high level of attention to each small transaction and the resulting accumulation of knowledge, trust and customer loyalty further strengthens Amazon's brand and business.

It is not only the customer facing systems at Amazon that are decentralised. Jeff Bezos has always pursued the idea of a decentralised organisation where small autonomous groups are free to innovate and test their ideas independently and he came up with the famous notion of the 'two-team pizza', if you can't feed a team on two pizzas the team is too large. In practical terms this limits teams to five to seven people, which not only ensures effective decision making but safeguards the company against becoming too internally focused. This strong company focus on the external environment (particularly customers and competitors) rather than the internal comes directly from its founder and is deeply embedded in Amazon's culture. As Jeff Bezos puts it, 'some people are internally focused, and if they reach critical mass they can tip the whole company.' Small autonomous teams help Amazon avoid this all too familiar fate. In addition, this structure fosters an attitude within Amazon to test and challenge assumptions, particularly when decisions are 'fact-based', which not only promotes initiative but also enables more grounded and objective decision making. Again, this can be traced directly back to the founder:

'The great thing about fact-based decisions is that they overrule the hierarchy ... the most junior person in the company can win an argument with the most senior person.'

Jeff Bezos, President and CEO of Amazon [52]

In the early years of online retailing there were many organisations that could have emerged as market winners, one of which was the highly successful book retailer Barnes & Noble. When it launched its online site in 1997 there were many who forecast that Amazon would soon be soon eclipsed, including Forrester Research who famously predicted that Jeff Bezos' venture would be 'Amazon.toast'.[53] In fact, Amazon has gone from strength to strength and now operates retail web sites on behalf of companies such as Target and Sears Canada as well as being the host site for many others including the large book retailer, Borders. It is continuing to diversify its product portfolio by moving steadily into non physical product categories such as music and movie downloads and DVD rentals. However, perhaps the most symbolic achievements to date are the co-ordination of the massive sales and distribution events that happen each time a new Harry Potter book was released. In June 2003 Amazon *pre-sold* over 1.3 million copies of 'Harry Potter and the Order of the Phoenix' worldwide, with some 250,000 delivered to the customer on the first day of release in the US alone, matching a similar number of first day deliveries for 'Harry Potter and the Goblet of Fire' in June 2000. 'Harry Potter and the Half-Blood Prince' set a new record in July 2005 with *advance* orders of some 1.5 million worldwide, 919,000 of which were ordered through Amazon.com alone, paving the way for the largest single product distribution in Amazon's history. This record was smashed again when the final Harry Potter instalment, 'Harry Potter and the Deathly Hallows', was released in July 2007 when pre-orders exceeded 2 million copies.

---

[52] I am indebted in this section to an article by Alan Deutschman, 'Inside the Mind of Jeff Bezos', which is a fascinating and informative read (and from which the quotes are sourced). The full text is available at FastCompany.com (Issue 85, August 2004) at www.fastcompany.com/magazine/85/bezos_1.html

[53] Source: Alan Deutschman 'Inside the Mind of Jeff Bezos' as above.

Distributed intelligence

'Significant changes always arise from lots of small, almost invisible changes.'

Eckart Tolle[54]

Part of the reason for Amazon's success lies in its decentralised systems and the use of distributed intelligence as the backbone of it knowledge base. As we have seen this allows Amazon to excel at process driven innovation, whether the ideas have been developed internally or adapted from other organisations. Since Amazon is an externally facing organisation it is particularly good at keeping abreast of what is happening in its industry and the wider world and quickly incorporates developments that can support or enhance its business. In a similar manner, eBay, the world's largest online auctioneer, operates a collegiate structure based around the combined knowledge brought together by all the traders and customers who participate in the auction process. This has made it one of the truly iconic web pioneers and a formidable business as we shall see when we discuss it in relation to the importance of focus and keeping things simple in chapter seven.

Wikipedia, the online encyclopaedia that is written collaboratively by volunteers provides a third powerful example of distributed intelligence. Created in 2001, Wikipedia has quickly become the largest multi-lingual free content encyclopaedia on the internet and an outstanding example of the successful application of an open source business model, since almost all the articles can be edited by anyone. By June 2006 Wikipedia was getting more visitors each day than the New York Time's site and in early 2007 it was able to boast of over 75,000 active contributors and over five million articles, available in more than 120 languages. Like Google before it, it has achieved the ultimate accolade of business success, becoming a verb as well as a noun. It seems that no research topic can now be completed without the need to first 'google' the subject and then to 'wiki' it – no matter how 'sniffy' academics may be about the reality of the matter! Three or four years ago I used to warn my growing high school boys that internet research required more than simply clicking on the first thing that appeared on a search engine. These days the superior algorithms that underlie search engines have significantly improved the quality of searches and the relevance of the best matches found. And one

---

[54] Eckart Tolle, 'The Power of Now', published by Hodder and Stoughton, 1999

of these best matches is inevitably a Wikipedia entry, which has now become the backbone for so much of the school-based research that my sons do.

This is a far cry from initial expectations in the mid 1990's when it was widely expected that it would be Encarta, developed by Microsoft, which would be the natural successor to the Encyclopaedia Britannica. Indeed, the early reaction to Wikipedia was scepticism that the standards of the content would able to match that of traditional encyclopaedias (compiled 'top down' from a central pool of expertise) or even remain accurate! However the collaborative system has proved remarkably robust in both maintaining high content standards from its wide body of contributors and as a self-policing system. Even though there are still limitations in scope and accuracy of some of the content, Wikipedia is very open and upfront about limitations that exist, which reinforces trust and usage (the scope of research can always be extended or checked elsewhere). In addition, the fact that content available from Wikipedia is largely freely distributable and reproducible has proved an enormous boon to teachers, students and parents alike, throughout the course of the entire education journey from elementary school to university! The wide spread adoption of Wikipedia by teachers is one of the strongest competitive advantages that the system possesses and has produced another example of a virtuous cycle as this loyalty is passed through usage from teacher to student and, vicariously, to parent!

While it is clear from these examples just how powerful distributed intelligence systems can be in promoting constant innovation and process driven change (incremental improvements to the way that we do things over time) it is perhaps less obvious that it also plays an important role in alerting organisations to deeper and more significant changes that are emerging within their environment. The larger the pool of contributors the more likely it is that some will spot small anomalies and unusual feedback from the environment, and this is often the forerunner of much larger changes. These oddities can be evaluated and the subsequent learning from the process can be integrated into the system from the 'bottom up'. This is a very powerful way of increasing adaptability and flexibility within organisations but is nothing new. There is an old adage in English that points to the importance of looking carefully at things which act in a contrary manner to generally accepted expectations: 'the exception proves the rule.' Interestingly, the modern interpretation of this adage (that exceptions should be expected so we need not be unduly concerned) is exactly opposite to the original meaning, where 'prove' meant to test! The adage actually means that exceptions test the rule and by examining these exceptions we are able to see whether the rule still applies or whether we need to develop a new understanding that more accurately reflects a changed environment.

Ideas into action

'Never doubt that a small group of thoughtful, committed people can change the world. Indeed, it is the only thing that ever has.'

Margaret Mead.

We have seen the power of 'thinking small' in entrepreneurial, corporate and web-based environments but it is equally appropriate to other contexts including not-for-profit and public sector organisations. A particularly good example is the additional educational needs support at the high school that my sons attend in Wiltshire, England. St John's School and Community College in Marlborough is a large split site school with some 1,500 students with an enviable academic record, a very positive learning environment and a happy student body. It has developed a very strong reputation as a caring school that sets high academic standards in a disciplined environment, but what sets it apart is the emphasis placed on the individual child at the centre of the teaching and learning experience. At one level this should be obvious but the difference with St John's is that the school lives its values, using a broader curriculum that includes helping children develop a sense of values based on respect for self, their peers and the community and environment around them. As part of this strong emphasis on the individual child the school attaches a great deal of importance on supporting additional educational needs across the broad educational spectrum from children with special learning needs to those who are particularly gifted and able. As all teachers know there is no simple template that can be applied in this area! My youngest son, Jamie, for example, is classified as both 'special needs' (as he is mildly autistic) and gifted and able! That is the reality of seeing each child for who she or he truly is and helping them to fulfil their potential.

When I met with Toni Brodie, the Director of Teaching and Learning, to discuss how the school achieves such a high level of individual learning support I was fascinated by how much of our discussion was around themes that are reflected in this chapter. We talked about the core objectives of her role, which are to ensure inclusiveness and achievement and to promote independence in all children by providing support for each one in the most appropriate way. The underlying touchstone of our conversation was around respect for every single person and the foundation of her work is very much at the individual level, preparing each child to take responsibility for themselves in a complex and uncertain world, starting with the school learning environment that they are in right now. Toni Brodie is incredibly passionate about her work and this undoubtedly gives her the energy to make things happen and deal constructively with the inevitable resistance to change that occurs within a school of this size, just as it does in any large organisation. In common with all strategic leaders she has the capability to hold a compelling vision of the future and act fully in the moment, giving it her complete attention. This has nothing to do with the size of the matter at hand but whether it is focused on core purpose; improving the teaching and learning experience for each child in the classroom and within the context of the school as a whole.

There is nothing 'small' about Toni Brodie's vision for the future. As part of her specific remit she is quickly moving the school forward in building more effective additional learning support across the board and changing structures and systems where necessary. However, at a broader level she is seeking to make a dramatic shift of the learning process from the traditional model based on a homogenous learning process for all the students to one where each child is fully recognised as an individual and the learning process is personalised accordingly. This is a huge shift in thinking, not least because it moves from a place where both students and teachers are comfortable to one which is much less so for both parties, requiring students to take far more responsibility for their learning and teachers to adapt accordingly. To make this vision a reality, however, each teacher in the school must be firmly focused on managing and optimising the learning environment in their classroom, in other words providing the most solid foundation for the individual learning process at the most specific personal level. This also provides a solid practical foundation for driving forward positive changes in the way in which children experience their school life, the extent to which they feel included and their ability to achieve their potential. In other words, each child will only experience a difference if the vision is matched by practical action and commitment on a day by day basis.

Anyone who has worked in a school will know how difficult it is to make significant headway in an environment where teachers already have very high demands placed on them. Toni Brodie has already made a dramatic difference in the two years she has been with the school (although, like many people with the capacity to make a real change she minimised her achievements during our discussion and concentrated on what she feels still needs to be done). She has managed this through her passionate belief in having a vocation, of being called to be a leader, her high energy levels and a very great deal of hard work. She also has the complete support of the Head Teacher, Dr Patrick Hazlewood, who is deeply committed to continuously improving the teaching and learning environment at St John's and establishing the school as a clear strategic leader in its field and as a national example of best practice. Both teachers care very deeply about what they do and share a sense of evangelism about honouring the greater potential of each child and putting in place the environment and processes that will allow them to reach their potential. Both talk of working towards a more collegiate structure ('a hotbed of collegiality') where levels of hierarchy might be reduced and staff at all levels have a more equal say in decision making to help achieve the best teaching and learning environment. They also both share an incapacity to sit still and rest on previous achievements. Like so many strategic leaders they have a strong sense of mission but an acceptance of the day to day challenges that need to be surmounted to achieve this mission. They shoot for the sky but live in the real world. When I asked Toni Brodie what her aspirations were for the future, her reply was simple, 'my own school'.[55]

Making a difference

'If you ever think you're too small to be effective, you've never been in bed with a mosquito.'[56]

Anita Roddick

Once we accept that there is no such thing as a small act we no longer have to worry about whether we can make a difference, we know we can. There is a powerful philosophical concept called the holographic universe, which argues that the wisdom of the entire universe is contained within the smallest element. Just for a moment accept that this is true. It puts an end to any meaningful discussion of the concepts of 'big' and 'small', all that is left is the intent with which we do something. Most of the strategic

---

[55] Further information on St John's School can be found on its web site, www.stjohns.wilts.sch.uk

[56] Although this quote is normally ascribed to Anita Roddick, founder of the Body Shop, I have also seen it attributed to Wendy Lesko, the Executive Director of the Youth Activism Project in the United States.

leaders that I know have never heard of the holographic universe but they act as if they had. They combine that rare ability of seeing a better way of doing things at the same time as giving full attention to what is immediately before them, the next small step along the way. They are passionate and energised because they believe they can make a difference. And because their actions are grounded in reality, they do.

4

GO SLOWLY

'There is so much to do; there is so little time. We must go slowly.'

Taoist saying

The tortoise rather than the hare

Of all the concepts in this book, the idea of taking things more slowly is perhaps the least intuitive. All around us is the clamour to achieve *more*, to be more efficient in the time we have, to fit more things into our life. The idea that we should slow down and do less seems to be completely at odds with our modern world. Yet, it is one of the most important concepts in this book, for the alternative is to slip further into the collective madness that is so destructive to our world. We would be wise to concentrate less on more *efficient* approaches to doing things and more on more *effective* ways of achieving our aims and objectives, in other words, finding the right solution in first place. Ironically, the result of our preoccupation with time efficiency is that we often embark on projects that have destructive side effects at a systemic level, which we have to cycle back and deal with later. Short term decision making without due foresight translates into long term systemic problems.

Enshrined in 'The Toyota Way', is the principle, 'make decisions slowly by consensus, thoroughly considering all options; implement decisions rapidly.'[57] Toyota is one of the largest and most successful global

---

[57] I am indebted throughout this section to Jeffrey Liker, Professor of Industrial and Operations Engineering at the University of Michigan, whose landmark book, 'The Toyota Way: 14 Management Principles from the World's Greatest Manufacturer', published by McGraw-Hill in 2004, explores how these 14 core principles create a culture of continuous learning and improvement at Toyota and underlie its success. The quotes in this section from the 14 principles are taken from his summary (and are also available on Wikipedia at http://en.wikipedia.org/wiki/The_Toyota_Way). Further information on Jeffrey Liker is available on his home page at www-personal.umich.edu/~liker

companies today and it has always looked to the long term. Its leaders understand the importance of taking time within the decision making process to reflect on the broader consequences of action taken today, and that beginning in haste does not necessarily win the race, especially if it results in going off in the wrong direction and having to begin again! This is captured in another principle in the 'Toyota Way', one that it very familiar to us, 'work like a tortoise, not the hare.' This principle of taking time to think ensures that decisions taken by Toyota reflect its deeper values and underlying purpose and are consistent with accumulated experience and learning. It does *not* mean that we will not make mistakes, rather that we can learn from those mistakes as part of a conscious process, adapt and move on. Soichiro Honda, founder of Honda, expressly linked this reflection to an iterative process of learning as follows, 'success ... can be achieved only through repeated failure and introspection. In fact, success represents 1% of your work, which results only from the 99% that is called failure.'[58] As the Japanese economy has languished over the last 15 years it has become fashionable to assume that western corporations have absorbed all the big lessons to be learned from Japanese business practice. As we shall see when we look in more detail at Toyota and Honda below nothing could be further from the truth.

Taking a longer term perspective

Take a moment to think about the environment in which you work. It is highly probable that you are very busy and quite likely that the boundary between work and personal life is becoming ever more porous. It may be that you feel stressed and over-worked by this or it may be that you are one of those fortunate people who actually thrive in a busy chaotic environment. However, there is one aspect of your working life that you are almost certain to share with others, a growing frustration with the amount of unproductive time associated with activities that are not core to what you are there to do. At one level, there are the administrative requirements that have always been a feature of large organisations such as meetings, internal emails, reporting and legal requirements, health and safety matters and so on. What is much more debilitating is the cost of constant fire fighting and changes in direction, often implemented through

---

[58] Source: Edward de Bono and Robert Heller, www.thinkingmanagers.com, 'Japanese Business Culture: Soichiro Honda, manager and entrepreneur.' The full article is available at www.thinkingmanagers.com/management/japanese-business-culture.php

the most dreaded word in business, a new 'initiative', combined with a tendency to use technology to micro-manage all aspects of organisational decision making. This internal control orientation together with increasing complexity in the external environment often means that the process of managing change has become formalised within the organisation, adding yet more levels to decision making. In commercial organisations things are bad enough (one look at email traffic is normally a good indicator of the problem) but in the public sector it has reached the level of an epidemic. Scott Adams, the creator of the Dilbert cartoon, and an astute observer of trends, ends one of his cartoons with the line, 'never before has so little been measured so much'[59], and this nicely sums up the frustration of many working in the public sector today. Ironically, our single-minded pursuit of productivity without a deeper reflective process has resulted in a work environment that is actually becoming *less* productive as well as unrewarding, since it is often devoid of underlying meaning or purpose. In the public sector, where work still means a sense of vocation for many, this can be absolutely soul destroying.

Decision-making is also becoming increasingly short-term in a world that calls for deeper *long term* thinking to resolve complex structural and systemic issues. This is also reflected at a broader level within society where, despite increased wealth and higher standards of living, there are increasing numbers of people who feel isolated and disconnected, effectively cut out of the community altogether. Given the complexity and scale of some of the problems we now face, at political, environmental and community levels, as well as within the commercial world, we need to redress this balance urgently. We might begin by recognising the importance of focusing on long term thinking, which implies having an implicit sense of direction, based on our core sense of purpose and values. In other words, we need to take a deep breath, pause and go slowly. In doing so we may find the strength and clarity to begin to dismantle some of the control structures that are increasingly strangling us. Only then will we find that we have the space, time and emotional stability to tackle the more deep rooted issues and problems that we face. We will finally have the opportunity to look in the shadows and find the solutions that lie hidden there. All we need then is the courage to do so.

Ironically, once we have put a more reflective thinking process in place

---

[59] Although I am not sure which of the many Dilbert compendiums contains this particular cartoon all are highly recommended! A good starting point for more information on Scott Adam's work is the official Dilbert web site at www.dilbert.com

we can make specific decisions very rapidly indeed, because we don't need to do extensive analysis and review on every small thing. This is the very opposite of so much of the 'rapid fire' decision making that is happening today, which is based on a very superficial understanding of the bigger picture and the need to meet short term deadlines. We can also develop one of the most important strategic abilities of all, the capacity to say, 'no'; 'no, we are not doing that because it is not within our strategic remit.'

Establishing firm foundations

'Planning is an unnatural process – it's so much more fun to do something. The nicest thing about not planning is that failure comes as a complete surprise rather than being preceded by a period of worry and depression.'

John Harvey Jones [60]

It is common now to draw a distinction between planning and strategy. Planning may be defined as a structured process of looking at the future, normally associated with the formulation of steps necessary to achieve an objective, whereas strategy is a process rooted at the deeper level of understanding on what makes an organisation unique and how this uniqueness can be translated into advantage in the marketplace (or in the case of not-for-profit organisations, into the way services are provided into the community). Strategy is thus often expressed in terms of three basic questions:

- Where are we now?
- Where do we want to be?
- How do we get there?'

It is not difficult to see that in order to answer these strategic questions we need to adopt a more reflective thinking process in order to access a deeper level of understanding. In reality, however, the distinction between strategy and planning is somewhat artificial because the starting point in *both* cases should be addressing the question, 'where are we now?' It is our understanding of our present environment that provides the solid foundation necessary on which to move forward. And, of course, this is the

---

[60] Source: John Harvey Jones. See also his classic texts, 'Managing to Survive', published by Arrow Books in 2003 and 'Making It Happen: Reflections on Leadership', new edition published by Profile Business in 2003

stage that we are most tempted to skip! If we are heading to Paris (our objective), fully equipped with city street maps (our detailed plan) but don't know where we are starting from we won't get very far. This is the point at which we need to invest time, to slow down and look more deeply at where we currently are and determine our overall sense of direction. In doing this we begin to look at time more as a compass rather than a clock.

Reframing our understanding of time

A clock gives us the linear measurement of time that we are most familiar with, something that the Greeks called 'chronos'. Clock time measures the movement of minutes, hours and years and is the kind of time found in our diaries where things are marked as 'urgent'. This linear sense of time reduces our ability to think because it does not encourage reflection, let alone time actually spent not 'doing' things (an essential part of a process of deeper thinking). We live in a world dominated by clock time, which is partly why our society seems more concerned with efficiency (the productivity aspect of what we do) rather than the effectiveness of our actions (whether we are doing the right thing in the first place). We are besotted by the modern mantra of 'saving' time, although, ironically, the more time we save the less of it we seem to have! In fact, at a deeper level, the more we concentrate on managing the scarcity of time, the more likely it is that we will experience being time pressured in our daily lives. Sadly, despite all our clever inventions the truth is we cannot save a single moment of time, we can only choose to live in each moment and experience it. As the old aphorism says, 'Yesterday's the past, tomorrow's the future, but today is a gift. That's why it's called the present.'

The Greeks have another sense of time, which they call 'kairos' and it is best described in the form of a compass, since it gives a sense of direction or trajectory that is aligned to the underlying sense of who we are. We experience it when we recognise something is 'important', often from a space where we are 'being' rather than 'doing'. Being in this space allows the possibility of transformation, of developing new ways of thinking and acting. However, we are not necessarily in control of this process and this is difficult for us to accept in our control-dominated world.

Try this exercise. Take a couple of hours off one morning to walk in the park or in some other natural environment. Before you leave think of a problem or issue that you would like to work on and simply put it at the back of your mind. Then take a small notepad and a pen and let the matter drop away. Just enjoy your time in the fresh air. As you walk, thoughts will come to you, some of which may appear to be relevant to the issue in hand and others that may not. Jot down anything that seems important, relevant or not. I cannot promise that you will definitely find a concrete solution to the specific issue or problem that you have highlighted but you will be amazed at just what does come to you! Even if you find yourself thinking about other matters entirely, don't dismiss them too readily. What you draw to you may reflect a deeper truth; that there are other areas of your life that need to be addressed *before* you can resolve the specific issues or problems that you chose to think about.

Kairos also means the time (or the moment) when we respond to a situation and take a risk, trusting our instinct to move us forward even though our common sense (and even our detailed analysis) may tell us to hold back. This kind of time cannot be measured like clock time because it works in different way. Rather than being driven by the clock, we sense that there is a right and significant moment for action or change. Entrepreneurs do this all the time since they often have an astute sense of timing, of sensing opportunities in the moment. In fact, for most of us intuition plays a very significant role when we are making important decisions, especially those that matter to us most. Indeed, the more difficult and complex a decision is, the more likely that we will make it using our 'gut feel'. We may thoroughly research our new DVD player but ask an office colleague out on a date on the spur of the moment! Shakespeare expresses the same sense of intuition and 'right timing' in the words of Brutus in the play, Julius Caesar:

> 'There is a tide in the affairs of men,
> Which, taken at the flood, leads on to fortune;
> Omitted, all the voyage of their life
> Is bound in shallows and in miseries.
> On such a full sea are we now afloat;
> And we must take the current when it serves,
> Or lose our venture.'
>
> *Brutus in Julius Caesar (Shakespeare)* [61]

We are often faced with a decision between something that is urgent and something that is important and, sadly, most of us normally respond by addressing the issue that is urgent. However, there are times when we override our cultural conditioning and chose what is important. It is the

---

[61] Julius Caesar, Act 4, Scene 3

time we watch our son play soccer when we know we will miss our report deadline. It is the occasion when we call an old friend we haven't spoken to in years when we know that the ominous rain clouds will put an end to cutting the overgrown lawn in our backyard. It is the moment that we admit that we are wrong even though it means going back to square one. Behind these decisions something important is going on and it is this that we need to capture consciously in our day-to-day decision-making. It is in this space where we slow down and take time to reflect that we find the key to thinking long term.

The National Trust

No organisation demonstrates more clearly the advantages of long term thinking than the National Trust, which is one of the largest conservation organisations in the world and has one of the largest charitable membership bodies in the United Kingdom. Set up in 1895 the National Trust preserves and protects coastline, countryside and buildings in the UK on a permanent basis. In addition to owning thousands of properties throughout England, Wales and Northern Ireland it also has significant land holdings of over 600,000 acres (nearly 1,000 square miles or 2,500 square kilometres), which cover nearly 1.5% of the total landmass of the country including 600 miles of coastline in England alone. It has a total income of some £250 million a year, which includes membership subscriptions, legacies, enterprise income (catering, retail services, licensing and holidays) and appeals and gifts. This makes it a very significant organisation in its field in terms of size and resources alone, resulting from its conspicuous success in becoming one of the most trusted organisations in the United Kingdom today. The need for the National Trust to plan for the long term and balance conflicting demands (for example the tensions between conservation and access) has made it an exemplary demonstration of reflective thinking in a complex environment. We can learn a lot from its approach.

As an independent charitable body the National Trust is freed from both the politicised position that accompanies being critically dependent on government funding and the short term reporting requirements of publicly quoted commercial organisations. As a result, it is able to take a much longer-term perspective that is strongly aligned to its core purpose and values (in a very similar manner to Toyota and Honda below). In addition, because its mission is relatively simple and adaptable it is able to be flexible and change without losing its core identity. However, it is the principle of permanence, more than anything else, that lies at the root of the National Trust's long term orientation and makes it so unique. This sense of permanence is captured in its strap line, 'forever for everyone', in addition to being stated specifically in its general purpose statement:

The National Trust shall be established for the purposes of promoting the permanent preservation for the benefit of the nation of lands and tenements (including buildings) of beauty or historic interest and as regards lands for the preservation (so far as practical) of their natural aspect features and animal and plant life.

National Trust Act 1907, paragraph 4(1)

An important corollary of this long term orientation is an enormous attention to detail within the National Trust and a wealth of practical experience about balancing the conflicts and tensions that go to the heart of our attempt to both live in harmony with our natural environment and to make our mark upon it. As a result, the National Trust now has an increasingly important role in education, including areas such as studying the effects of climate change, recognising the significance of an area or building within its community and passing on the practical knowledge and experience that comes with balancing conflicts and tensions between the natural environment and human aspirations. There are, for example, few organisations that are faced with a decision to let their natural assets erode away, as the National Trust is with respect to areas of coastline threatened by significant erosion by the sea. As a result, there is a profound depth of experience in the organisation; both in terms of managing core processes and in the quality of thinking that underlie the choices made. Far from being an organisation obsessed with the maintaining the status quo the National Trust is, in fact, managing a complex process of change, not only in terms of influencing attitudes towards the natural environment and our historical heritage but also in determining what our legacy will be to future generations. This is anything but simple stuff!

These are areas of interest both to society as a whole and also to commercial organisations, which are increasingly being asked to demonstrate their awareness of their corporate social responsibilities. This is far more subtle than it appear at first sight. It is easy to see that the experience and capabilities of the National Trust will be relevant to housing corporations, which are being pressurised to build new developments on a more environmentally sustainable basis. However, it may not be quite so obvious that the work that the National Trust does on studying the impact of an area or building within its community (resulting in a 'statement of significance' for each one) is useful for any organisation that is looking at the process of establishing its impact on the community around it. In particular, the National Trust is adept at looking at the full costs and benefits of different policy approaches that specifically include externalities (those economic effects of decisions and choices not reflected in market prices), which many commercial organisations are only just beginning to get to grips with.

Government also has much to learn about how long term improvements can be achieved in social areas, where the political process itself so often sabotages long term sustainable gains. As a public institution the National Trust is used to being in the media spotlight and being criticised for some of its actions. However, it is salutary to think of what might have happened if the work of the organisation had been taken over by government at some point of time. The success of the National Trust (and other bodies like it) offers a wealth of opportunity to learn how aspects of public service provision might be improved, including the importance of focusing not just on the grand design but on the small steps of implementation. The National Trust not only works successfully towards its long term mission but it also does small things extraordinarily well. It does this without compromising its purpose and vision because it recognises that grand social projects take time, *lots* of time, and are judged on progress made step by step. The short term decision making process is tightly linked with its long term aims and guided by them. The most significant example of this is what is known as the '50 year rule', which is applied to any new purchase that the National Trust makes. In essence, what this rule says is that before any acquisition can be made, the organisation must have sufficient funds available to maintain it for 50 years, determined by a conservative formula that includes a significant contingency for potential but unknown costs at the time. This approach is an anathema for most governments, which remain fixated on what can be done in the short term, normally in relation to the period of time before the next election. The long term perspective that lies at the heart of the National Trust points to a much more effective way to maintain aspects of our social and community services and environment than the short term policy orientation of many government bodies.

There is also much to be learned from an organisational culture where 85% of people who work for the National Trust say that they are proud or very proud of the organisation and what they do. This is particularly true in public sector where many people are starved for the recognition that they do what they do as a vocation rather than simply a job. I have yet to find a single teacher or nurse who is motivated solely by the financial rewards of their position! There is another critical point too. When I met with a colleague, who is a senior member of the legal team in the National Trust's Head Office in Swindon, I finished our discussion by asking him what he considered to be the most important threat to the organisation. Almost automatically, he replied, 'climate change', but then stopped and reconsidered. 'No,' he said, 'that would affect us all ... loss of trust ... that would be devastating.' He is absolutely right because the National Trust can continue to do what it does only if it maintains the high levels of trust that it has established in members, employees and within society as a whole. There is a deep lesson that can be drawn from the National Trust's success in maintaining this trust, which it has achieved partly through its vision of a better world, partly by focusing intently on each small element of the execution of its strategy and partly by 'thinking slowly' and building strong foundations for long term sustainable change. In a society where we are rapidly losing our trust in our political institutions and public bodies there is a great deal to be learned here indeed.[62][63]

Toyota and Honda

Toyota and Honda are among the largest and most successful organisations in the world. In 2007 Toyota had revenues of some $203 billion and net income approaching $14 billion. Honda had revenues of some $94 billion and net income of approximately $5 billion in the same period. In the first quarter of 2007 Toyota outsold General Motors for the first time selling 2.35 million cars compared with GM's 2.26 million. It is expected to formally overtake GM in 2008 to become the world's largest automotive company by annual sales (a position that GM has retained since 1931 when it passed Ford) but this is largely symbolic as Toyota has maintained a position of strategic leadership in the industry for many years. Toyota's famous 'Total Production System' was dubbed 'the

---

[62] Extensive further information on the National Trust is available on its web site, www.nationaltrust.org.uk

[63] My thanks to Tim Butler at the National Trust for his invaluable help with this section.

machine that changed the world'[64] and its principles have been widely adopted throughout and beyond the automotive industry. As the Economist bluntly put it, 'it taught the modern car industry how to make cars properly.'[65] At the heart of the production system there lies a determination to eliminate waste and an absolute concentration on consistent high quality by a process of continuous improvement (called kaizen in Japanese). One the best known aspects of this system, the 'just in time' inventory strategy that caused so much attention in the west in the 1980's, was actually introduced by Toyota on a full scale basis as early as 1938, just one year after the company was itself established.

In addition to its world-leading manufacturing base Toyota excels at rapid product development and maintaining very high levels of customer satisfaction, both key indicators of customer loyalty. The company has also developed a culture that motivates employees to consistently hit demanding targets in the constant pursuit of excellence. This relationship between management and employees is much more than mere words. It results in uncompromising customer and product standards, which puts Toyota models consistently at the top end of customer satisfaction surveys. Although there has been a significant shift away from the concept of a job for life in Japan, reflecting similar social changes in other countries, Toyota still emphasises the long term partnership between management and employees as one of the key elements of its success:

> **Management should take care of employees, encouraging them to work lively, respect their rights and give them an environment that makes workers want to work ... Japanese manufacturing is generally trouble-free, high quality and has a good finish ... loyal employees make good products. There is a certain reason why Japanese cars have high quality. If we fired employees recklessly, the quality of our cars would drop.**
> *Fujio Cho, Chairman and Representative Director of Toyota* [66]

Like Toyota, Honda also commands enviable customer loyalty based on similarly high standards of production and customer satisfaction. Its

---

[64] James P. Womack, Daniel T. Jones and Daniel Roos, 'The Machine That Changed the World: The Story of Lean Production – Toyota's Secret Weapon in the Global Car Wars That Is Now Revolutionizing World Industry', published Free Press (Reprint Edition), March 2007
[65] The Economist, 'Special Report, Toyota: The car company in front', January 29th 2005
[66] Kiyoshi Tsukamoto, 'Toyota-to-Honda' (Toyota and Honda), reviewed by Takanori Kobayashi in an article in Japan Today, 'Corporate Culture, One Key to Success of Toyota, Honda', available at www.japantoday.com/jp/book/99

legendary founder, Soichiro Honda, established strong engineering and production values, which are reflected in Honda's corporate vision statement, which is refreshingly practical:[67]

1. Quality in all jobs – learn, think, analyse, evaluate and improve
2. Reliable products – on time, with excellence and consistency
3. Better communication – listen, ask and speak up

Although Honda's roots lie in engine manufacture and its success is arguably due primarily to leadership in the technology of the internal combustion engine (it manufactures a diverse range of products including marine and jet engines, scooters and lawn mowers) it is best known for its highly successful expansion into motorcycles and cars. Indeed, its success in penetrating the US market has become the basis for one of the best known business school cases of all time. The early explanations of Honda's success (founded on traditional economic reasons such as scale economies) have quickly given way to a realisation that it was Honda's culture and adaptability that enabled it to succeed. Hard work mattered far more than strategy, a point neatly summarised by management writer, Richard Pascale (currently an Associate Fellow of Oxford University) when he described Honda's story as one of 'miscalculation, serendipity and organisational learning'.[68] Interviews that Richard Pascale had with managers at Honda about its initial entry into the motorcycle market back this up with comments such as 'in truth we had no strategy other than the idea of seeing if we could sell something in the United States', and, more poignantly still, 'we were entirely in the dark for the first year.' When a break finally came it was not for the big bikes that Honda had hoped to sell but for the 50cc run-arounds that Honda employees were using to run errands around Los Angeles!

Honda's later successful entry into the US automotive market with the Civic in the early 1970's shares a similar pattern. Few took Honda seriously as a competitor (the same fatal mistake that the British motorcycle manufacturers had made earlier) and many laughed at the idea that the small Civic could possibly compete in North America. This mental blindness

---

[67] Source: Edward de Bono and Robert Heller, thinkingmanagers.com, 'Japanese Business Culture: Soichiro Honda, manager and entrepreneur.' Full article available at www.thinkingmanagers.com/management/japanese-business-culture.php

[68] Richard Pascale, 'Perspectives on Strategy: The Real Reason Behind Honda's Success', California Management Review, Spring 1984. For further information on Richard Pascale see his web site at www.sbs.ox.ac.uk/faculty/Pascale+Richard/Pascale+Richard.htm.

is captured humorously by Richard Rumelt, currently Professor of Business and Society at UCLA when he describes how the US automotive industry misjudged Honda. In 1977 he set a final MBA exam on the Honda Motorcycle case and asked 'Should Honda enter the global automobile business?' He calls it a 'giveaway question' and continues that 'anyone who said "yes" flunked.' Conventional wisdom dictated that markets were saturated, efficient competitors already existed and Honda had little experience in automobiles and no automotive distribution in the US. He finishes his story by stating that 'in 1985 my wife drove a Honda.'[69]

At the root of the success of both Toyota and Honda lies a capacity for long term thinking that is based not simply on the practice of manufacturing high quality products and services but on making a unique contribution to society in doing so. The remarkable philosophy called 'The Toyota Way'[70] summarises the managerial values and business methods that have given Toyota a source of competitive advantage as a result of the values, beliefs and business practices that have arisen over the years based on this core principle of making a unique contribution to society. If we look at the language used in the 14 principles of the document we can very clearly see the explicit long-term orientation, a commitment to organic growth and continuous improvement and a decision making process that incorporates a strong emphasis on reflection (thinking before acting). Seven of the 14 principles are centred around achieving effective production processes rather than efficiency (under the heading 'the right process will produce the right results') and this includes an overt recognition that innovation depends on bringing problems and issues to the surface and resolving them as part of day to day practice. In other words, organisational learning is driven by bringing root problems into consciousness by identifying, understanding and resolving them rather than trying to fix them after the event. For illustrative purposes, I have

[69] Source: Richard Rumelt, , Professor of Business and Society at UCLA, reported by Henry Mintzberg, Bruce Ahlstrand and Joseph Lampel in 'Strategy Safari: A Guided Tour through the Wilds of Strategic Management', published by Free Press in 1998. Different Interpretations of Honda's US success are discussed further in 'the Many Hands of Honda', an excellent paper by Richard Rumelt which is available at http://www.anderson.ucla.edu/faculty/dick.rumelt/Docs/Papers/HONDA.pdf. For further information on Richard Rumelt see his home page at http://www.anderson.ucla.edu/faculty/dick.rumelt/rumelt.htm

[70] Source: Jeffrey Liker, Professor of Industrial and Operations Engineering at the University of Michigan, 'The Toyota Way: 14 Management Principles from the World's Greatest Manufacturer', published by McGraw-Hill in 2004. The 14 Principles are also available on Wikipedia at http://en.wikipedia.org/wiki/The_Toyota_Way).

selected a few of the principles below, although the document is best read in its entirety.

Selected Principles from the Toyota Way

Principle 1   Base your management decisions on a long-term philosophy, even at the expense of short-term financial goals.

Principle 2   Create a continuous process flow to bring problems to the surface.

Principle 4   Level out the workload. Work like a tortoise, not the hare.

Principle 5   Build a culture of stopping to fix problems, to get quality right first time.

Principle 7   Use visual control so no problems are hidden.

Principle 8   Use only reliable, thoroughly tested technology that serves your people and processes.

Principle 12   Go and see for yourself to thoroughly understand the situation.

Principle 13   Make decisions slowly by consensus, thoroughly considering all options; implement decisions rapidly.

What makes Toyota and Honda strategic leaders is that they combine the capacity for long term vision with an intensely practical culture that emphasises the short term processes that ensure uncompromising product standards and customer satisfaction. This culture reinforces their ability to meet demanding targets through a combination of innovation, determination, perseverance and hard work that relies on 'thinking slowly' and then acting quickly. Moreover, both companies do not give up easily, they persist until their objective is achieved or a better way forward has been found. They have developed inclusive employee cultures that allow them to embrace change and move forward rapidly, partly because their deliberative thinking approach helps them do things right first time. This is, perhaps, best summarised in the words of Hiroyuki Yoshino, President and

CEO of Honda Motor Co:

'Honda is a people-centred company. In short, each individual working within Honda can fully show his or her abilities, which is how we progress. This is Honda's strength.'

Hiroyuki Yoshino[71]

These distinctive values and business practices explain why both companies (and Toyota in particular) currently lead the automotive industry in the development and adoption of greener technologies, including the development of hybrid electric technology (with full scale fuel cell electric cars to follow) and increasing fuel efficiencies, critical to both the development of a more environmentally sustainable product and to competitive advantage within the industry. In 2007 Toyota sold its millionth hybrid car and the company predicts that by 2010 hybrids will account for about 10% of production and by 2020 'just about all Toyotas will be hybrids.'[72] There are few organisations in the world that actively look at a 50 year planning horizon at Board level as Toyota apparently does. And there are few organisations that share this driving long term vision and determination to make the world a better place, with an obsessive attention to detail, to getting things right. Toyota takes its slogan, 'we put our entire soul into each and every car' very seriously indeed.

Inevitably, such a prolonged period of growth and success brings its own problems. During 2007 quality control problems have emerged which threaten to undermine Toyota's rock solid reputation for high quality. The company has responded vigorously by introducing new controls, hiring more inspection engineers and beginning a mammoth re-training programme. In 2003, anticipating a shortage of key inspection supervisors (who have the power to stop the line before a production error is passed on) Toyota established its Global Production Centre ('GPC') in Japan, with branches also being set up overseas. By the end of 2007 some 10,000 people have graduated from the GPC, although even this has not been enough to match the global expansion of the business over the last four years. Yet, Toyota remains completely committed to both maintaining its

---

[71] Kiyoshi Tsukamoto, 'Toyota-to-Honda' (Toyota and Honda), reviewed by Takanori Kobayashi in an article in Japan Today, 'Corporate Culture, One Key to Success of Toyota, Honda', available at www.japantoday.com/jp/book/99

[72] Source: The Economist, 'Briefing Toyota: A wobble on the road to the top', November 10th 2007

leading edge in quality and moving the automotive industry into a more sustainable relationship with the environment. An engineering colleague of mine, who is currently working in China, sent me an email the other day with the title 'Toyota – Urban Myth'. In it was the question, 'How many times did Toyota design the cruise control for its cars? Answer: once. The urban myth is that the equivalent number for a major global competitor is 83.[73] Western corporations, it turns out, still have much to learn from Japanese business practices.

Ideas in action

Many of the issues that we face today are complex, systemic and extend beyond national boundaries. This is not only true of climate, environmental, political and social issues but also in the commercial and economic sphere as a result of increasing global interdependence. Just think of the complexity of major supply chains today, which stretch half way round the world and back again. As a result, the kind of long term thinking capabilities that have been developed by organisations as diverse as the National Trust, Toyota and Honda are very relevant to us all. By 'thinking slowly' and acting quickly we can open a space to understanding the deeper patterns and relationships that underlie complex issues. Linking the day to day activities of employees to an underlying sense of meaning and purpose, a difference that they can make over the long term, provides continuity and stability for the organisation and a 'robust container' for individuals (giving greater certainty based on consistent clarity of expectations). Allowing employees to surface problems and issues, as Toyota and Honda do, and then take time to deliberate the best approach for resolution makes for better decision making and greater loyalty over the long term. We may go more slowly at first but we do not need to return to the starting point so many times. In short, we build for the long term.

Although the world is still very much dominated by short-term thinking there are an increasing number of organisations that dare to do things differently. A good example is the not-for-profit organisations that deal directly with protection of the environment, such as the Wildlife Trusts in the United Kingdom. These trusts are set up on a geographical basis to create and enhance havens for wildlife in their areas and to take on a broader educational and lobbying role, helping to reduce our 'ecological footprint' in general. Much of their work is small scale, establishing and

---

[73] I am indebted to John Simpson for this insightful 'urban myth'.

looking after specific havens and, unsurprisingly, their strategy is often similar to that adopted by the National Trust. Like the National Trust they seek to achieve their aims over the long term and need to carefully balance conflicting demands (for example, conservation and the needs of the local communities). This approach is working well, both in terms of successful projects undertaken and in their ability to recruit significant numbers of members, some 726,000 by the beginning of 2008.

In addition, the natural suspicion and antipathy that once characterised the relationship between environmentalists and the commercial sector is beginning to change. Indeed, it is becoming increasingly common for commercial companies and environmental concerns to work together on developing long-term solutions to thorny issues. Jane Goodall, the well-known conservationist, tells the story of plans for a new rapid transit line in Taiwan, where the new line passed through the only major remaining breeding ground of the rare pheasant-tailed jacana. At first there was an outcry but environmentalists quickly accepted that the route was the only one that was economically viable and chose to work with the company to find a solution, in this case by moving the breeding ground. Water was diverted back into former wetlands nearby and suitable vegetation was replanted. In 2000 five birds hatched in their new home and more birds had moved to the site by the time Jane Goodall visited the following year. This may be small beginnings, perhaps, but it is an important example of the power of a collaborative approach, which brings together the experience and resources of both parties and leads to an innovative and, hopefully, sustainable solution for humans and pheasant-tailed jacana alike.[74]

Think slowly, act quickly

'Recognition is the change from ignorance to knowledge.'
Albert Einstein

Naturally, the successful move of the breeding grounds of the pheasant-tailed jacana is very small scale but that is actually the point. If we want to make a major difference to our impact on the environment we must be prepared not only to dream of a better world in which we live in greater harmony with our natural surroundings but also to take practical action. Even the biggest plans begin with the first small step. Ultimately, that is the

---

[74] Source: Jane Goodall, Time Magazine, 'The Power of One'. September 2nd, 2002

only way to gain real momentum over time. A seed spends almost half its life underground, invisible to the world, before it bursts through the soil into the sunlight. We don't think of this time spent underground as wasted because we know that it is vital to the seed's future growth! Chinese bamboo provides an even more dramatic example. After it is planted 'nothing' appears to happen, not only in the first year but in the second, third and fourth years. There is no evident sign of growth, not even the smallest of green leaves. It is only in the fifth year that it suddenly shoots up, sometimes reaching 90 feet in height and all in the space of just six weeks or so. To some it may appear to have grown 90 feet in six weeks but the truth is that it has taken five years. So often we are impatient and so eager to move ahead that we are unwilling to take the time to really think things through and develop an understanding of our venture or the effects our actions will have on the communities and environment around us. In the short term this can work, particularly if economic conditions are favourable. However, in time, we will be tested in our endeavour; economic conditions may turn against us or the going may simply get rough. If we haven't built solid foundations based on a strong sense of purpose, and we don't have clarity about the nature and intent of our actions, we may wish that we spent the time putting on our bathing suit before we went out for a swim.

5

SERVE OTHERS

'To laugh often and much; to win respect of intelligent persons and the affections of children; to earn the approbation of honest critics and endure the betrayal of false friends; to appreciate beauty; to find the best in others; to give one's self; to leave the world a little better, whether by a healthy child, a garden patch, or a redeemed social condition; to have played and laughed with enthusiasm, and sung with exultation; to know even one life has breathed easier because you have lived – this is to have succeeded.' [75]

Ralph Waldo Emerson

The illusion of independence

When my family wants to go away for a short inexpensive break we head for the Isle of Wight, a small island off the Southern coast of England. Although only a relatively short distance away, crossing that small stretch of water makes us feel as if we are leaving our daily troubles behind and really going somewhere. When we arrive we are greeted with the fresh smell of salt in the wind and the prospect of many happy hours of walking across downs and coastline, normally followed by a good dinner in one of the lovely village pubs on the island. These are simple pleasures but it always seems like heaven to me. Before we do any of this, however, we normally stop at a small café called the Leafy Bean for a quick cup of coffee and a piece of home-made cake or toasted tea cake. The café is small, seating only 16 people and is it located in the centre of Shanklin, a small

---

[75] Although this quote is widely attributed to Ralph Waldo Emerson (and may indeed be his) it is particularly difficult to source. One possibility is that it is based on a similar quotation in a poem published by Bessie Stanley in 1905. For those who are interested more information on the origins of the quote is available at transcendentalists.com, page reference, www.transcendentalists.com/success.htmed.

seaside town located on the south side of the island. Lennie, the proprietor, greets us so warmly that we may as well be long lost friends and before we know it we are seated with a feast before us. We can take a deep breath and relax for our vacation has begun. For this is a very special place.

It is not the multitude of coffees and teas available that makes the Leafy Bean special or even the home made cakes, although these are all very good indeed. It is not the location (on a street corner with a supermarket car park opposite) or even the warm and friendly atmosphere created by the proprietors, Lennie and Audrey, who have run the café since 1997. It is not even the constant flow of island double-decker buses that pass by regularly on their way to the nearby bus station, although these especially delighted my two sons when they were younger! It is because the Leafy Bean is an oasis of community, where locals gather to pass the time, chat, share tables or simply shelter from the rain. This little café is part coffee shop and part social club, a news gathering service and a community centre all rolled into one. Everyone is greeted with a smile, engaged in conversation, listened to and ... acknowledged. Not simply made welcome but acknowledged. I once saw Lennie help an aged customer work out what monies were due, carefully putting the change back into her purse and then reminding her to take it with her when she was ready to go. As he helped her to put her things together and put on her coat he gave a very small hug, almost imperceptible, but the message was clear, that age and infirmity was not an issue here; she was important, cared for, part of the community; she mattered. It makes no sense trying to analyze the Leafy Bean simply as a coffee shop; it is far more than that. It is a local institution that makes a big difference in the lives of its customers.

Nothing exists in isolation; all things are in relationship, both with each other and with the whole. We all know this profound truth yet for much of the time we behave as if we are independent, each one of us on our own personal island. The Leafy Bean is a success because it is a relationship-based business and customers know that they are valued, cared for, in that relationship. The quality of coffee is important but secondary. Yet, so often we forget how critical relationship is in defining success in any endeavour. We may feel like an island but is worth remembering what we would see if the tide were to go out completely; that we are all outcrops from the same bedrock.

Pull versus push

'We discover who we are in service to one another, not the self …
Our humanity is diminished when we have no mission bigger than
ourselves.'[76]

Bono

Rick Jarow, author of *'Creating the Work you Love'* and currently Assistant
Professor at Vassar College in Poughkeepsie, New York, has some sage
advice for those of us preparing to start our own businesses or follow a
new career path. He suggests that we do not commence by analyzing the
market to assess whether there is sufficient demand for the output of our
endeavours. Instead, he advises us to ask ourselves the simple question,
'what is my community?' It is by knowing who we are and where we are
from that we align ourselves with those who are naturally drawn to the
products and services that we wish to provide. This distinction between a
'pull' strategy (meeting the needs of the community and the wider world
around us) rather than the more familiar 'push' strategy (pushing our
products and services into the marketplace) brings the concept of serving
others to the centre of our work. It reinforces clarity of purpose and
provides access to the deeper roots of the community, which often
translates into help, advice and resources.

It may simply be a product of my age and the natural passage of time
but I have been in a lot of meetings during my life where decisions have
been made that are fundamental to the future course of a business or an
endeavour. I have noticed that those decisions that have successful
sustainable outcomes have something in common and it is this. They result
from a meeting of minds based on a shared passion of making some
element of the world a better or more exciting place. It may be a decision
on a new business venture (such as a new and innovative retail format) or
the development of a specialized university course for a market that is not
currently being served. It may relate more overtly to improving community
care; for example, a new intensive approach to a 'detox' program for drug
addiction. The bottom line is that it doesn't really matter how exciting or
innovative an idea or concept is in its own right. Excitement and creativity
alone will not do it. To succeed, the idea needs to be rooted in serving real
tangible needs. If it is not, it will be desperately difficult to communicate to

---

[76] Bono, writing in Time Magazine, 'A Time for Miracles', published on March 22nd 2007. The
full article is available on Time Magazine's web site at
www.time.com/time/magazine/article/0,9171,1601932,00.html

others, let alone muster up the energy to get it off the ground and attract like-minded souls to the venture. A business model needs two elements for it to succeed; firstly, the profit and loss needs to add up and, secondly, it needs a narrative to pull it together. Without a good story we haven't got a hope!

Adopting a clear focus of serving others reinforces our clarity of purpose, the prime reason for our endeavour. We saw this in chapter two when we looked at the importance of the quest for justice that underlies much of the work of the Pierian Centre, founded by June Burrough in the heart of Bristol. A strong sense of service to the community not only builds strong relationships that translate into intense customer loyalty but it also taps deeply into the roots and resources of that community. As with all successful and rapidly growing enterprises the Pierian Centre had an insatiable appetite for cash in its early years and was often operating on a financial knife-edge. It survived and prospered because June was able to find all kinds of resources from within the community itself including staff, volunteers and financial funding. Loyalty to the Centre from employees, associates and customers alike is fierce with much of the new business coming from word of mouth based on personal experience. I vividly recall discussing with June how she would recruit a new staff member for a vital position with no financial resources to do so. She decided to email details of the position to those associated with the Centre in one way or another, with the hope of at least saving the fees that would be charged by a recruitment agency. Within a couple of days she had no less than 35 applicants, almost all of whom she would have been ideal for the position. People want to work for the Pierian Centre, not only because they identify with what it stands for but also because they are already part of the wider community it serves.

The discipline of seeing things from the perspective of service to others is critical to developing our ability to think strategically. It helps us to be absolutely clear in our vision for the future (the bigger picture of what we are trying to achieve) and links that future directly with our capacity to act right now, rooting it in the messy operational detail that will provide the foundation to move forward. But it is actually more than this. It is a fundamental capacity to look at things from more than one perspective, from a place outside of ourselves, and from that place comes all manner of insight and opportunities that remain hidden from us if we are shuttered within our own world. The old adage, 'try walking in somebody else's shoes' contains a great deal of practical wisdom.

Redefining customer loyalty

In 1995 Thomas Jones and W. Earl Sasser published a landmark article in the Harvard Business Review that suggested that conventional ways of interpreting customer satisfaction were simplistic and encouraged erroneous conclusions. The authors found that loyalty is not related to satisfaction in simple linear terms and that it takes high levels of emotional involvement from customers before loyalty actually kicks in. In fact, if we plot the build up of loyalty in relation to customer satisfaction on a graph, we see that it takes the form of a curve rather than a straight line. Initially, customer satisfaction will increase steadily without a corresponding increase in loyalty but at very high levels of satisfaction loyalty begins to build rapidly (the underlying relationship is exponential). In practical terms, this means that we need to do exceptional things or do things exceptionally well to win real customer loyalty. In reality, our customer satisfaction indices are normally over-optimistic, since a rating level of 'good' or a score of four out of five brings very little substantive loyalty. The dramatic consequences of this are summarized by the authors when they state that the 'gulf between satisfied customers and completely satisfied customers can swallow a business.'[77]

Almost all organisations that have achieved high levels of loyalty are obsessive, either about customers directly or about the products and services that they provide, or in some cases both. Apple is obsessive about sleek product design and simple and effective functionality. Its products work, in an industry where that simple equation cannot be taken for granted. Pizza Express and Pret A Manger (a national sandwich chain in England) are obsessive about consistent customer standards, demonstrated by an attention to detail in *all* aspects of the retail proposition; still sadly uncommon in an industry where standards frequently vary widely from location to location. Innocent, a producer of very high quality natural fruit juices, is obsessive about the quality of its natural ingredients in an industry that has often compromised quality to reduce costs, ensure longer shelf life or simply meet the vagaries of fashion. In the case of Innocent what you see is what you get, quite literally in this case as the ingredients are shown on the side of the box as pictures, in proportion to the actual mix. Traditionally, we are accustomed to a distinction being made between a 'product oriented' company and a

---

[77] Source: Thomas O. Jones & W Earl Sasser, Jr, 'Why Satisfied Customers Defect', Harvard Business Review, November – December 1997

'customer oriented' one. What these examples demonstrate is that it is the deeper connection made with customers that really matters. Whether this is expressed in customer or product terms is not important, what is critical is that all these companies share an obsession about serving customer needs, about making a real difference. In many cases, successful companies, such as Virgin, actually redefine the customer experience entirely, effectively leading customers into new territory in doing so!

Starbucks

'It's a pretty arrogant thing to say 'we changed the world' ... I don't know if I'd say it like that. I think we have managed to, with a simple cup of coffee and a very unique experience, enhance the lives of millions of people by creating a sense of community, by bringing people together and recognizing the importance of place in people's lives.'[78]

Howard Schultz, Chairman, President and CEO of Starbucks

By any measure Starbucks is one of the most successful organisations in the world, expanding at breathtaking pace over the past decade (with store count growing in some years by 40% to 60%). It possesses one of the few truly iconic global brands despite very little advertising and promotion, relying instead on its store fronts to build awareness. It has even been lampooned in the animated sitcom, 'The Simpsons', a sure sign of success![79] Yet, the truth is that there will be few 'brownie points' for my decision to use it as a strategic leader, however well deserved it is. Since the final quarter of 2007 the company has experienced intense media scrutiny as its share price has plummeted (falling 55% between May 2006 and April 2008), it has experienced poor trading results and acknowledged mistakes made by over-expansion and the increasing commoditization of its core proposition. For the first time in its history, comparable store sales fell in the quarter ending September 2007 and in January 2008 Howard Schultz was reinstated as CEO to revive the company's fortunes. On top of that, success has brought Starbucks many detractors who have blamed the company for everything from environmental abuse, mistreating third world

---

[78] Source: Taylor Clark, 'Starbucked: A Double Tall Tale of Caffeine, Commerce & Culture', published by Sceptre in 2008 (comments made in an interview between the author and Howard Schultz, CEO of Starbucks).
[79] 'Simpson Tide', originally aired on March 29th 1998 on Fox, written by Joshua Sternin & Jeffrey Ventimila and directed by Milton Gray.

producers, wiping out independents and homogenizing the coffee drinking experience. In short, Starbucks has become a 'whipping boy' for many of the problems and issues that people associate with large corporate organisations. The very ubiquity of its stores is now held against it.

In spite of all of this, Starbucks remains an excellent example of a strategic leader and a particularly good illustration of the power of acknowledging and working with community. Strategic thinking does not guarantee that mistakes will never be made or that an organisation will be successful in perpetuity, no matter how attractive this thought might be! It is *how* an organisation deals with its mistakes that determine its leadership credentials and Starbucks has acted swiftly and dramatically to deal with what The Economist has called 'the most serious crisis in its history' as we shall soon see.[80]

Passionate beginnings

Starbucks was founded in 1971 by three partners as a retailer of high quality coffee beans and expanded into coffee shops after it was acquired by entrepreneur, Howard Schultz, in 1987. It is currently the largest chain of coffee shops in the world, with close to 16,000 locations in 44 countries by April 2008. Moreover, unlike most other large chains, it has achieved this degree of success without being a franchise business since its stores are either company owned or joint ventures and licensed outlets. Although the majority of stores are still in the United States a sizeable minority (some 29%) are now in other countries making Starbucks a truly international brand. With revenues reaching some $9.4 billion by 2007 and close to 2000 employees by April 2008, Starbucks is both very large and very successful. The company has also had a profound impact on the way in which coffee is viewed in contemporary society, which is every bit as important as the successful business metrics. The Economist has even gone as far as saying that Starbucks has 'created a mass taste for good coffee'[81], a comment echoed by Taylor Clark, author of 'Starbucked: A Tall Tale of Caffeine, Commerce & Culture', when he says that 'this is a company that forever changed the way people consume the most popular beverage on the planet.' Starbucks itself tends to stress its influence on the way in which that coffee is drunk, in other words the community and

---

[80] Source: The Economist, 'Coffee Wars, Starbucks v McDonalds', January 12th 2008.

[81] Source: The Economist, "Face Value: Staying Pure, Howard Schultz's formula for Starbucks', February 25th 2006.

neighbourhood aspects of its coffee shops.

Despite its size and success, Starbucks remains very committed to acting like a small company, tapping into the tradition of the independent coffee house as an intimate social gathering place. The organisation holds on fiercely to its decentralized ethos, its belief that the best decisions are made store by store. As former CEO, Jim Donald, put it, 'you see the banter, the customers knowing the people behind the counter ... it's part of the reason they go.'[82] At the same time, Starbucks knows that it has to continue to work hard to maintain its success and adapt where necessary. Chairman and CEO, Howard Schultz, has long stressed the difficulties of combining rapid growth with maintaining the community orientation of its stores. 'The battle within the company' he says, 'is making sure growth doesn't dilute our culture' and the common goal of leadership is to ensure Starbucks continues to act like a small company.[83] It was Schultz himself that drew public attention to the consequences of the diminution of the 'Starbucks experience' when he wrote to the company's top executives on Valentine's Day in 2007 expressing his concerns that 'over the past ten years ... we have had to make a series of decisions that, in retrospect, have led to the watering down of the Starbucks experience' leading to some customers finding Starbucks stores sterile 'cookie-cutter' places that no longer reflected a passion for coffee.[84] These challenging statements tell us a lot about the Starbucks' culture; that it remains strongly service oriented, focused on the customer and resilient. In addition, it can be flexible and adaptive to change, without compromising its core purpose and values, which include a very broad sense of service to all of its partners as well as a passion for coffee. It is this cultural dimension that lies at the very heart of Starbuck's success as we shall see.

Living service values

A couple of years ago I was shopping in the Eaton Centre, a large shopping mall in downtown Toronto, and took the opportunity to stop at the Starbucks coffee shop that is located within a very large book store there.

---

[82] Source: Time Magazine, 'The Big Gulp at Starbucks', December 18th 2006.

[83] Source: Time Magazine, 'The Big Gulp at Starbucks', December 18th 2006.

[84] Source: The Economist, 'Coffee Wars: Starbucks v McDonald's, January 12th 2008 and Time Magazine, Global Business Management, 'Wake-Up Time', April 21st 2008. The comments made by Howard Schultz began life as an internal memo to senior executives but found their way on to the internet. The full memo is available at
http://starbucksgossip.typepad.com/_/2007/02/starbucks_chair_2.html

My mind was on other things when I placed my coffee order so it took a little time for me to comprehend the barista's response, a simple 'no'. As I stood there, not quite knowing how to respond to this, she corrected herself, apologized and said she would brew some fresh coffee immediately. She was clearly *not* having a good day and whilst I was in the process of paying for and collecting my order her team worker quietly intervened and a hushed conversation ensued. I cannot be sure exactly what passed between them or what was said in a telephone call that followed. I only know that this was one *very* unhappy person indeed and that she left some ten minutes later when a replacement barista arrived. However, it is what happened as she departed that has left such a lasting impression on me. Her mood and demeanour had been transformed; it was literally as if she was a different person leaving the store. Ironically, I had the good timing to be collecting more milk at the precise time that she was on her way out so I did catch the last words of the parting conversation, which were that she was welcome to come back at any time and that she needed only to make a phone call. She left with a broad smile on her face.

To this day I have no idea how this transformation took place but I believe that it is no small thing. It is indicative of the culture of service that underlies Starbucks, not just towards customers but also for employees, growers and other partners alike. It is noticeable that the baristas and staff (who are all called partners at Starbucks) appear better trained, more attentive and more alert than so many others who work in retail or other service occupations. I describe this as a sense of aliveness that enables them to communicate and interact with customers and embodies the 'sense of humanity'[85] that is deeply engrained within the company. In this, Starbucks is similar with other leading retail organisations such as Pret A Manger and Waitrose (the supermarket arm of the John Lewis Partnership). All offer premium quality food propositions, have strong customer facing cultures and offer caring and rewarding work environments. The result is that they have developed high customer loyalty and strong brands. All three organisations *care* and customers pick that up instinctively; not just from their direct customer service experience but also from the myriad of signals that they tune into every time they shop or visit a location. Each smile, half-heard conversation, stock-out, tidy

---

[85] Source: The Economist, "Face Value: Staying Pure, Howard Schultz's formula for Starbucks', February 25th 2006.

or untidy shelf, even the dirt on the floor, tells part of the store's story and customers know very quickly whether the organisation is living by the values it espouses or not. Starbucks understands this and one of its defining features is an extraordinary attention to detail, whether that is waiting times for a drink, resolution of order problems, table clean-up or washroom cleanliness.

This attention to detail is achieved partly by placing such a high level of importance on firmly keeping the culture of the company small scale and promoting independent decision making at local level. But it is more than simply this. Starbucks places a priority on cultivating a relationship with its customers. Its aim is to be the 'third place' in its customers' lives, filling the gap between home and work and overlapping with both. In doing so it is filling the same role as drinking establishments have always done, whether they are Italian coffee houses, Viennese cafés or traditional ale houses. As we saw with the Leafy Bean, this relationship is based on a much broader definition of a coffee shop which includes a strong social and community orientation. The relationship with customers at Starbucks is fostered by a set of values that are summarized in the 'Green Apron Book', which all partners are given. This puts into words some of the core 'ways of being' that enable a partner to be successful at Starbucks including 'be welcoming', 'be genuine', 'be knowledgeable', 'be considerate' and 'be involved'.[86] It would be very easy to be cynical about this corporate philosophizing if it were not for the fact that Starbucks lives these values day in and day out and they can all be witnessed at any one of its coffee shop locations. Naturally, there are other very good coffee shops but it is the consistency of standards across such a large chain that marks Starbucks out as different.

The bottom line is that the customer experience, including the overall ambience of each location, really matters to Starbucks. The company will frequently reject a time saving process if the 'Starbucks experience' is compromised. As Jim Alling, President of Starbucks in the US puts it, 'as much as we want to meet people's desire to produce beverages quickly, we also realize that people want a smile with their drink that they don't want to feel rushed.'[87] Moreover, there is an acknowledgement that the company has to redress the balance between efficient throughput and ambience still further. Howard Schultz has initiated a radical programme of

---

[86] Source: Joseph A. Michelli, 'The Starbucks Experience: 5 Principles for turning Ordinary into Extraordinary', published by McGraw Hill, 2007.
[87] Source: Time Magazine, 'The Big Gulp at Starbucks', December 18th 2006

changes that include a return to grinding beans in-store for drip coffee and the introduction of new expresso machines that give baristas more control over the process and make them more visible. To allow the company to redress this balance and maintain a long term orientation Schultz has also announced that Starbucks will stop reporting comparable store sales to Wall Street. The company has put an exemplary coffee experience right back centre stage with long term shareholder value tied directly to creating long term customer value. The most dramatic example of this change was the decision on February 26th 2008 to close all 7,100 of its company-owned US stores for three hours to retrain 135,000 baristas. As Time Magazine reported:

> **Part of the training involved the correct way to pull an expresso: into a shot glass, not a paper cup, a shortcut that had evolved to move the line more quickly. It was a strong statement that Starbucks cares about quality – with a clear shot glass a barista can make sure the expresso correctly settles into three layers – and isn't led by a fast-food-style obsession with throughput.'[88]**

Joseph Michelli, a management and training consultant in the US, recently worked within Starbucks in order to write a book that summarizes the five key philosophies that underlie its ability to maintain this consistency of customer experience. Interestingly, each philosophy speaks of an open organisation, willing to learn and adapt. The key principles are:

1. Make it your own.
2. Everything matters.
3. Surprise and delight.
4. Embrace resistance.
5. Leave your mark.

Starbucks lives its values with all of its partners. It offers generous employee benefits, giving all US employees who work at least 20 hours a week a package that includes stock options and comprehensive health insurance. The latter was almost unheard of for a food retailer when it was introduced and was instigated at Howard Schultz's insistence. As a child he had witnessed first-hand the devastating effect an injury can have on a family's income when his father broke an ankle as a delivery-truck driver. In many ways, his goal has always been to 'build the sort of company that

---

[88] Source: Time Magazine, Global Business Management', Wake-Up Time', April 21st 2008.

my father was never able to work for.'[89] The company also pays growers, on average, 23% above market prices[90] (which equates to some $1.26 per pound of coffee) and is one of the largest, if not the largest, purchaser of fair trade coffee in the US. It is also committed to increasing the amount of fair trade coffee that it sells (currently about 4% of sales) provided that quality levels can be maintained. It operates an evolving set of guidelines and practices for buying coffee called C.A.F.E. ('coffee and farm equity practices') that enable buyers who meet certain criteria to negotiate long-term premium prices for the coffee that they sell. These criteria include working on environmentally friendly practices and constantly improving the living conditions of their labourers as well as maintaining a high level of product quality. The company is also very active in both local and wider communities with a whole range of activities from recycling books to local schools to working with SEED, a network supporting women in business, founded by Lynne Franks.[91] All this indicates that Starbucks is serious about its community values. As Jim Alling comments:

> **'There is something a little magical about founding a business that aspires to enrich the human spirit. That's actually part of the Starbucks core purpose ... Sure, one of our principles is to recognize that profitability is essential to our future success. But it's not the first item on the list; it's the last one. And when you live and work according to those kind of principles, good things seem to come your way.'[92]**
>
> *Jim Alling, President, Starbucks US Business*

Staying the course in the real world

Naturally, consistently living the values that Starbucks espouses in the real world is going to be challenging at times. There are numerous practical issues. One example is the question of whether Starbucks should significantly increase the share of fair trade coffee that it uses. The

---

[89] The Economist, 'Face Value: Staying Pure, Howard Schultz's formula for Starbucks', February 25th 2006.

[90] Source: The Economist, "Face Value: Staying Pure, Howard Schultz's formula for Starbucks', February 25th 2006. This is some time ago and Starbucks may be paying a larger premium today.

[91] For more information on SEED please see its web site on www.seednetwork.com

[92] Source: Joseph A. Michelli, 'The Starbucks Experience: 5 Principles for turning Ordinary into Extraordinary', published by McGraw Hill, 2007 (extracted from the foreword by Jim Alling).

company argues that it is difficult to do this quickly without compromising its total commitment to quality (and some growers are unwilling to pay the costs of fair trade certification which can amount to $20,000 to $30,000). At the end of 2006 Starbucks was publicly lambasted by Oxfam, the development charity, for not sufficiently supporting the Ethiopian government's attempts to trademark three types of local coffee bean. These matters are important to Starbucks because they are a challenge to the company to be seen to be living its 'sense of humanity' in its day to day business practices. In practice, the issues are also complex and easily distorted (there are always two sides of a story and this one had a happy ending) but Starbucks is perceived to be big enough that it needs to be beyond reproach. This is a tough remit and it is not one that many of Starbucks' competitors would necessarily take on board. It is, however, a direct cost of strategic leadership, of not only adopting an ethical stand in principle but also making it work in the real world in a very public arena. This is the point where practice meets theory!

Starbucks has come a very long way since it was founded in 1971. It is now a huge organisation with sales of almost $10 billion. To have come this far and maintained its core community values is an exceptional achievement and one that lies at the heart of its success. Maintaining this delicate balance between operational effectiveness (and the financial performance expectations that lie beneath) with maintaining a unique customer experience will certainly be difficult. But Starbucks has probably already gone further than any other organisation of its size in proving this possible. In many ways, as it continues to grow it is entering into genuinely new territory, one of the hallmarks of true strategic leadership. Can it be done? Only time will tell!

The voluntary sector

'The world is precious, every bit
Please don't make a mess of it!'
A refrain from a Christmas play at Kennet Valley School [93]

Adopting a mindset of service to others is a key element of strategic

---

[93] Kennet Valley School is based in Wiltshire in England. I believe that the words to this refrain are taken from the book 'Lottie' by Gordon Snell and Peter Bailey, published by Orion in 1997 in which Lottie has an important letter to write to the Queen of the World about the damage done to animals by people and pollution. All the animals want to sign it with their own special marks.

thinking in *any* endeavour because it enables us to 'step into somebody else's shoes' and adopt a bigger perspective than we can hope to develop when we simply look through our eyes alone. Nevertheless, it is in the voluntary sector that it has its most obvious application. After all, most voluntary organisations are set up specifically to deal with broader societal issues that are not addressed commercially through the marketplace. In practice, however, things can be more subtle and complex than they appear on the surface. We may need to look more deeply into the culture of a voluntary organisation, rather than simply rely on its mission statement or core purpose, to see how the philosophy of service actually manifests.

We live in a small village and both my sons went to our local primary school, which looks after the education needs of local children between the ages of five and eleven years old. Naturally, this is a very broad remit and despite government attempts to harmonize and raise standards across the country there is still a great deal of difference between schools in terms of academic orientation and attainment, the socio-economic background of pupils and even the approach to learning and development. All parents know that the choice of school can make a very big difference for their children and few subject areas are quite as emotive. In our case, the decision was not especially difficult as Kennet Valley School not only has a good reputation but the lower school also happens to be just opposite our house! I must confess, however, that I didn't really appreciate at first what a special experience this would be for our boys. In fact, if I am honest, in the early days I was more concerned about whether the academic standards would measure up. Having previously lived in both London and Toronto I considered myself both cosmopolitan and sophisticated and I wondered whether my children's education would live up to my expectations. Looking back I can see just how little I understood about what really matters in a teaching and learning environment.

Kennet Valley School has some 70 pupils split between two village sites, managed by three class teachers and a Head Teacher. As it turns out I needn't have worried about the academic side as the school achieves solid, if not exceptional, results and the children have a broad curriculum, which is very much enriched by being part of the village communities. What I completely failed to take into account was the caring ethos of the school, which has given both my boys a sense of self-esteem and of being valued for who they are. This is the specific sense of serving others that underlies everything the school does and it is based on appreciating the whole child and helping them develop a sense of their unique place in the world. The school practices an 'apprentice model' where the older children take responsibility for the younger ones. As classes cover a two year age group this is built into the structure of school life from the very beginning with the older children acting as 'mentors' to help the younger ones in each class. It is also built in through formal events such as the 'switch day', when older and younger classes switch sites and work alongside each other and the social games afternoon, where the older children 'invent' games for the younger children to play together on the school field. There is nothing more heart-warming than when your eight old describes, with an expression of great worldly wisdom, how he has been helping the younger ones with some task because 'they're not old enough to know how to do it yet.' Most important of all, they learn it through everyday informal activities such as helping the younger children get safely on the bus at the end of the school day.[94]

The children also learn about how to live in a community, to respect each other and to consider others less fortunate than themselves. In a gentle way, they also start to become aware of the significance of some of the 'big' issues that we face such as environmental degradation and poverty. As with all the best learning this is done as much by the teachers modelling behaviour as through direct input. Both my sons care very much about the state of the world (although being teenagers they have learned not to show it sometimes) and this is part of the gift that the school has bestowed on them. This connection with community and the world in which they live is embedded deep within them. Only much later did I realize that these core values, lived and practiced by the teachers, overrode even government policy when necessary! This is strategic thinking at its best, achieving the most important result for those that you are there to serve, even when the system itself undervalues and sometimes impedes your ability to carry out the task. It also raises a critical point; that much of the really important work in organisations today, particularly in the public sector, goes on unacknowledged and is sometimes even actively discouraged. This is as true for nurses and police officers as it is for teachers. These are our modern day heroes and heroines, those who are changing the world for the better by doing ... simply what they do.

---

[94] My thanks to Paul Burrowbridge, formerly Head Teacher of Kennet Valley School, for providing me with background information on the school. For further information please see the school's website on www.kennetvalleyschool.org

Care for the Family

Care for the Family is a national charity, which was set up in the United Kingdom in 1988 to promote strong family life and to help those hurting because of family breakdown. Care for the Family's work is motivated by Christian compassion, but its resources and support are available to everyone, of any faith or none. It currently has revenues of some £3.5 million and has recently taken on its one hundredth member of staff. At a simple level it serves its community by offering a wealth of support through seminars, events and resources. This includes a single parents' network and pen pal scheme, support for bereaved parents, single parent breaks, befriending networks, marriage and friendship seminars, a parent toddler group network and much more besides. Over half a million people have attended Care for the Family events such as *'It Takes Two'*, a course designed to help people gain insights and skills to strengthen their marriage. What enables Care for the Family to really make a difference, however, comes from a deeper place. It is the recognition that service to others means getting alongside them, not dispensing advice 'from above', no matter how well intentioned. This may simply be to listen, it may involve specific help or support in some way but it is always without judgment. The charity expresses this as follows:

'We're a charity whose heart is to come alongside you and your family in the good times, and the tough times, too – bringing you hope, compassion, help and encouragement.'[95]

Care for the Family lives these principles each and every day. The Executive Director, Rob Parsons, talks of the time when Care for the Family was running a big Conference that included a number of invited speakers. Beforehand, Rob spoke to each of the speakers. He told them that if they felt that they had everything 'sussed' or were hoping to pass on all that they knew to others – if, for example, they were dying to impart the secret of a perfect marriage – then they were not the right person to speak at that conference. What is most needed in Care for the Family's work, he stresses, are people who are broken, who have 'cried a little' and whose motto is 'me too'. If we want to give expert advice we have to recruit those that are best at providing it. Care for the Family takes a different view. It is looking for people who can come alongside somebody in need and be

---

[95] Source: Care for the Family website, now amended. For further information on Care for the Family please see its comprehensive web site on www.careforthefamily.org.uk

vulnerable, which means being wholly authentic, being ourselves. This is the place where healing can begin. There is no better way of illustrating the power of this approach than through a story.

Loving Against the Odds – A Letter to Care for the Family [96]

Let me share one great encouragement with you. Some of you may recognise the following letter. I quoted it in my first book, *Loving Against the Odds*. It was from a woman who attended one of our first marriage seminars. Although I received it years ago, I have never forgotten it:

Dear Rob

On Saturday, my husband and I attended the Marriage Matters seminar. It was a day that changed our lives. In the morning, before leaving our home, I said to my husband, 'I think this seminar is our last hope; if nothing good comes of this day, I think we may have to part.' You see, after fourteen years of marriage, he had an affair. I've not been able to forgive him; however sorry he said he was, I simply could not. That was until Saturday. But when you spoke of God forgiving us, I thought, 'How can I not forgive?' And your words made me think so much about my children, my little girl and my little boy; they deserve a happy life, a mother and a father to love and care for them. The whole day made us look at our family, and we talked so much that night, and we're still talking. We laughed a lot and at the end of the day, we cried together.

Thank you. Saturday changed our lives; we're both looking forward to a happier, brighter and more loving life together. Here's to the next fourteen years.

That letter is now years old, but just this month that woman wrote to me again. She enclosed a family photograph and next to her and her husband, two teenagers smiled out at the camera:

---

[96] Source: Care for the Family. I have always found this letter deeply moving and I am indebted to its author for sharing the powerful message of hope that it conveys.

... and I enclose a recent photograph of our family. Who would have thought that eight years on we would still be in touch with you. We both thank God every day for the day you touched our lives. Jo is now sixteen and Ben is fourteen and they are a real pleasure to be with and have grown into such lovely children. We are both so glad that we have both been here to watch them grown into the young adults they are now. Sound proud, don't we ...

I confess that as I read that letter, I was very moved. In fact, I got on my knees in my office and said to God that I would have done everything we have attempted over the past ten years – all the seminars, the videos, the books – done it all just to see those two children smiling out at me with their mother and father by their side.

Rob Parsons, Executive Director, Care for the Family

Ideas in action

There are many areas in life that fall between the private and public sectors, where the commercial incentives are not strong enough for private organisations to provide services but the community served is not significant enough (or powerful enough) to justify access to sufficient levels of public funding. These include issues as diverse as the closure of rural post offices, the fate of redundant churches, the provision of youth services and facilities, the treatment of alcohol and drug addiction and many other local community services. Many of these areas have access to some level of government funding while others are supported by charitable or other voluntary bodies (sometimes both). Normally, however, funding is tight and often haphazard, and certainly falls short of allowing comprehensive solutions. In these areas the community orientation of serving others often provides strategic insights and highlights additional resources that may be available. One powerful example is the emergence in the United Kingdom of community owned village stores.

Threatened with the continued closure of village shops, pubs and post offices, village communities are grouping together to form community owned stores that not only provide local access to essential goods and services but also function as an important social hub for the village. These initiatives can be surprisingly complex and are always lots of hard work.

They normally involve raising funds through a mixture of local shares, fundraising events, loans and grants and also require considerable market research to determine what kinds of goods and services are needed and the likely level of local support. Moreover, applications for grants and loans need to be supported by fairly detailed and realistic business plans. Finally, a scheme can only come to fruition if local people can be found with the aspiration to fulfil the central roles in the provision of goods and services. What these schemes have in common is serving others; they will only work if they are set up to meet the real needs of the local community. This may mean acting as a café during the day, light food restaurant at lunchtime and early evenings, and running as a general store and post office as well. Alternatively, a pub may serve as the hub for providing services by broadening its fare and extending its hours (and quite probably its premises) in order to do so. Running this kind of operation is always very hard work and can involve some complex logistics (since it involves running several separate businesses simultaneously). However, it can also enable the business to tap into the deeper resources of the community in terms of funding, staffing and support.

One example of a successful creative solution to these complex issues can be found in the small village of Urchfont in Wiltshire, which lies just South of the North Wessex Downs. In response to the closure of both the village store and post office, the villagers set up a new community shop as a 'not for profit' social enterprise owned by the community, with over 180 shareholders. The business consists of a shop, sub post office and Information Centre and was expressly set up for the wider benefit of the community. The villagers recognized the importance that the shop would play as an active central meeting point within the village to share information, meet friends and provide community services (displaying notices, giving directions, helping with local fundraising by selling tickets and so on). To meet these needs they decided to locate the venture in a separate building next to the local pub, the Lamb Inn, so that it could cater for amenities such as lunches, morning coffee and afternoon tea. Although, by necessity, the range of the convenience store is fairly limited, it has a distinctly local flavour since it stocks produce and products (such as pottery and stationery) from the area. The owners are very responsive to the needs and comments of local customers; for example, adding fresh vegetables soon after the store had opened. Interest and support for the venture is high and the shop manager is supported by over 50 volunteer shop assistants. It is expected that the business will have annual sales of some £100,000 and will make a small surplus after the first year. This is a creative and responsive community solution and has inspired similar villages to look into establishing their own ventures.[97]

Social enterprise

The power of this approach to social enterprise has been recognized by the introduction of 'community interest companies' in the UK, which can be set up to address the needs of specific communities, without all the legal requirements associated with becoming a charity. There are currently some 15,000 social enterprises that specifically recognize social aims as part of their core purpose and mission. One of the most successful of these is Cafédirect, a charitable business created by Oxfam to sell coffee, tea and cocoa for which growers have received a fair wage. The organisation works in partnership with small-scale growers across the developing world, buying from 37 producers in 12 countries and covering over a quarter of a million growers. It has been hugely successful in building distribution, both within the UK and more recently overseas, and it now sells through most of the major supermarkets and directly to the service industry. Its remit is simple. As CEO, Penny Newman, puts it, 'we're about one thing and one thing only – quality products that bring a better quality of life to people around the world.'[98] The organisational structure reflects this remit with growers holding shares in the company and sitting on the Board of Directors so that they can have a say in how the business is run. This tight focus on serving the needs of a well defined specific community is critical to Cafédirect's success.

Making a deep impact

We can never truly measure our impact on other people. It is an irony that

---

[97] I drew on a number of sources for this, most notably the article 'Urchfont Community Shop and Post Office' available from Community First's magazine (www.communityfirst.org.uk), an article by Lesley Andrews, 'Open for Business: The Village Shop Makes a Comeback', published in View Magazine in 2006 and a number of topical articles contained in Wiltshire Life Magazine between 2005 and 2007. For further information on the Urchfont Village store today see the web link for Urchfont Community Web (www.kennet-communityweb.com/site/Urchfont-Community-Web/index.htm), Wiltshire World Changers (www.wiltshireworldchangers.org/star-projects.php?id=14) and the Village Retail Services Association (www.virsa.org/index.cfm/villageshop/Directory.Details/shop_id/264)

[98] Source: Cafédirect web site, an excellent source of further information on the organisation, available at www.cafedirect.co.uk

when we begin to put service to others at the centre of our lives we very quickly become conscious of just how little we see of the full effects of our actions. The impact of most of what we do remains invisible to us. If we are wise we learn to accept this. We live more in the moment and concentrate on the small things in front of us, seeing what we can do at the day to day operational level and doing it really well. All the organisations explored in this chapter do just this. They are all obsessive about detail at the same time as being fully committed to their long-term visions. They take pleasure in the small things as well as moving forward on the 'grand plan'. We should, however, never forget that there is always a bigger picture even if we do not see it ourselves. We are connected in more ways than we can imagine.

There is a story of a school teacher who sets her class an exercise to draw something that they are thankful of around Harvest Festival (or Thanksgiving). As the children present their work she smiles as she sees many of the familiar images; parents round a table, fruit and vegetables and even a lovely picture of the nearby woods. She is taken aback, however, when Joseph presents her with a simple picture of a hand. The class is captivated by this picture and the children start to guess whose hand it might be. There are all sorts of suggestions; one child suggests it might be 'a local farmer', another that it is 'Joseph's mother', and a girl at the back thinks it may be the 'hand of God, who brings us all the food'. But Joseph just shakes his head. Finally, the class gives in and the teacher asks, 'well Joseph, whose hand is it?' 'It's your hand' he replies. And only then does the teacher remember how she has so often taken Joseph by the hand, when he is shy, looking lost or simply in need of encouragement, just as she does with all the children. She has never given it a moment's thought, it is just her job. How could she have known just how much it meant to Joseph?[99]

---

[99] There are quite a few variants on this story. One is contained within 'Chicken Soup for the Soul', written and compiled by Jack Canfield and Mark Victor Hansen, published by HCI (Health Communications, Inc) in 1993.

6

REFLECT

> 'The quieter you become the more you will be able to hear.'

Zen Proverb

The illusion of control

Things are not always what they seem on the surface. We all know that the French Revolution of 1789 to 1799 was created by a combination of factors including high unemployment and food prices, inequitable taxation, resentment of royal absolutism and other privileges of the nobility and, finally, the ineptitude of Louis XVI to deal effectively with any of these problems. Food scarcity in the months immediately before the revolution seems to have tipped the balance unleashing a period of political and social upheaval that spread from France into Europe as a whole. It was this that ushered in the principles of the enlightenment including democracy, citizenship and the concept of inalienable personal rights. What is generally not in the history books is an event that happened six years prior to the revolution several hundred miles to the North in the volcanic island of Iceland. In June 1783 a 17-mile split appeared on the island and the volcano, Laki, erupted sending out 122 million tons of sulphur dioxide into the atmosphere over an eight-month period. A choking cloud spread south, killing a quarter of Iceland's population and three quarters of its livestock. It drifted across the North Atlantic to Britain where it was reported by newspapers to be like thick smog with the dull sun 'coloured like it had been soaked in blood'. The cloud lasted weeks, if not months, and engulfed much of Western Europe causing vegetation to wither and millions of people to suffer from severe chest pains and blinding headaches. The high levels of sulphuric acid attacked the lungs of victims causing them to choke and sometimes to die. The Hertfordshire poet, William Cowper, wrote of the distress that it caused in Britain in the following graphic terms:

'Such multitudes are indisposed by fevers … that farmers have great difficulty gathering their harvest, the labourers having been almost every day carried out of the field incapable of work and die.' [100]

Significantly, water and food supplies were contaminated across Europe and weather patterns changed too. The summer of 1783 was the hottest ever recorded and the following winter was the coldest. French scientists now believe that these events may well have contributed to the 'tipping point' of scarcities that led directly to the discontent and uprisings that grew into the French Revolution. There is no doubt that Louis XVI and his advisors did not deal effectively with the many problems and issues that led to the revolution in 1789. But, perhaps, we expect too much of them. There was little direct precedent for what happened in France at the time and no one could have anticipated the effect of a natural disaster such as the eruption of Laki. What Louis XVI *could* have done, however, was to have been more receptive to what was happening in France at that time. He could have listened more attentively to the signals around him and adapted accordingly. Small changes at the right time would have probably gone a long way. He could have done all this had he not suffered from the illusion that he was in control.

Like the unfortunate Louis XVI we too suffer from an unhealthy belief that we can control the world around us and, if anything, the ubiquitous availability of modern technology has deepened this illusion, making it easier for us to override the warning signs around us. The effect is to make us more reckless. This is ironic given that we often explicitly build in elaborate safeguards and controls to help us minimise unexpected consequences. However, we consistently underestimate the complexity of our environment and fail to take into account the long term consequences of our actions. This is partly because we do not take the time to evaluate the systemic consequences of our decisions, the effect that our actions have on the whole. We don't see the relationships that exist within complex systems. In short, we have lost the ability to reflect.

---

[100] Source: BBC News Online, 'When a Killer Cloud Hit Britain', January 19th 2007. The full article is available at http://news.bbc.co.uk/1/hi/sci/tech/6276291.stm. I have also drawn on an article in The Economist, '18th Century Climate Change: The Summer of Acid Rain', published on December 22nd 2007 and a brief article in Ozone Magazine, 'BBC Two, Time Watch: Timely Reminder', Winter-Spring issue 2007.

The power of reflection

'There could be a day of reckoning when you wish you had connected the dots more quickly. Future generations may ask … what were our parents thinking? … Why didn't they wake up when they had the chance?'

Al Gore, on climate change in 'An Inconvenient Truth'[101]

Reflection is the lynch pin of strategic thinking, all else depends on it. Although we look at the seven key disciplines of strategic thinking separately in this book, they are, of course, all part of one holistic process. We have already seen that the capacity to 'go slowly' and 'think small' both require a space for reflective thinking. Now we can acknowledge that *all* the seven key disciplines rest on the foundation of reflection. Reflection is simply *that* important. In practical terms we can summarise this in a simple four-stage thinking process to guide us in any situation. It works as follows:

The Universal Four Stage Strategic Thinking Process

SLOW DOWN, OBSERVE, REFLECT AND THEN ACT

Ironically, following this simple process not only enables us to act more effectively but also more decisively and quickly over the long-term. By opening up a reflective space at the beginning of the process we allow ourselves to take a broader look at the systemic factors, which will define the overall context within which our decisions will be made. We take a look at the whole and our relationship to it. We have given ourselves the opportunity to step back and reconsider both our objectives and the choices available to us to meet those objectives. We spend this time upfront to bottom out issues and really think things through, to seek a secure footing to move forward. Critically, creating this space gives us the opportunity to challenge our expectations and assumptions at the very beginning of our endeavour. If we do so we will find it considerably easier to embed reflective thinking into our daily business practice; indeed, our daily practice, period. We may take longer making our initial decisions but thereafter we have a firm foundation for future action. As a result, those actions can be taken more quickly as our pathway is both secure and, more

---

[101] Al Gore, 'An Inconvenient Truth: A global warning', available on DVD, released by Paramount, 2006

importantly, pointing in the right direction. As Steven Covey, author of 'The 7 Habits of Highly Effective People', remarks, it is one thing to climb to the top of the ladder of success but another to find that it is leaning on the wrong building![102]

It doesn't really matter *how* we choose to open space for reflection, it matters far more that we do so in the first place. Our aim is to pause before we act and take the time to consider things from a deeper level. In many ways this is the very opposite to the 'normal' thinking process that we are used to, where our mind is constantly busy. Instead of generating thoughts, we are creating a space to quiet the mind and letting thoughts come to us. If we acknowledge this space we open up to the very real possibility of new insights, pictures, ideas and even aspirations being able to emerge. We tap into a creative source that is often buried under the weight of our over active minds. It is interesting that, at first sight, what emerges may appear to be somewhat random and fragmented. However, we normally find that we possess a strong intuitive sense of what is important and this guides us in the process of pulling the insights together into a whole and integrating this into our decision making process.

BP

'Business, as an integral part of society, can and should act as lead agents of change and progress. People expect big profits, but they also expect a willingness to engage and address society and the world.'[103]

John Browne, former Group Chief Executive, BP

BP had revenues of some $291 billion and profits of $20.8 billion in 2007, making it one of the largest and most profitable corporations in the world. It has some 115,000 employees and serves about 13 million customers each day in over 100 countries. Although it lost ground within the oil industry during 2007 (both Exxon and Shell were more profitable) it was

---

[102] Stephen R Covey, 'The 7 Habits of Highly Effective People: Powerful Lessons in Personal Change', published by Simon & Schuster, 1989 and 2004. For those interested in the work of Stephen Covey see also 'The 8th Habit: From Effectiveness to Greatness', published by Simon & Schuster in 2004 and Stephen Covey's web site at www.stephencovey.com

[103] Press release by John Browne, former CEO of BP, on November 19th 2006, reported on the School of Natural Resources and the Environment website of the University of Michigan (www.snre.umich.edu). The full text of the release is available in archive form at www.snre.umich.edu/news/details.php?id=1512&gclid=CLCSh8aAmIsCFSUySAodVB1fRw

still ranked fourth in the world in the 2007 Fortune Global 500 (on the basis of sales) and seventh in the Forbes Global 2000 in 2008 (based on a mixture of four measures; sales, profit, assets and market value). Clearly, even in difficult times, BP is a highly effective and profitable organisation. It is this ability to excel in terms of operational excellence and also to lead the industry in strategic terms that marks it out as a true strategic leader. BP's financial and market performance has been driven by operational effectiveness, size and scale economies (through acquisitions and increasing energy reserves) and a lean, decentralised organisational structure. It has an enviable record of long-term operational excellence with a strong emphasis on upstream strategy and effectiveness (for example, the ability to 'dig wet holes', striking oil first time and minimising the number of dry runs). There is a strong emphasis on maintaining reserve capacity (finding more oil than is used up) with the focus currently on seven key strategic global fields including the Gulf, Indonesia, West Africa, Venezuela and Russia. This upstream strategy, built around seven key geographical areas, is not only clear and simple but it is also consistent. It has been in place for over six years and has acted a powerful driving force for resource allocation, contributing to an impressive build up of productive upstream assets. These critical upstream capabilities (including both development and distribution) are core competencies for BP and important elements of its competitive advantage. As the costs of exploration activities are enormous these capabilities play a fundamental role in underpinning its operational effectiveness and financial performance.

Oil prices are also fundamental to BP's profitability and the increasing price of oil between 2006 and 2008 (when oil reached over $100 a barrel) certainly explains part of BP's performance. However, the company is acutely aware that it is in a cyclical business and that it cannot necessarily rely on continued high prices for sustained profitability. As a result, its goal is to ensure that levels of operational efficiency will enable a sustainable profitable business at prices as low as $30 a barrel. This provides clear reassurance that the profitability of the company will not evaporate in the event of low oil prices during a downturn. Living in this cyclical environment encourages both long term thinking and strong attention to operational detail. Both are critical strategic factors and BP has strong capabilities in both areas. At the same time, the organisation has very effective decision making processes that result from its lean and flat structure (with minimal levels of hierarchy) and its consistent drive for both efficiency and effectiveness. BP's objective has been to create an integrated global company with central strategic direction but with real authority and accountability at local level. This combination of a devolved structure and lack of middle management levels gives BP the ability to make tough decisions and it also gives it that all-important capacity to reflect. It does this by effectively opening up the space and the direct communication lines to engage in a deeper thinking process. At the same time, BP's leadership model stresses the importance of the formal process of creating space for reflection in decision making. This has the benefit of enabling collaboration and challenge to flourish and incorporating diverse points of view into the decision-making process. This combination of a decentralised structure and formalised time for reflection is a key reason why an organisation as large as BP has been able to commit itself to delivering a major step-change in its core business through its move towards a more diversified green energy company.

Foundations for success

'Just over a year ago we lost 15 people and injured many more in the accident at our refinery in Texas City in the United States. That was an event that we are absolutely determined should never happen again. In the last twelve months a great deal of work has been done to identify exactly what happened and why.'[104]

John Browne, BP's AGM in April 2006

The organisations that we have looked at up to now – Toyota, Honda, Starbucks, Amazon, the National Trust, Virgin – are all strategic leaders in their fields but none is in an environment as complex as BP. It operates in a highly politicized global industry where the scale of operations is huge, the strategic remit is very broad and competition is intense. In addition, BP's commitment to green energy implies a more complex and diversified business than some of its 'oil and gas' competitors. Not least, it stands at the forefront of environmental and climate change. Few organisations operate in such a challenging and complex environment as this and even fewer can legitimately claim that they have established a position of strategic leadership in their industries. BP has much to teach us from that

---

[104] Source: remarks made by John Browne, former CEO of BP, at BP's AGM on April 20th 2006, sourced from BP.

perspective alone. However, we can also learn a great deal from its reaction to when things do not go well, from the specific challenges and failures that inevitably result from managing such a large and complex business operation around the globe.

BP has had a particularly tough couple of years. It has been roundly criticized for failing to spend enough money on safety after the explosion at its refinery in Texas City in 2005 killed 15 employees and injured another 180. In the same year the company suffered corrosion and oil spills in Alaska, delays in developing new oilfields and two investigations of its trading arm for price-rigging. BP has reacted quickly by improving the personal, process and environmental dimensions of safety, with significant ongoing financial investment. Between 2007 and 2010 it is committed to spending $7 billion on safety upgrades at its US refineries and in replacing infrastructure in Alaska. Indeed, it intends to go even further and 'take a leadership position in process safety in the years to come.'[105] This cannot bring back lives that are lost or reduce the level of human tragedy that lies behind the statistics but it is a significant statement of intent for the future. In its 2006 annual report BP reaffirms its core values including the responsibility to act fairly and honestly in all its dealings. It talks about the importance of its code of conduct (the policies and standards that provide the framework for conduct in the millions of relatively small transactions generated each year) in providing a foundation to realize these values. The report notes that 'if behaviours and outcomes fall short of those standards, then we act decisively to learn and to improve. That is our commitment.'[106] This reflects a broader commitment ingrained within BP to learn from its mistakes and integrate this learning back into the day to day operations. This can only come from a culture that is receptive and open. Most importantly, it requires the capacity for reflection, one that is deeply embedded within the structure of the organisation and within the day to day decision making process.

'Beyond Petroleum'

'No enterprise ... no institution ... perhaps no individual can really succeed without a sense of purpose – a purpose which explains and guides every step ... A sense of purpose that gives meaning to every day of your life ... which motivates and carries you through

---

[105] Source: BP Annual Report and Review, 2006.
[106] Source: BP Annual Report and Review, 2006.

the hard times ... which transcends the trivia and the grind ... Our purpose ... our fundamental objective, is to be one of the world's greatest companies.'[107]

John Browne

John Browne was the first oil executive to acknowledge the link between carbon dioxide and climate change. As early as 1997 he gave a speech in California in which he expressed his concerns about environmental degradation and climatic change. He talked about the need to strike a balance between development and environmental protection and he recommended that action be taken to address the genuine and growing threat to the earth. Thereafter BP began to seriously address the issue of finding new forms of low carbon energy and reducing what would now be known as its internal 'carbon footprint'. By 2000 the company was ready to make a major declaration of its intention to move towards a diversified green energy company and it adopted the Helios symbol (a green and yellow sunburst named after the sun god of ancient Greece) as part of a major re-branding exercise. This was accompanied by the slogan 'Beyond Petroleum', which spoke clearly of BP's aspirations. Interestingly, this was originally accompanied by three other 'BP's; 'better people', 'better products' and 'big picture', all of which are areas in which the company has invested heavily. Although many were cynical at the time about BP's intentions this was far more than mere re-branding hype. It was the organisation making good on its commitment to take a leading role in meeting the environmental and climatic challenges that John Browne had talked about consistently since his first speech on the topic in California. In 1997 he declared that 'we are all citizens of the world, and we must take shared responsibility for its future'[108] and by 2000 he was even more emphatic stating that 'the issues of global warming and of air quality in the word's cities are real ... the risks are there and to ignore them would be foolish as well as arrogant.'[109] BP was preparing to play its part. That part is likely to be very critical indeed, not only for BP as a company but for our world as a whole.

---

[107] Remarks made by John Browne, former CEO of BP, at Morehouse College in the United States on September 29th 2000, sourced from BP.

[108] Source: BP's website (www.bp.com) under the section 'About BP/millennium', page reference www.bp.com/sectiongenericarticle.do?categoryId=9014445&contentId=7027526. BP has an excellent web site with very comprehensive coverage on its history, strategy and current priorities.

[109] Remarks made by John Browne, former CEO of BP, at Morehouse College in the United States on September 29th 2000, sourced from BP.

BP has made substantial progress in the last five years towards its green energy goals including investing significantly in alternative and renewable energy businesses, reducing greenhouse gases in internal operations, looking at sustainable transportation options and also funding significant research activities. It is dedicated to investing in and applying new energy sources that are both low-carbon and neutral, with its core focus on energy for the power sector, which currently generates around 40% of the world's man-made emissions of carbon dioxide. BP is committed to make low-carbon power generation a profitable business and is moving ahead rapidly with carbon capture and sequestration projects (which effectively replace carbon emissions into the ground and have the potential to make a dramatic difference in carbon reduction world-wide). In all areas it is striving to make a significant reduction in its own carbon footprint (with a symbolic reduction of carbon activities by 10 per cent within the organisation itself). In addition, BP is actively investing in a whole range of alternative energy technologies; the company is the currently the largest manufacturer of solar panels in the world and a leading player in the markets for both bio fuels and wind generation.

It is not only in renewable energy and reduction in carbon emissions that BP is making great strides. It is actively involved in research and development. In 2006 it announced plans to invest $500 million in the BP Energy Biosciences Institute, a dedicated bioscience laboratory researching new fuels for transportation. It is also taking an increasingly active role in influencing government policy, regulation and research. In November 2006 John Browne called on governments to play their part in what he called the 'environmental sustainability drama', making the point that only governments can create the 'global framework in which business can go to work making changes.'[110] This is an example of BP taking a pro-active role that goes well beyond the conventional remit of business, one that sees business as a major change agent for good in society. It combines the conventional commercial objectives of business (where profitability is the market signal that resources are being effectively used) with a much broader social role in creating a better future.

The power of one

BP is a unique organisation. It has built a very profitable and effective

---

[110] Remarks made by John Browne, former CEO of BP, at Columbia Business School in New York, 'Energy Security and Climate Change', on November 17th 2006, sourced from BP.

business in conventional terms and done so in a highly complex and challenging environment. It operates in a global arena under the watchful eye of governments. In fact, few environments could be more demanding. BP has a very strong sense of purpose and a healthy capacity for reflection embedded throughout the company. It took on board the seriousness of environmental and climate change issues long before it became fashionable to do so and it continues to champion the need for radical international action. It has done all this by mobilizing the energy and support of a great many people throughout the organisation to make major changes in almost every aspect of the business. It has managed to make these changes remarkably quickly, particularly given the size of the company. Naturally, this would not have been possible without the combined efforts, skills, ingenuity and sheer hard work of many, many, people throughout the organisation. Yet, there is also a strong sense that it is due, in no uncertain measure, to one man. It is hard to imagine that BP would be where it is today without the drive and single-purposefulness of John Browne and the unique sense of mission that he has brought to the company. Not only does he exhibit the now familiar characteristics of strategic leadership; the combination of vision and the capacity to act, but his background as a development engineer has enabled him to remain firmly rooted in operational reality at the same time as taking on an almost evangelical role in promoting a new balance between development and the environment.

I have never met John Browne but I would like to do so.[111] I know from a good friend who works for BP that he has enormous energy and he is obsessive in his work life (during his tenure as CEO he generated enough output to keeps three PA's constantly busy!). I also know that his background and experience keep him firmly rooted in the real world and operational reality, yet he is completely genuine in his commitment for a better world. Like all the strategic business leaders that I have met he is very serious about leaving a legacy for future generations. My colleague at BP expressed John Browne's personal philosophy in a very simple statement, that 'BP should be a force for good.'[112] That may be a simple statement but it is also a very powerful one. It is one thing to talk about the unique qualities of BP's infrastructure and culture and suggest that this enables the company to have a capacity to reflect that underpins its

---

[111] While I have never met John Browne I am, however, indebted to him for finding the time to look over the material in this section of the book and for his kind note of support.
[112] I am indebted here to my good friend at BP, Simon Taylor, who provided so much help with this section of the book.

strategic leadership, both in its industry and in leading the global response to changes in the environment. But it is only half the story. The culture at BP reflects the commitment and passion of the man who was at the top for 12 years from 1995 until May 2007. BP's ability to reflect deeply is also the product of another story, that of John Browne himself.

Reflection practices

'Every profound innovation is based on an inward-bound journey, on going to a deeper place where knowing comes to the surface.'[113]

W. Brian Arthur, Economist, Santa Fe Institute

There are a number of formal processes that can help us to enter a reflective space including meditation, a short period of silence, practicing becoming more conscious in the moment (often simply by taking a series of deep breaths) and many other reflective or metaphysical practices. The most important thing to remember about these practices is that their effectiveness depends not on the length of time that we spend on them but on whether we do them regularly. A little each day will make much more of a difference than long sessions every now and then! In practice, this is easier for some of us to achieve than for others so the good news is that we don't actually have to do anything special. As we have seen, walking, spending a little time in nature, exercise, sports or other areas of intense concentration can have the same positive effect of clearing the mind and allowing in new ideas, insights and inspiration. In fact, almost anything can be used to this effect if it does the trick for you. It may be through a practice or hobby such as yoga, music, art, dancing or martial arts. Or it may simply be a question of checking our breathing at regular intervals, becoming more conscious of the individual breaths, particularly before making important decisions or attending meetings. All it needs is a reason for us to 'stop' for a moment, recalibrate and open some space to let in the new.

Some close friends of mine attended a course held at a monastery a few years back and the monks had the practice of ringing the bells every

---

[113] W. Brian Arthur is an economist, presently on the external faculty at the Santa Fe Institute and a Visiting Researcher at the Intelligent Systems Lab at PARC. He is credited with creating the modern theory of increasing returns and specializes in developing a 'more realistic economics', technology and innovation and complexity theory. For more information see his web site at www.santafe.edu/~wbarthur.

6. Reflect

couple of hours for two minutes silence.[114] Just as the group would be on the brink of coming to a decision on some 'important' matter the bell would inevitably go and everything would have to stop. How frustrating! Two minutes had never seemed so long. It reminded me of my early school days when we played football during the breaks. Wasn't it always the way that when we just about to score that perfect goal the bell would inevitably go? And then there's that universal temptation. 'Just another minute', 'I know I can get that ball in the back of the net ... if only I had that extra minute.' And here's the funny thing about that bell. Our frustration subsides during the silence. We don't pick up where we left off, or at least not exactly where we left off. We ask ourselves instead, 'now why were we talking about that, surely it's a side issue?' 'Maybe that decision wasn't one that was worth having. Let's get back on track and do what we are here to do.' We reframe, we reconnect to the central purpose of what's in hand. That's all it takes sometimes, one or two minutes of reflection. It was the same for me with football. I really wasn't very good at scoring goals. In fact, my soccer skills were quite limited altogether. I was much more effective in defence and by racing up the field I was normally over-extending myself and making my team vulnerable. Formal lesson time allowed me the time to reframe my tactics and return to where I was least damaging from my team's perspective!

There is another way to clear the mind that takes the very opposite approach to the practices we have discussed so far. It is particularly useful for those of us who are more action oriented by nature and who bridle at the prospect of time spent 'passively' in inner contemplation. Instead of adopting a practice to consciously quiet the mind, we engage fully in an active pursuit. In fact, we immerse ourselves in it. This is most powerful when it involves service to others. As we have seen in chapter five, a practice of service to others allows us to distance ourselves from our own issues, problems and challenges. By gaining space and distance from our own 'stuff' we not only gain a different perspective but we also open up to the possibility of new insights and approaches emerging. By stepping into somebody else's shoes, by engaging fully in the service of others, we temporarily 'shut off' the constant stream of thoughts that clamour for our attention, allowing the space for deeper insights and creative solutions to come through. It is strange but when the issues we face are most intractable (and the temptation is therefore to throw more time and effort

---

[114] I am indebted to Peter and Jill Chandler for this example of reflective thinking and for much else besides!

at them) it is often helpful to withdraw for a short while and immerse ourselves in something else entirely. Ironically, this withdrawal often open up the space to be able to challenge the closed loop of self limiting assumptions that have held us back from seeing a wider picture. Although we can do almost anything this process is particularly powerful when we are in service to others because it is through relationship with others that creative insight often occurs. In my own case I often find that the problems that I am working on with my clients mirror my own and I can apply the creative insight gained directly to my own life.

Narrative tools

Several years ago I was asked by a colleague who was Finance Director of a large charitable concern if I would work with him on introducing a strategic planning system into the organisation. As part of my remit we held a weekend strategic workshop for the senior executives in a very pleasant country hotel. It was the only pleasant thing about the event, which was a disaster. Political intrigue and almost open warfare between various members of the executive certainly did not help and our joint approach to the event, which was too directive and relied far too much on PowerPoint presentations and plenary group discussions, quickly ran aground. As facilitator I was left in the uncomfortable position of having to scrap almost all of my prepared agenda and simply work with what was in front of me. And that, as it turned out, was an unspoken but implacable opposition to the introduction of any strategic planning system.

Luckily, before the event, I had managed to persuade my colleague that it would be useful to do some work around scenarios. So, on the second day, I went ahead with these, splitting the team into three small groups and sending each group off to work on developing a response to a number of potential future events. The object of scenario analysis is to learn from the thinking process that occurs when we consider how we would react to a hypothetical set of circumstances rather than develop a concrete plan of action. I use it not only to work with the alternative possible outcomes developed by teams ('scenarios') but also to challenge them to look more deeply at the implications involved. In this case, given the way that the weekend had developed to that point, I must confess did not have very high expectations on the outcome. However, I quickly realized that I was wrong. The executive team rapidly engaged with the process and the exercise became the highlight of the weekend. In fact, by engaging the team around a narrative they were capable of challenging some of the core assumptions of the organisation and defining many of the key challenges that they faced. It was the only time during the weekend that the overt workshop activity took precedence over the underlying political infighting!

I learned a very valuable lesson that day and I now use narrative tools a lot in my work, whether I am facilitating an event, holding a seminar or teaching. The more complex a situation is the more valuable these tools become because they often bypass the linear thinking that bedevils our society. More importantly, we can use these tools to go into a deeper reflective place where we are able to challenge assumptions that we would normally take for granted or explore different approaches to a situation that might be considered too risky or inappropriate in the practical business context. As we become caught up in the story we begin to draw from a deeper creative well and that can be very powerful indeed. Scenario analysis and story-telling also help us to surface assumptions and belief systems that otherwise are likely to remain hidden (what some call the 'shadow side' of organisational life) and to perform a basic 'reality check' for where we are.[115] I am always amused when a group presents a response to a scenario and their colleagues accuse them of cheating! 'You can't do that', they say, which always leads to a very interesting discussion of why they think this is the case! Looking at what is permissible, and what is not, is every bit as illuminating as examining the different approaches and knowledge used by different groups when formulating their responses to a potential future event.

At an individual level story-telling is immensely powerful, so much so that I am almost always humbled by the outcome. And because it is so powerful it needs to be handled with a great deal of respect. Personally, I believe that it should only be used on an explicitly voluntary basis and it is always important to ensure that there is an adequate 'safety net' for participants (somebody trained to deal with anything that might arise for participants, preferably an accredited counsellor). Ideally, there should be no overt or covert pressure for individuals to participate or reveal anything that they don't want to. This all requires considerable skill on the part of the facilitator, not only in terms of process but also to make sure that the use and context of story-telling is appropriate in the first place. As with all of these tools, however, story-telling offers the potential to go to a much

---

[115] If you are interested in exploring the implications of the 'shadow side' of organisations I would recommend 'Working on the Shadow Side: A Guide to Positive Behind-the-Scenes Management' by Gerard Egan, published by Jossey-Bass in 1994.

deeper place and can offer great insight either in an individual or a corporate setting. But surely it goes way beyond this. Story-telling is no technique. Telling a story goes to the heart of what it means to be human. It is, and always has been, fundamental to who we are and how we communicate with each other. So it should come as no surprise that story-telling can play such a powerful role at the very heart of our ability to reflect, at the very foundation of strategic thinking.

Ideas in action

The ability to reflect is critical in any complex environment, particularly in relation to the deeper relationships that underlie the bigger system. If we run a coffee shop, for example, it is wise not to protest about the arrival of a national competitor until we think things through. Coffee shops and restaurants are often subject to 'clustering' effects where additional competitors can actually increase demand by making an area more attractive as a whole to potential customers. A similar rational explains why some shopping mall owners actually pay anchor stores to locate in their malls. The attraction of the anchor store pulls in customers so that smaller niche players (who may also be competitors of course) also benefit from increased footfall as a whole. The net effect is that there is an opportunity for everyone to gain, providing that they are competitive in the first place! Unfortunately, many of us see the world as a 'zero sum game', where the gain of one person or business must mean a corresponding loss to another. This not only prevents us from embracing change as an opportunity but it reduces our ability to be flexible and adaptable because we cut ourselves off from learning from others. Even if the new coffee shop opens directly opposite ours it is very likely that we will be able to learn significantly from their approach; changing and adapting where appropriate while strengthening those parts of our proposition that make us unique. Even loyal customers like to have choices!

The more complex the environment the more critical the reflective process is. In public transport initiatives, for example, there are a very large number of factors that will affect an individual's choice of transport. Moreover, there are very significant time delays in changes to behaviour. It may take a couple of years, for example, for a new lower-fare bus tariff to increase demand for services because many potential passengers use bus services only on an occasional basis, if at all. Lower fares will also be ineffective unless timetabling, safety and convenience factors also meet customer needs. If we are seeking to make changes to long term customer behaviour (for example, encouraging people to travel by bus for certain types of journeys instead of by car) we will need to look at the system as a whole and make sure all the factors are aligned. In practice, this is very difficult, as anyone involved in public transport knows!

Sometimes, however, technology can help. In the rural area in which I live scheduled bus journeys are increasingly being enhanced by the ability to book on demand (either by phone or internet).[116] This demand-pull system is not only more convenient for passengers but allows the transport company to run services only when necessary and adjust the size of the bus accordingly. Instead of running large double-decker buses that are largely empty outside peak periods, it can run smaller more cost effective vehicles, which allows it to offer more frequent journeys and better value   Even then, uptake of the new service is slow. Changing customer behaviour takes considerable time and it is hard to compete with the convenience of using our own car, sitting conveniently at the end of the drive. In practice, word of mouth or personal experience becomes the best advocate to change behaviour. This means concentrating on improving services at times and in places where it is often least convenient for the transport operator (for example, late night services for those eating out or extended service to hospitals and other public institutions). It means looking at every 'park and ride' trip as a potential 'moment of truth' for a customer who is currently wedded to their car. It involves increasing effectiveness and reducing costs to be able to extend services at good value and reduce the *in*convenience factor of not using one's own car (and recognizing that using public transport is often an inconvenience for many of us). However, most of all, it means truly understanding the web of relationships that underlie the needs of the community and meeting them. Those needs include a desire for many of us to be more environmentally responsible in our transport choices. That ought to be a big opportunity for public transport companies in the future. A more powerful incentive still for consumer change is rapidly increasing fuel costs, which provides us with a classic example of opportunity hidden within the shadows!

---

[116] A very good example of this is the Connect2Wiltshire transport service, which offers door to door transport in to and from many areas of Wiltshire for people living in or visiting the county. Further information is available at www.bookaride.net/c2w/index.html.

Starting at the beginning

There is a story that has been circulating on the internet for some time, which adds something important to our discussion on the importance of reflection. It is called 'rocks in the jar' and I am indebted to Rick Jarow, Assistant Professor at Vassar College, for this particular version.[117] A business guru was tackling the subject of time management in a seminar. He pulled out a big jar and filled it with large stones until no more could fit in. He asked the participants whether the jar was full and they agreed that it was. In response he pulled out a bag of smaller stones and began to add them to the jar until no more could fit in. Again he asked his audience if the jar was full and again most of the audience replied 'yes'. This time, however, there were quite a few dissenters who said 'no', although they couldn't quite put their finger on why the jar might not be as full as it looked. The business guru smiled and pulled out a bag of pebbles and began adding them to the jar, until once again no more could fit in. Again he asked 'Is it full?' By now the audience had got the point and hesitated, some saying 'yes' but most answering 'no'. 'Quite so,' said the teacher and he began to add sand until no more could fit in. 'What is the morale of this story?' he asked the businessmen. 'Oh, that's easy' they responded, 'no matter how busy you are, you can always fit in more to your schedule!' 'No,' replied the guru, the moral is simple, 'first things first!'

Talking about the power of reflection is a very conceptual matter. In practice, either in a business situation or in our personal life, it is sometimes difficult to know where to begin. The answer, as our business guru demonstrated above, is 'first things first'. Begin with what is most important, the central purpose of an undertaking or endeavour. Begin with what is most important in your life, those things that would make your life full even if all else was lost. This provides the rudder for everything else. We begin by putting the biggest stones first into our jar because otherwise they will be crowded out by other things! There are many other variants of this story. In some the business guru goes one stage further and adds water into the jar. In one version it is beer rather than water. When asked what the meaning of the beer is the teacher replies, 'no matter how full your life may seem, there's always room for a couple of beers with a

---

[117] Rick Jarow, 'Creating the Work You Love: Courage, Commitment, and Career – The Complete Anti-Career Book' published by Inner Traditions, 1995 and 'The Ultimate Anti-Career Guide: The Inner Path to Finding Your Work in the World', CD/tape box sets, published by Sounds True 1998/2000. See also Rick Jarow's web site at www.anticareer.com

friend.' Now, personally, I like that version![118]

I believe that my friend and colleague who works for BP is an exceptionally effective manager. I *know* that he is both highly intelligent and capable and I imagine that he makes a formidable difference at his job. But, like many of us in middle age he has been in the organisational world for a long time and he can be sceptical about the benefits of many of the changes that he sees take place. There is a sense of world-weariness that affects all of us after a time. 'Surely not another initiative,' we say to ourselves, only in much less polite terms. We might add, 'we've been around this loop before' or more likely, 'when will they ever learn?' Certainly my friend is no fool and he is the last person you would call naïve or gullible in any way. However, when we talked about BP and, in particular, the legacy of John Browne, there was an unmistakable sense of pride in his voice. That's what happens when we put 'first things first'. That's the 'secret' of how an organisation as large as BP has managed to change so quickly and so effectively.

---

[118] My thanks to Ed Austin for sending me this version

7

BE SIMPLE

An innocent approach

In 1998 three Cambridge graduates, Richard Reed, Jon Wright and Adam Balon, wondered whether they should leave their 'proper jobs' and start a new business venture selling pure fruit smoothies. They had developed the smoothie recipes but it still seemed a big step. So they put up a stall at a little music festival in London with two dustbins, one marked 'yes' and the other 'no'. Then they put up a big sign saying 'Do you think we should give up our jobs to make these smoothies?' and let the customers decide. By the end of the day the 'yes' bin was overflowing and they promptly resigned their jobs. So began Innocent Drinks, a company formed with a very simple idea, that every product it sells contains 100% pure, fresh ingredients and no fruit concentrates. By 2007 it was one of the fastest growing food and drinks companies in the UK, turning over some £76 million and claiming a 70% market share for its smoothies. That equates to selling some two million smoothies every week! Innocent has always believed in keeping things simple and straightforward and this applies to its product range, quality and ethical standards and its brand definition. At the heart of the company is its promise that anything that it produces 'will taste good and do you good. We promise we'll never use concentrates, preservatives, stabilizers, or any weird stuff in our drinks'.[120] Around this

---

[119] William of Ockham was an English Franciscan friar and scholastic philosopher from Ockham, a small village in Surrey, near East Horsley. He is remembered primarily for formulating the principle of parsimony in explanation and theory building that became known as 'Occam's Razor' (a variation on his name).

[120] Source: Innocent Drinks packaging

business definition it has committed to making the world a better place with initiatives on recycling, reducing carbon emissions, ethical procurement and charity work. Innocent expresses this as follows:

> **'It's all a bit Miss World, but we genuinely want to leave things a tiny bit better than the way we found them. First and foremost, this means we'll always make 100% natural, healthy drinks in a responsible, sustainable way.'** [121]

Innocent was built on the simple premise of providing an easy way to make every day a bit healthier. From the beginning the founders pursued a non corporate culture with a friendly image, a quirky logo (an apple, affectionately known as 'the dude' with a halo) and casual, humorous labelling. They were convinced that with a 'sincere commitment to the cause and creative thinking', it was possible to 'create a fast growing company that acts responsibly.' [122] This culture has attracted a very talented work team as the company sought to employ experts in every relevant field from employment strategy to web design (a strategy which earned it a 'top employer' accreditation from the Guardian newspaper). This combination of passion, commitment, creativity, service and raw talent has enabled Innocent to achieve both mainstream commercial success and stay true to its wholesome brand values. These include the procurement of all ingredients ethically, the use of ecologically sound packaging materials and the simple act of leading by doing good things at its head office, 'Fruit Towers'. One obvious such initiative is giving away 10% of its profits through the Innocent Foundation to create a sustainable future for local communities in the countries from which it sources its products. However, the company also does a host of other things from continuously improving the environmental sustainability of packaging materials to providing drinks for the homeless. In addition, few companies are as responsive to customers as Innocent, which relies heavily on customer feedback to drive its products, brand values and strategic direction.

The straightforward and almost irreverent approach of the company is felt by customers (both users and retailers), suppliers and other partners of

---

[121] Source: Innocent Smoothie Recipe Book: 57½ recipes from our kitchen to yours', published by Fourth Estate, London, 2006. Please also see the company's web site (www.innocentdrinks.co.uk) for more information on core philosophy and principles, particularly at www.innocentdrinks.co.uk/us/ethics.

[122] Source: Innocent Drinks case study by the Design Council available at www.designcouncil.org.uk/en/Case-Studies/All-Case-Studies/Innocent-Smoothies

the business alike, especially through its simple down-to-earth communications, which incorporate the same no-nonsense honesty of its brand values and products. There is something reassuring familiar with Innocent as it mirrors the attention to detail that we have seen in other strategic leaders in this book. The company is focused on getting the small things right. Dan Germain, who joined in the early stages as Copywriter, expresses this as follows, 'We give a damn about the small stuff. We obsess about details. It's the only way to keep everything Innocent. It's weird – big stuff almost takes care of itself, but it's the little things that you need to keep an eye on.'[123]

There is nothing small about Innocent's vision for a better world or in its undoubted commercial success. The company's achievements rest on a remarkable sense of clarity and simplicity. It is focused on a clear unambiguous proposition supported by strong values and its famed no-nonsense culture and communication style. This strategic clarity binds together all those who are involved with the company in a common endeavour. It also allows Innocent to identify trade-offs and boundaries and act accordingly. In short, it knows what it here to do and what it does not do! One example is in the company's ethical procurement policy. It will only procure fruit from suppliers who sign up to the minimum standards of the International Labour Organisation. In what it calls 'having zero tolerance with the basics',[124] it simply won't trade with suppliers if they are not signed up to the ILO. And that is it! No 'ands', 'ifs', 'buts' or 'maybes'. These simple rules, based on Innocent's strong core values and sense of purpose, provide a clear and focused decision-making framework that allows the company to define its direction without confining it. As a result, it retains its creative and innovative approach (which gives it flexibility and adaptability in the marketplace) but maintains its strong sense of identity.

---

[123] Source: Innocent Drinks case study by the Design Council available at www.designcouncil.org.uk/en/Case-Studies/All-Case-Studies/Innocent-Smoothies
[124] Source: Innocent Drinks web site, under ethics, now redrafted. Innocent has a wonderful web site (www.innocentdrinks.co.uk), which is well worth looking at as a model of what a good web site should be!

Less is more

Innocent provides a wonderful example of the importance of simplicity in defining strategic and competitive advantage. Indeed, the more complex our world becomes the more important it is for organisations to maintain clear focus and boundaries. My good friend, David Snowden, Founder and Chief Scientific Officer of Cognitive Edge (and formerly a Director in the IBM Institute for Knowledge Management)[125] draws a nice distinction between *complicated* strategies based on *simplistic* thinking and the *simple* frameworks that are called for in *complex* environments. Over-complicated solutions are one of the curses of modern life. In commercial organisations there is the inexorable temptation to provide new things for customers (or new levels of administration to make life 'easier' internally). Each decision, viewed in isolation, may make sense but from the viewpoint of the whole this often translates into an enormous build up of systemic cost. There is a price to pay for added levels of complication (sometimes known as 'complexity creep'). Mark Gottfredson, a partner at consultancy Bain & Co., studied 75 companies in 12 industries and found that as firms become more complicated growth slowed. Those companies that were lowest in complexity grew 1.7 times as fast as their average competitors, even taking firm size into account.[126] Government is even more susceptible to the lure of unnecessarily complicated solutions, often yielding to the temptation to micro-manage aspects of the economy, service provision or its own administration. The result is normally ineffective and sometimes disastrous, leading to the build up of cost without any definable improvement in services, or worse still, an actual decline in service standards. As the Economist summed up in an editorial on the record of the UK government in April 2006, 'the lesson is to do more by doing less.'[127]

---

[125] For further information on David Snowden please see his web site (www.cognitive-edge.com) and/or visit his blog at www.cognitive-edge.com/blogs/dave

[126] Source: Mark Gottfredson, partner and co-head of Bain & Company's capabilities sourcing practice, quoted by Time Magazine in the article 'The Big Gulp at Starbucks', December 18th 2006. For further information on Mark's work please see Bain & Company's web site (http://www.bain.com)

[127] Source: The Economist, 'Britain's Government: Labour's Black April', April 29th 2006.

eBay

'One of the great attractions of eBay is its entertainment value; like any great flea market you never know what you will find ... Serendipity is a powerful force that eBay is keen to play on, so that almost anything ... can be found either by chance or design.'[128]

The Economist

Few organisations are as iconic as eBay, the world's largest online auctioneer and marketplace. It was founded in 1995 in San Jose, California and currently has a global presence in 39 countries with 276 million registered users worldwide. Users trade goods in over 50 categories, with over 40% of sales now being fixed price rather than the traditional auction format. Unlike many e-commerce organisations eBay has been profitable since its inception, partly because it carries no inventory and operates by facilitating direct exchanges between buyers and sellers. By 2007 revenues stood at $7.7 billion and income from operations was over $2.1 billion, dwarfing most other internet based companies and placing it alongside Google, Amazon and Yahoo! as one of the key global web-based players today. The business has clearly come a very long way since its inception as a site to trade collectibles such as Beanie Babies.

The statistics behind eBay tell a compelling story. In 2007 the value of goods traded over eBay amounted to over $59 billion, which translates into more than $2,000 worth of goods traded every second. At any given time there are approximately 113 million listings worldwide, with some six to seven million listings being added each day. By the end of 2007 there were a staggering 532 million stores hosted by eBay worldwide (of which approximately 46% were on the company's international sites) and a study conducted by AC Nielsen International Research in 2006 estimated that there are approximately 1.3 million sellers around the world who use eBay as their primary or secondary source of income.[129] By any definition, eBay is a cultural phenomenon. Its success spreads throughout its community of users to a degree unprecedented in almost any other organisation. As

---

[128] Source: The Economist, 'Leader: Anniversary Lessons from eBay' and 'Meg and the Power of Many: Special Report on eBay', June 11th 2005.

[129] Source: eBay web site (www.ebay.com) under 'fast facts' (http://news.ebay.com/fastfacts_ebay_marketplace.cfm). Staggering as these statistics are, transaction volumes are increasing rapidly as I found out when I edited this section of the book nine months after the first draft was finished.

former President and CEO, Meg Whitman, put it, eBay is 'still the best place in the world to start a new business.' More than anything else, eBay has pioneered the concept of online communities based on commerce, sustained by trust and inspired by opportunity. It has done this using a surprisingly simple business model and allowing a remarkable degree of self regulation. Again, Meg Whitman summarizes the eBay approach. 'We make a small number of rules and get the heck out of the way, because the entrepreneurial talents of our users will solve a lot of the problems.'[130]

Sustaining a community business

As eBay has grown it has become both an economy and a community in its own right by delivering the efficiency of a global market to buyers and sellers no matter how small they might be. By providing the technology platform for others to trade in such a simple and intuitive way it has drawn large numbers of buyers to its sites, reinforcing its preeminent position as the world's most successful auction site. eBay stores can be set up in a few minutes, have relatively low subscription fees and can be easily customized by the owner including the choice of whether to sell by the traditional auction method or using a fixed 'buy it now' price. In essence, success is a self reinforcing system and eBay has been able to capitalize on this by providing a ready market for even the smallest of niches, based on its core competence of aggregating many buyers and sellers in one place. It has reintroduced the joy of the flea market into the modern world, for buyers and sellers alike. Indeed, eBay recognizes that many people enjoy the 'haggling factor' found in traditional markets and has introduced new features such as 'Want it Now' (which acts like a wanted ad) and 'Best Offer' (which allow a seller asking for a fixed price to entertain a best offer) that capitalize on the 'time-honoured tradition of trading'.[131]

eBay certainly had the advantage of being one of the first in the online marketplace but the company's success is a result of much more than simply 'first mover advantage'. What truly distinguishes eBay as an organisation, and makes it very special, is the strong sense of community that has developed between the community of buyers and sellers. This is

---

[130] Meg Whitman, former CEO of eBay. Both quotes from The Economist, 'Meg and the Power of Many: Special Report on eBay', June 11th 2005.
[131] Bill Cobb, former President of eBay in North America, quoted in The Economist, 'Meg and the Power of Many: Special Report on eBay', June 11th 2005.

only possible because of the high levels of trust that bind the system together. This trust has led to formidable self policing policies including feedback systems, user 'neighbourhood watch' groups (which help guard against misuse or violations of site etiquette) and lots of open and honest communication between the company and community. Although eBay is sometimes criticized for being too devolved (normally around specific instances of trading inappropriate goods or for lack of central customer service facilities) this community based model is remarkably powerful in maintaining honesty and integrity and enabling the organisation to adapt and evolve. The users have always been vociferous and noisy because eBay becomes part of the lifestyles of its members and issues can go to the centre of their lives. The company has used this to its advantage, even allowing some user groups direct access to corporate email systems to alert category managers when things go awry. As Bill Cobb, former President of North America, puts it 'the passion meter runs high' and this level of commitment and involvement is a highly beneficial thing for the company. He has no doubts about the importance of the eBay community as a foundation for the company's success:

'Managing is the wrong word ... We enable, we listen, we respond ... Generally in a company the employees know the most about the business. In eBay, our community knows more than we do.'[132]

Keeping it simple

At its core eBay has a very simple proposition; to be the world's largest online auctioneer and marketplace. It manages product and operational complexity by devolving much of the detailed operational decision making to buyers and sellers and regulates its business through a limited number of simple rules. It is a wonderful example of the power of simplicity in creating one of the world's most successful businesses and one of its largest communities. eBay's proposition is not only clear and focused but its business has also operated within recognizable industry boundaries. Like Amazon it taps into the huge body of expertise of its community in exchange for providing them with the technology umbrella under which to operate. This enables it to draw on the distributed intelligence of its

---

[132] Bill Cobb, former President of eBay in North America, quoted in The Economist, 'Meg and the Power of Many: Special Report on eBay', June 11th 2005.

members, bringing in their expertise at the all important level of individual products and services. In addition, users do most of the work including photographing their goods, writing their listings, communicating with their buyers and dispatching their sales.

It is at this operational level that we find the obsessive attention to detail that we have seen as a hallmark in many other organisations that we have identified as strategic leaders in their fields. It is also at this level that we find the product passion that is a characteristic of all great retailers, and which here also serves to bind buyers and sellers together through common interests. The strength of this community is apparent from the length of time that people spend when visiting eBay and the number of visits they make. According to a Nielsen survey in March 2007 visitors to eBay UK spent an average of two hours on the site and viewed 266 pages a month. In the same survey Nielsen concluded that eBay UK accounted for a staggering 11% of all time spent by UK users on the internet. All this adds up to extensive customer loyalty and a very powerful business model that belies its simplicity.

The challenge for the future

The greatest challenge for eBay is to keep this clarity and simplicity in the future. As the company has expanded it has begun to diversify away from its original auction based approach. Not only does it now sell over 40% of items at fixed prices but it has also acquired a variety of businesses to support or extend its proposition. These include shopping.com (a shopping comparison site), PayPal (an online payments company) and Skype (an internet telephony company). In April 2006 it launched its new eBay Express site, which is designed to work in much the same way as standard internet shopping sites and provides customers with the opportunity to buy selective eBay items from multiple sellers through a conventional shopping cart system. This trend is likely to continue with more of the company's revenue coming from fixed price sales and from new rather than used goods. This strategy, however, brings the company more closely into direct competition with other internet powerhouses such as Amazon and Google, which are also aiming to expand and diversify, causing the boundaries between the businesses to dissolve rapidly. We are witnessing the beginning of increasingly bloody internet turf wars, not only between the existing web-based giants, but also with emboldened traditional retailers that are ready to resume their advance onto the web.

Naturally, eBay cannot stand still, particularly as others advance into its territory. Google is increasingly using its search engine and advertising capabilities to steer specialist buyers directly towards specialist sellers, thus reducing the advantages of eBay's online marketplace. It is also adapting its customer-facing technology to be more shopping oriented with, for example, the purchase of Froogle (a shopping comparison site) and the introduction of a new payments system that rivals PayPal. These developments partly explain why eBay was so keen to purchase Skype, since its internet telephony technology makes it much easier for buyers and sellers to communicate directly. Even more important than specific competitive threats is the fact that online shopping is becoming relentlessly more competitive as the internet provides consumers with near perfect product and price visibility. Large traditional retailers such as Wal-Mart and Tesco are keen on exploiting their huge purchasing power online by offering multi-channel propositions that give customers the best of both worlds. Since many people are keen to have things immediately, and jump at the opportunity to save unnecessary shipping costs, the possibility of picking up goods from local stores becomes a clear source of competitive advantage. On the face of it, none of this is good news for eBay. Indeed, the price paid by the company for some of its acquisitions, (particularly Skype, which included an up-front payment of $2.6 billion in 2005 and resulted in a charge of $1.4 billion in October 2007), disappointing growth and a stagnating share price resulted in Meg Whitman stepping down as CEO in March 2008.

The saving grace for eBay is that its core business remains unique and its community-based structure has proved very adept at allowing it to survive and prosper. To compete in today's world firms need to be flexible and agile, maintain an open mind and listen carefully to the needs of their customers. eBay has proved that it has the capability to do all this and more. Unlike many competitors, its business has been uniquely moulded by its users, a large number of whom are actively involved within its community. One often sited example of this is the sale of second hand cars on eBay. The company was caught off guard when managers discovered them being listed under the toy cars category on the site. The senior team worried about risk, trust and safety and former CEO, Meg Whitman, recalls that there were '100 reasons not to do it.'[133] Nevertheless they followed

---

[133] Source: William Meyers, U.S. News, 'Keeping a Gentle Grip on Power', October 31st 2005. The interview is available at
www.usnews.com/usnews/news/articles/051031/31whitman.htm.

the customer initiative and car sales now lead all other product categories with a turnover of over $17.2 billion in 2007. Managers readily admit that customers continue to shape and influence eBay's business in all areas. This organic approach and the constant 'reality check' from within the community help to keep eBay on track; it helps to keep things focused and simple. When eBay received an offer from Yahoo to merge the companies it listened hard to its community and broke off negotiations when it concluded that buyers and sellers would not be served well by the merger. The financials were attractive but the company quickly concluded that preserving the independence of its community was more important.

Community leadership

The leadership style of CEO, Meg Whitman, reflected the importance of serving this community and the competitive strength that underlies this highly fragmented and participatory business model. During her tenure as CEO from March 1998 to March 2008 she oversaw the transformation of eBay from a small auction website with 30 employees and revenues of about $4 million into a hugely successful global commerce engine. She is an inspirational leader and the recipient of numerous accolades including the most powerful woman in American business by *Fortune* magazine in 2005 (and being nominated as one of the world's 100 most influential people in *Time* magazine in 2004 and 2005). Most importantly, Meg Whitman recognized that establishing simple community rules is by far the best way to run a business operating within a complex environment with such a wide and diverse body of stakeholders. In a US News interview with William Meyers in October 2005[134] she talked about the counterintuitive strands that made up her leadership style, which Meyers summarized as 'leads by not leading, bosses by not bossing and manages by not managing'. This included the understanding that:

- eBay does not own its community. Buyers and sellers don't report to the company and if they are dissatisfied they don't have to show up to 'work'!

- People are basically good so trust them. This philosophy can be traced back to Pierre Omidyar, the former software engineer who founded eBay in 1995.

---

[134] Source: The quotes in this section draw from an article by William Meyers in U.S. News, 'Keeping a Gentle Grip on Power', October 31st 2005. The interview is available at www.usnews.com/usnews/news/articles/051031/31whitman.htm.

- Management does not know more than the marketplace or community. Leadership involves listening and 'constantly changing the prism through which you view the business.' In this context, Tom Tierney, a director of eBay, sees the role of the CEO as a receiver rather than transmitter and calls it a 'discovery process not a dictatorial process.'

This consensual leadership style bodes well for eBay's future with the leadership baton passing to John Donahoe on March 31st 2008 when he took over as President and CEO. It is likely that he will maintain the open learning culture that has provided the foundation for eBay's success to date, which stresses building continual consensus and asking questions rather than providing answers. This involves sharing the learning within the community and taking very seriously the self regulating nature of eBay's business. Critically, it places a very high level of importance on earning and maintaining trust through transparency and acknowledging the need to experiment and sometimes fail. Meg Whitman summed it up as follows:

> **'It's different from traditional leadership … It's usually: What does the centre want to do? It's command and control. At eBay, it's a collaborative network … You are truly in partnership with the community of users. The key is connecting employees and customers in two-way communication. We call it "The Power of All of Us".'[135]**

Ideas in action

The nature of simplicity is widely misunderstood in our world. To be a 'simple person' should be a great accolade. Instead, it is often used as a derogatory phrase that might best be translated as naïve and unsophisticated, or perhaps somebody whose mental facilities are not quite up to scratch. If we look at our best businesses, however, we see just how misguided this view is. Great endeavours, like eBay, have simplicity at their core. They know what they are about and what they stand for. They have a clear appreciation of boundaries and trade-offs, know what they do and what they don't do! They don't attempt to have their cake and eat it by trying to be all things to all people, the kiss of death to any endeavour. As a result, they don't fall into the strategic trip of getting 'stuck in the

---

[135] Meg Whitman quoted by William Meyers, U.S. News, reference above.

middle' with a proposition that neither leads the industry in terms of operational excellence nor is clearly differentiated from competitors.[136] In short, they become strategic leaders and not 'me too' players. It is always interesting to look at stores that have recently closed in a high street or mall. How many times can we actually remember the business that used to be behind those shuttered doors and whitened panes of glass? In many cases it takes time to pin down who has gone missing because the harsh reality is that the store had no clear sense of identity. And a memorable sense of identity is almost invariably simple and easy to understand. If it takes time to figure out what the business is all about, the chances are that it will not last. It is hard to miss something that is not relevant to our lives. And it is a salutary reminder of just how difficult 'simplicity' can be to achieve in today's world.

It is often surprisingly difficult to put into words a simple proposition. What is it about Starbucks, for example, that makes it uniquely Starbucks? That is because a business proposition communicates to us through *all* our senses not just through our mind. We interpret our experience through our physical, emotional and spiritual dimensions as well as our mental facilities. Sometimes, for example, we just know we 'like' the feeling of one retail outlet but can't wait to get out of the door of another. It might be the spatial layout (physical), the friendliness of staff (emotional) or the deeper purpose behind an endeavour (spiritual) rather than a purchase made strictly as a result of a favourable price comparison. But while we may have difficulty expressing what makes a retail experience rewarding for us we normally know it when we see it, feel it and occasionally touch it. The more clearly focused and straightforward the proposition, the more that all the parts fit nicely together, the easier it is for us to understand and identify with it. If we buy a 'premium' product and discover average quality we are disappointed and will not repurchase. If we lunch at a new restaurant with food to die for, but service that makes us feel like we might as well be dead, we will not return. Simplicity, consistency and something a little bit special (a point of uniqueness) make for a good retail offer.

We see these principles at work at Waitrose, a premium grocery

---

[136] Michael Porter, who heads the Institute for Strategy and Competitiveness based at Harvard Business School, has long argued that there are three fundamental ways in which an organisation can gain sustainable competitive advantage; through cost leadership, differentiation or niche strategies. A good starting point for further understanding is 'Competitive Strategy' By Michael E Porter, published by Free Press, 1980 or one of the author's many articles on strategy. For further details see Michael Porter's home page at Harvard Business School on http://www.isc.hbs.edu

retailer in the UK, which is owned by the John Lewis Partnership. While some competitors attempt to market a variety of store brands reflecting different levels of quality, Waitrose practices a policy of consistent quality and exceptional service across the board. If it fails to deliver in the execution of its high standards, it acts quickly to learn from the experience and improve. It listens to its customers and makes them feel important because it believes that they *are* important. It walks the talk. There is no muddle about what it is seeking to achieve. Because it knows what it stands for it doesn't get into the some of the difficulties that competitors inflict upon themselves, such as launching premium store brands and then yielding to the temptation to improve margins by reducing product quality. This consistent commitment to a straightforward quality proposition has worked exceptionally well for Waitrose. In 2006 sales amounted to £3.7 billion and the chain is expanding rapidly in terms of its reach within the United Kingdom. Although it has a relatively small share of the UK market overall (some 4%) its share is considerably higher in its heartland of the South of England (some 7%) and, tellingly, higher still in premium product categories such as organic food (16%) and wet fish (10%). This success is due to both the clarity of its proposition and outstanding execution.[137]

At the other end of the price spectrum, Wal-Mart has also been very clear about its core offer, which is best summarized as providing reasonable quality goods at prices that everyday folk can afford. It is important to phrase Wal-Mart's proposition in terms of its customers because this reflects the core values that have driven it to become one of the most successful businesses of all time. This philosophy can be traced directly back to the company's founder, Sam Walton, and is acknowledged explicitly on its web site, which states that 'at the heart of Wal-Mart's growth is the unique culture that "Mr Sam" built.' His business philosophy was based on the simple idea of making the customer No. 1.'[138] For a while, many questioned whether this approach was enough as customers became less cost conscious (with the share of income devoted to food and household products steadily decreasing over time) and customers 'traded up' to competitors with more up market propositions. However, as the US

---

[137] More information on Waitrose is available on its web site at www.waitrose.com, including the key values, philosophy and proposition that lie at the heart of the organisation (www.waitrose.com/ourcompany/index.aspx) and, in particular, the pages on the 'Waitrose difference' (www.waitrose.com/ourcompany/thewaitrosedifference.aspx), corporate social responsibility etc.

[138] Source: Wal-Mart's wet site (www.walmart.com), 'An Introduction to Walmart.com', available at www.walmart.com/catalog/catalog.gsp?cat=542413

economy slipped into recession in 2008, the core strengths and sharp focus of Wal-Mart have once more proved decisive and its fortunes have dramatically turned. Between November 2007 and April 2008 its share price increased by over 20%, while some of its premium food competitors (such as Whole Foods Market) saw corresponding declines in value. Clarity and consistency pay at both ends of the market spectrum.

Simplicity and the clarity and focus that it brings are not the exclusive remit of single product businesses. When I visit Toronto I always keep an evening free for a family visit to one of Shopsy's deli restaurants and no visit would be complete from the perspective of my two boys without us occasionally yielding to the temptation to pick up a Shopsy's hotdog or two from a street vendor. In fact, the restaurant business and the meat product distribution business are now under separate ownership but product quality and customer experience remain true to the concept originally started in 1921 by the husband and wife team of Harry Shopsowitz and Jenny Shopsowitz. The Shopsowitz Delicatessen became a Toronto institution as a result of the 'unsurpassed flavour of its deli meats' and began using the 'Shopsy's' brand name in the mid 1940's. Owners of both sides of the business have retained this unique identity created by the heritage of the brand and the consistent product quality associated with it. As a result, Shopsy's has thrived and remains a unique Toronto 'institution'. Like many businesses that have survived the test of time Shopsy's core proposition is disarmingly simple. Successful execution, on the other hand, takes a lot more work![139]

Pret A Manger

'If Pret were a TV show (and sometimes I wish we were) we'd be Monty Python over Big Brother .... any day.'[140]

Julian Metcalfe, Co-Founder of Pret

The retail sector provides many inspirational examples of businesses that have got it right. One of the best is Pret A Manger, a UK sandwich retailer that was founded in 1986 by two college friends, Sinclair Beecham and

---

[139] Source: Shopsy's web site and product information. Further information on Shopsy's is available at http://www.shopsys.ca and on Wikipedia at http://en.wikipedia.org/wiki/Shopsy's. Better still, visit one of the locations and see for yourself (www.shopsys.ca/locations.html).

[140] Source: Good Stuff: Home Truths, Menus and Stuff', a booklet written by Julian Metcalf, which is available at Pret A Manger outlets

Julian Metcalfe. From the very beginning Pret, as it is informally known, has been fanatical about good food, insisting that its sandwiches are fresh and use only natural, preservative-free ingredients. To do this, all but the very smallest stores has its own kitchen and all ingredients are delivered fresh before dawn each day. The company minimizes use of additives and preservatives, sourcing free range and organic ingredients wherever possible. All sandwiches are packaged in cardboard to emphasize the fact that they cannot be kept overnight. At the end of the day anything that is left is given to charities for the homeless. As a result, Pret is able to claim that 'in many of the world's cities you'll find places pretending to be Pret but missing it. The characteristics that make Pret unique are hard to copy.'[141] It is right. The obsessive commitment to detail, to getting the small things right, combined with the fanaticism to freshness and quality ingredients is very difficult to replicate indeed. In many ways Pret operates more as a restaurant/café than a sandwich store, which contributes greatly to its unique ambience. To maintain the integrity of its approach the company does not franchise its proposition. In fact, it is as passionate about not losing control as it is about its food. The web page dedicated to franchising on its web site simply reads, 'Franchising – sorry we don't. Please don't call us and ask for a franchise because we don't; we really don't. We don't franchise. The fact is, we don't like to franchise, so we don't.'[142] The result is a uniform consistency of high quality product and service with no compromise.

Pret's fanaticism to freshness and quality ingredients has paid off in terms of commercial success. By the first quarter of 2008 annual sales exceeded £200 million and the company had 200 stores in the UK, US and Hong Kong and employed almost 4,000 employees. Somewhat controversially, it attracted a 33% non-controlling stake from McDonald's in 2001 but this has done nothing to diminish the quality or integrity of its operation as some critics had feared. On the contrary, future developments are very much in line with its passion for producing exceptional, natural, fresh food. Interestingly, Pret has been content to take things slowly, building its business one step at a time. This, as we saw in chapter four, is one of the other key disciplines of strategic thinking. Some 30 new outlets are planned for 2008 as well as an expansion of the delivery service and new local format, simply called 'Local Pret'. Yet the

---

[141] Source: Pret A Manger's web site (www.pret.com) at www.pret.com/about/franchising.htm
[142] Source: Good Stuff: Home Truths, Menus and Stuff' as above

message is the same, 'we must go one step at a time, no rush.'[143]

Pret is remarkable for something else too. The passion it has for food is translated into customer service. I know of no other retailer that comes close to achieving the dynamism, passion and service commitment of its 'team members'. It invests heavily in training and development as part of its culture of making Pret a 'better, kinder, easier place to work and shop.'[144] It also values the cosmopolitan feel that results from employing people from many different nationalities. By 1998 it employed some 1,400 people, of whom only 19% were from Britain and 60% were from other European countries, mainly from Eastern and Central Europe. The company also promotes heavily from within, with some 60% of managers beginning their careers as team members. This approach gives the outlets a very special feel, full of local personality and colour, despite its total commitment to maintaining uniformly high standards throughout the chain. When my oldest son, Scott, was 14 we arranged for him to do his school work experience placement at Foyles, a large book retailer, in central London. Each day he bought his lunch at the local Pret A Manger and he was quickly 'adopted' by staff as a member of the store community. Commuting into work in Central London each day was quite a challenge for a 14 year old boy who had grown up in a peaceful village in Wiltshire so having a safe, friendly place for lunch was really important. In fact, it has since become one of the most treasured parts of his experience. This is the magical aspect to Pret, which is very hard to define. It is part staff culture, part food culture. And it has something to do with the fact that outlets have the ambience of a café as much as a sandwich store. Whatever it is, it is unique.

This is a critical time for Pret as it prepares to expand significantly beyond its core territory around London. In February 2008, 22 years after founding Pret, Julian Metcalfe and Sinclair Beecham announced that they were selling the company to a private equity firm, Bridgepoint, and the US investment bank, Goldman Sachs, for £345 million. They are, however, keeping a 25% minority stake in the company together with management. Bridgepoint announced that it intended to change Pret 'from a domestic to an international business through controlled expansion of its already profitable but small US presence'.[145] Can it stay true to its core values and

---

[143] Source: Pret A Manger's web site at http://www.pret.com/about
[144] Source: Pret A Manger's web site at www.pret.com/about/good_jobs.htm
[145] Source: The Daily Telegraph Online (www.telegraph.co.uk), 'Pret a Manger to be sold to private equity', February 23rd 2008. The full article is available at http://www.telegraph.co.uk/money/main.jhtml?xml=/money/2008/02/23/cnpret123.xml

quality commitment as well as expand more rapidly? Can it retain its uniqueness? The signs are that it can. The new 'Local Pret' is intended to take the concept into smaller towns, central business districts, suburban areas and other smaller catchments, providing a more relaxed 'softer' environment where customers can linger as well as take out. 'Local Pret' is intended to 'develop strong, trusting relationships with landlords and customers alike' and tellingly will grow 'one shop at time'.[146] Moreover, although Pret acknowledges that the new 'Local Pret' will have a different, more relaxed, feel about it, the traditional obsession with food quality and commitment to staff will remain:

> **'The foundations, non-negotiables, indeed the lifeblood of Pret, remain steadfastly in place: proud staff; fabulous recipes; on-site, preservative free production; fast, efficient service ... Pret was a racy sports car, it's now a family saloon as well.'[147]**

Beyond the commercial world

Sadly, simplicity and government are not two words that we normally use in the same sentence! Yet, nowhere in today's world is simplicity more important. I have always believed that one of the clearest signs that a society is in a deep state of malaise is its inability to use resources effectively. The collapse of communism is a classic example of how a 'command and control' system of resource allocation rotted from within. Thankfully, most of us live in countries that are nowhere near the excesses of the communist system. However, across the world, we are building up huge levels of systemic cost within public services and administration that is not directly related to the front line provision of services. Indeed, it is the customer-facing services that most frequently suffer when funding becomes tight. Again, individual decisions may make sense in isolation but when viewed as a whole we see that the whole system is increasingly under pressure. This is not only putting very considerable strain on those working in public services but it is also disabling us, as a society, from committing the resources necessary to address the systemic global issues that we now face. These issues, which include environmental degradation, poverty, climatic change, disease, rising global inequality, substance

---

[146] Source: Pret A Manger's web site at www.pret.com/pdf/pret_local.pdf
[147] Source: Pret A Manger's web site at www.pret.com/pdf/pret_local.pdf

addiction and other forms of 'anti-social' behaviour and the corrosion of 'social cohesion' as result of family and community breakdown, require not only significant funding but also our time. In order to do this, we need to radically simplify the way we do things to release the resources that are required. This may seem impossible but it would prove surprisingly easy in a time of crisis. We don't lack the capability, we simply lack the will. We *can* act now rather than wait until the crisis hits us. We owe it to future generations to do so.

Starting with us

I have a 'portfolio career' that includes teaching, writing and client based work. One of the activities that I find most rewarding is working with people who are making significant changes in their lives or careers. Often my clients have a good sense of their future direction and my role is principally one of providing a 'sounding board'. However, this clarity is sometimes lacking and it can be difficult to know quite where to begin. This is especially the case when a 'period of transition' has not been initiated by them! In these cases I have learned that a good starting point is to recommend a 'simplicity practice', a fancy term I use for doing something concrete to simplify our lives. I normally start with physical clutter. 'Begin to give away, sell or throw away your surplus possessions,' I tell them. 'Decide on a reasonable percentage (say 20%) and go for it.' Now, I must be very honest here and admit that I do not always practice what I preach and my own house is full of all sorts of unnecessary stuff that has accumulated throughout the years including large numbers of books, piles of CD's and innumerable toys that my growing teenagers cannot bear to part with just yet! However, I persist with my recommendation because I know that simplifying our lives is one of the most effective ways in which we can create the space to bring in new ideas, creativity and energy. Not only will we literally create more physical space (and save ourselves from tripping over all the junk) but we will also have much fewer distractions.

I sometimes suggest following the physical clear-out with a review of subscriptions, memberships and other commitments that have accumulated over time with a view to eliminating those that are no longer important. I did this myself several years ago and I can vouch for what an enormous relief it was when the contents of my mailbox started to shrink dramatically. Not only did this generate much more free time but it is amazing how little I missed of what I had given up. If we lighten our load the journey becomes surprisingly easy! For those of us who find it difficult to give up that golf club membership I recommend a device that I find useful. Pretend that you are moving to a new country and ask yourself what *new* commitments you would undertake and use this as a guide. If you wouldn't commence the activity today the chances are that you will not miss it. Musician and writer, Jim Brickman, suggests a number of other simplification practices in his book, *'Simple Things'*, including ignoring email for a day, removing one unused appliance from the kitchen counter, waking up 15 minutes early and using the time selfishly and vowing to listen rather than talk.[148] It may seem that you are not doing anything relevant or important with these practices but it will move your energy and, at a deeper level, create the space to allow new ideas, insights and opportunities into your life. The process is cumulative and it is also rather enjoyable. I follow up the simplicity practice by asking my clients to answer a single question and it is this. 'What is the *one* thing that you would like to achieve over the next six months?' Like many simple questions, it is harder to answer than one might think!

Simplicity is important. It is the foundation for clarity and focus in our lives and it begins with us. If we can master simplicity in our personal domain we can bring it into our working lives and into our business endeavours. If each time we send an email we stood back for a second and ask the question, 'Am I sending this because this person really needs to receive this information?' and act accordingly, we would dramatically increase the effectiveness of our working lives and all those around us. This is not as easy as it sounds. A colleague of mine has an exercise where he asks his clients to suspend all email activity for period of time to demonstrate the level of dependency and ineffectiveness of email culture. There are always howls of protest!

The power of a simple gift

You might think that a shoebox filled with small toys, schools supplies, hats and scarves and other gifts is not likely to change the world. However, to the 47 million children who have received such a box since 1990 it has made a profound difference. That is what Operation Christmas Child does. Each year it collects boxes of unwanted toys and gifts and sends them to hurting children around the world. They are delivered to children in hospitals, orphanages, refugee camps, homeless shelters and

---

[148] Jim Brickman, 'Simple Things', published by Hay House Inc, 2001

impoverished neighbourhoods. In 2005 the UK sent 1.18 million boxes to children in 13 countries. There is tremendous power in a small and simple idea. One simple act can make a very big difference. [149]

---

[149] More information can be found on www.samaritanspurse.uk.com/occ

8

DREAM

'The reason that you do something is because you can't not do it. It's hard to explain that to people without sounding like a lunatic.'

Alan Webber[150]

'Perseverance is a great element of success. If you only knock long enough and loud enough at the gate, you are sure to wake up somebody.'

Henry Wadsworth Longfellow

A family affair

I have known John Tucker, Founder of the International Centre for Families in Business for close to 15 years. He is one of the most passionate and energetic people that I have met and when he makes up his mind to do something he invariably achieves it. Whatever it takes to make something happen, John is up for it. He has a unique way of making things happen, of communicating his excitement about what *could* be, and so enabling a very diverse group of people, often from completely different backgrounds and perspectives, to come together around a common cause or endeavour. The Centre is his dream and I have watched that dream unfold over the last five years. I know that, in reality, this journey has been a rollercoaster of highs and lows and that there have been times when it seemed like the only person believing in the dream was John himself. Turning a dream like this

---

[150] Alan Webber was Co-founder of Fast Company and currently writes a regular column for USA Today. He specialises in writing on the information economy, change and innovation. Further information on Alan is available at www.leighbureau.com/speaker.asp?id=110 or on his blog at www.alanmwebber.com

into a reality is not for the fainthearted or for those looking for quick rewards. It requires commitment, perseverance and a level of obsessive behaviour and resolve not found in many of us. That deep commitment comes not from the head but directly from the gut. It is a fire that burns in the belly and provides the energy to follow though no matter what.

The International Centre for Families in Business was set up to offer family business a place for learning and education; a place where the family and other key personnel will be able to access information, seek advice and, above all, meet and share with other families in business. It offers a range of services for family business including resolving conflict, succession planning, creating an exit strategy and generational transition. In addition, it hosts CEO forums, providing a unique platform for family business managers to network and share best practice. Finally, it deals directly with professional intermediaries and family business advisers, providing training programmes designed to enable greater understanding of the unique issues facing the family in business. To do this it has established a network of professional partners including solicitors, accountants, business support agencies and academic partners. This enables it to run professional and academic programmes including the very first Family Business MBA at the University of Gloucestershire Business School. As a result, it is now the UK's most comprehensive source of support and education to families in business. This is a heady list of achievements but it is only the beginning of the Centre's journey. John is determined to put family businesses on the map. He works tirelessly with professional advisers to guide them into a far greater understanding of the unique issues that family businesses face. The Centre provides a special place of understanding for families in business but its influence is much greater as those who pass through its events, programmes and workshops come out with a changed perspective towards family business.

When I met John Tucker to discuss the Centre for this book we did not spend much time talking about its achievements. Like many strategic leaders John is not shy about acknowledging his success but his focus is forward looking, about what still needs to be done. We talked about the 'real stuff', the root of why John does what he does. He talked passionately about the need for families in business to have the frameworks and tools to deal with the issues that they face because 'too many are being destroyed by working together.' 'Sometimes,' he added, 'I drive home ... I can cry ... I can't believe that families can do this to each other ... I watch parents systematically destroy their kids ... through envy, greed, power and control ... they lose sight of the fact that they are parents.' This is the fire in the belly that underlies the Centre and all that it does, that gives it its unique perspective. It is why John Tucker is so restless because this simply matters far too much to him to put boundaries around, to fit into part of a 'lifestyle', to be limited in any way. He talks about his work taking him to places where families are 'stuck in a horrible place', where 'if they continue to behave as in the past … there is no future.' John's dream is to provide a space for those families to work out these issues so that a different future is possible. The Centre is his legacy to future generations. It is the beginning of developing a forum for a greater awareness of the family issues that lie at the heart of many family businesses and spreading that understanding amongst all those who work with families in business. It is about the creation of a comprehensive framework for dealing with the issues. John Tucker speaks from experience because he ran his own highly successful training company and knows the compromises that are made when business takes a priority over family in a busy working life. It is this burning passion that has enabled him to bring the Centre from a dream into reality.[151]

When John Tucker meets somebody new he often tells a story at the end of the meeting. It is the story of one of his clients; we will call him David, the youngest brother working in a family business. Unfortunately, a dispute within the family had resulted in both he and his sister exiting the business, leaving his older brother as Managing Director. When he met John, David had not seen his parents or his brother since that time. Periodically, John would suggest that it might be the right time for him to make contact again, to begin to build a bridge towards renewing that broken family relationship. They would talk occasionally about the possibility of David visiting his family home again but he was not yet ready to make that step. This situation continued for quite some time, with John bringing up the subject from time to time and David not being able to make the move. Then one evening John got an unexpected call from his client, who announced that he was actually at his parents' house. 'How is it going?' John enquired. 'It's not what you think,' David replied, 'I'm here because my brother died this morning. He had a heart attack as he stepped out of the shower.' There would be no time now for making peace with his brother; the door had closed on that forever. Thankfully, there *was* still time to heal other family wounds, but it came at an unthinkable price. John

---

[151] This section is drawn from a conversation with John Tucker in early 2007. For more details on the current work of the International Centre for Families in Business please see its web site at www.icfib.com

tells this story because David has asked him to. He has asked him to tell the story to as many people as possible so that others have the chance to make a different choice and not make the same mistake. 'Do you not know what you have?' is a question that John is often tempted to ask when he sees what families in business are capable of doing to each other. The Centre means that some families in business are, perhaps for the first time, able to answer 'yes' to that question. They will have the opportunity to create a new future that reflects what is best for *both* the business and the family.

The power of dreams

'People often ask me when they will they act on moving towards their dreams and aspirations. They remain frustrated because they cannot seem to make any progress. 'When you get angry enough' is my reply.'

Rick Jarow [152]

When we are called a dreamer at school it is a sure thing that it is not intended as a compliment! It is much more likely that we have been caught looking out of the window rather than paying attention to the teacher. Yet, it is the dreamers who change the world, by envisioning a better future and acting upon it. There are few speeches more famous than Martin Luther King's 'I have a dream' speech, which derives its power from its use of story to vividly paint a picture of the future with the sons of slaves and slave-owners walking hand in hand. The critical point is that we need both the boldness to imagine a better future and the capability to act. That is what distinguishes a dream from a daydream. Strategic leaders who manifest their dreams not only live in the future (with a powerful vision that draws people to them) but are also, paradoxically, firmly rooted in the world around them. Sir Richard Branson is a fine example. He is quite capable of imagining a world where space flights are a commercially viable business but he is also a pragmatic opportunist, very aware of the realities and opportunities before him.

Peter Senge, Chair of the Society for Organisational Learning and currently on the faculty of MIT, uses a model of two hands joined together

---

[152] Rick Jarow, currently Assistant Professor at Vassar College in Poughkeepsie, New York, 'Creating the Work You Love: Courage, Commitment, and Career – The Complete Anti-Career Book' published by Inner Traditions, 1995 and 'The Ultimate Anti-Career Guide: The Inner Path to Finding Your Work in the World', CD/tape box sets, published by Sounds True 1998/2000. See also Rick Jarow's web site at www.anticareer.com

with a rubber band to illustrate this relationship between vision and an accurate awareness of reality.[153] One hand lies above the other and this hand represents vision. The bottom hand is our connection with day-to-day reality, the anchor for our vision. The rubber band, of course, represents the connection between them. If we move our top hand, the lower hand also moves gently upwards, the rubber band stretching and keeping both hands together. Our vision is pulling us towards our desired goals but is being sensibly constrained by the nature of the reality around us. Our idea may, for example, be ahead its time and, realising this, we may need to develop support and gather further resources in order to move forward in a sustainable manner. Vision and reality work, literally, 'hand-in-hand'. Without a powerful picture of the future to lift and inspire us we remain embedded in our current state. Conversely, if we fail to remain connected to the real world, our dream quickly becomes hubris. The rubber band snaps and, like Icarus in the Greek myth, we may soar for a while but our search for the heavens ultimately takes us too close to the sun and we come crashing back to earth for a small lesson in humility. We find that an act of hubris (when we deviate from a point of balance due to exaggerated self pride, arrogance or self-confidence) is almost inevitably followed by nemesis (literally to 'give us what is due'), which brings us back into balance – most often in a rather unpleasant fashion!

The impossible hat

We see this paradoxical nature of dreams, the coexistence of the visionary aspect and an acute awareness of current reality, in many of our strategic leaders and businesses. This is what enables them so often to make the 'impossible' happen! Tilley Endurables, maker of the famous 'impossible' hat, is a good example. Located in Toronto, Canada, Tilley Endurables manufactures a range of travel and adventure clothing that is sold through five family-owned stores in Canada and over 2,000 associated retailers around the world. It was founded in 1980 by Alex Tilley who has a passion for travel and adventure. He had just taken up sailing and found himself constantly frustrated with hats that blew off, shrank, sank, discoloured and 'made me so darned mad I decided to make my own.' 'Fortunately, I knew

---

[153] Peter M. Senge, 'The Fifth Discipline: The Art & Practice of The Learning Organisation', published by Century Business, 1990. The best starting point for further information on Peter Senge is the web site for the Society of Organisational Learning (www.solonline.org) at www.solonline.org/aboutsol/who/Senge

nothing about headgear so I didn't realise that it was thought impossible to make such a hat.' Alex worked with a millinery designer and sail maker for months to perfect the hat that all the professional hat makers said couldn't be made. Tilley Endurables now manufacturers 250,000 such 'Tilley hats' a year and exports them all around the world. All hats are 'nearly indestructible' and carry a free replacement guarantee if they ever wear out. Tales of the 'impossible' hat abound. The most famous story is that of Michael Hackenburger, an elephant trainer at Bowmanville Zoo in Ontario, who had his Tilley hat snatched three times and swallowed by one of his 'students'. Each time Michael would allow a little time to pass before retrieving the hat, washing it and carrying on. Michael has donated his hat to the Tilley museum, which is located at the company's head office and flagship store in Don Mills, Toronto. Tilley Endurables is a business built on a vision, a standard of hat that simply didn't exist at the time, but it is also founded on Alex Tilley's detailed knowledge of the very down-to-earth and practical qualities required of the hat. Of course, there are many other factors that contributed to the success of Tilley Endurables, including exemplary customer service and an ability to learn from lessons along the way but it began as one man and a dream of a better hat![154]

Apple

'Death is very likely the single best invention of life. It is life's change agent. It clears out the old to make way for the new …Your time is limited so don't waste it living someone else's life. Don't be trapped by dogma – which is living with the results of other people's thinking. Don't let the noise of other people's opinions drown out your own inner voice. And most important, have the courage to follow your heart and intuition. They somehow already know what you truly want to become. Everything else is secondary.'

Steve Jobs, CEO of Apple [155]

---

[154] My thanks to Tilley Endurables for the promotional pack that it kindly sent me way back in 2005/2006 when this book was merely an idea, which subsequently proved very useful in preparing this section. For further information on the company please see its web site at www.tilley.com. Alternatively, if you happen to find yourself in Toronto visit the Flagship Store in Don Mills (full details at http://www.tilley.com/retail-stores.asp).

[155] Steve Jobs, CEO of Apple, Commencement Address at Stanford University, June 2005. The full text of is available at news-service.stanford.edu/news/2005/june15/jobs-061505.html. It is essential reading in its entirety.

The story of Apple is the story of Steve Jobs. It is the story of a classic 'garage' dream, in which he co-founded Apple along with Steve Wozniak and Ronald Wayne in 1976 and the company quickly became the very symbol of the personal computer phenomenon. But the dream then faltered. Despite its early success, built on an enviable reputation for high build quality, open architecture and colour graphics, Apple stumbled as Microsoft relentlessly built market dominance based on the hegemony of its Windows operating system. By the 1980's Apple was largely confined to the educational market and niches such as graphic design. When Steve Jobs was fired by the company in 1985, after a struggle with Apple's Board of Directors, it looked as if the dream was over. Mr Jobs is, however, not a man to give up easily or drift slowly into retirement. He took full advantage of the enforced redundancy to look deeply at what he wanted to achieve in life, remarking that 'the heaviness of being successful was replaced by the lightness of being a beginner again, less sure about everything'.[156] If anything, he became even more creative and founded not one but two companies; NeXT a computer platform development company, and Pixar, a computer-animation firm that was contracted to produce feature films for Disney. Pixar went on to profoundly influence animated movie making and scored a series of huge box office hits including *Toy Story*, *Monsters Inc.*, *Finding Nemo* and *The Incredibles*. Disney acquired the company in January 2006 in an all-stock transaction worth $7.4 billion that left Steve Jobs as its largest shareholder with a hefty 7% of the company's stock. He also joined Disney's board of directors. Meanwhile, in a twist of fate, NeXT was subsequently acquired by Apple in 1997 and Steve Jobs found himself back at the helm of the company he had founded over 20 years before.

Since regaining control of Apple, Steve Jobs has transformed the company beyond recognition, turning it in to one of the most creative and admired organisations today. Now a major force in consumer electronics through its product innovation, sleek empathetic design and easy functionality, Apple had revenues of some $24 billion in 2007 and employed over 20,000 people worldwide. It generates fierce consumer loyalty, partly as a result of its historical counter-cultural position in the marketplace, pitted as the underdog to Microsoft for so many years. It is also highly profitable, generating a net profit of $3.5 billion in 2007. In many ways, it is the quintessentially 21st century company, highly successful at a commercial level but also representing a subversive, almost rebellious attitude, forever prepared to challenge the status quo. Under

---

[156] Steve Jobs, Commencement Address at Stanford University, June 2005 (as above)

the leadership of Steve Jobs it has produced a relentless stream of sleek and user-friendly products and it has taken advantage of the innate superiority of these products to take on dominant established players in other industries such as music (the iPod music player), telecoms (the iPhone) and television (Apple's TV digital video system). It regularly challenges the established rules of the game as we saw in the introduction to this book when we looked at its entry into the telecom market with the iPhone. All these products represent major market opportunities.

Apple is now using the disruption caused by Microsoft's launch of its new 'Vista' operating system to mount an aggressive challenge to the dominance of its former nemesis in its core computer market. Vista has adopted many of the features of Apple's previous 'Tiger' operating system but the real test came when Apple launched its brand new 'Leopard' system in October 2007. Apple senses a remarkable opportunity at the moment and that can prove a dangerous thing for its competitors. Market share data can be difficult to interpret but many industry insiders believe that Apple could be on the verge of a significant 'breakout' in its penetration of the computer market. Recent data suggests shipments are well above its traditional share (below 5%) causing Steve Jobs to comment in an interview with Fortune in February 2008 that 'the Mac share is going up every single quarter. We're growing four times faster than the industry. People are starting to pay a little more attention ... I think a lot of people have finally started to realise that they don't have to put with Windows – that there is an alternative. I think nobody really thought about it that way before'[157] As I write this (in April 2008) Apple's share of both the US and global consumer electronics and computer markets is growing rapidly and it looks as if a 'trigger point' may indeed have been reached. Apple is very much the player to watch in its core computer market.

For the moment, music remains Apple's biggest and most iconic success, where it has established a dominant position in the online digital music market, with some 70% – 80% of the global market. In fact, the launch of the iPod music player was so successful that within months Apple had sold more downloads than the entire music industry had achieved up to that point. By September 2007 it had chalked up sales of 110 million iPod music players since its launch in November 2001 and by January 2008

---

[157] Source: Fortune Online, Steve Jobs, interviewed by Betsy Morris, Senior Editor of Fortune, in February 2008. The full text of the interview is available at
http://money.cnn.com/galleries/2008/fortune/0803/gallery.jobsqna.fortune/index.html
(page 11 of 15).

its online music store, iTunes, had sold in excess of 4 billion songs. Apple also holds a similarly dominant position in paid movie downloads. Not bad for a new entrant into the marketplace. When Steve Jobs was ejected from Apple in 1985 Andy Hertzfeld, a key member of the original Apple Macintosh development team, commented that 'Apple never really recovered from losing Steve ... [he] was the heart and soul and driving force ...they lost their soul.' It seems that the heart and soul of the company is very much back! [158]

The crucible

'I didn't see it then, but it turned out that getting fired from Apple was the best thing that could have ever happened to me ... it freed me to enter one of the most creative periods of my life.'[159]

Steve Jobs

Much has been written about Steve Job's management style and there is no doubt that he shares much in common with many of the other strategic leaders that we have looked at in this book. He combines being a visionary with a tireless capacity to act, our very definition of strategic leadership. He is remarkably persistent, using failure as an opportunity for deep learning and there is that obsessive quality that we have seen before in strategic leaders. There is no mistaking the fact that Apple is not run on the basis of consensual decision-making. It is, first and foremost, Steve Job's show, and he makes the rules even though the company has an extraordinary pool of talent. Like many other leaders his career has been forged through adversity. Being fired at 30 from the company that he founded acted as a painful crucible in his life and as a source of deep introspection. He admits that it was personally devastating, that the 'entire focus of my adult life was gone.' In June 2005 he talked to the graduate class at Stanford University about how he did not know what to do for months and how he felt that he had let down the previous generation of entrepreneurs. He was convinced that he had 'dropped the baton as it was passed to me', and even went as far as meeting with David Packard and Bob Noyce 'to apologise for screwing up so badly.' It was a very tough time

---

[158] Source: Wikipedia, 'Steve Jobs' using quotes obtained from the 1996 documentary 'Triumph of the Nerds', on the reaction to Jobs' famous firing from Apple by CEO John Sculley and the Apple Board of Directors. Please refer to http://en.wikipedia.org/wiki/Steve_Jobs
[159] Steve Jobs, Commencement Address at Stanford University, June 2005 (as above)

for him, particularly since it was such a public failure. [160] It is ironic that one of the reasons for his dismissal from Apple was the feeling that his aspirations for the Macintosh were out of sync with market reality. When he returned as CEO of Apple it was the incorporation of NeXT's technology platform within Macintosh that became the heart of Apple's renaissance.

After a while, Steve Jobs was able to transform this situation by going inward and realising that his rejection did not change things. It helped him become more aware of his deeper beliefs and values and he was able to summon the courage and commitment to start again. This 'trial by fire' has become the touchstone upon which he has built his dreams. When he later learned that he had pancreatic cancer he faced death in the same way and came back stronger than ever. He attributes much of his current success and personal happiness to the lessons he learned from these periods of trauma and failure and the internal reflection that they sparked. It is difficult to convey the profundity of these experiences as an outsider but I have worked in similar circumstances and seen this process first hand. I have worked with an entrepreneur who was similarly ejected from the business that she founded. Witnessing the degree of pain that she went through was one of the most emotional working experiences of my life. She 'left' the business with grace but the personal grief that she suffered at losing the business was no less devastating as a result. She chose to support her staff by 'blessing' her successor even though it was the most painful choice she could have made. She 'transcended' the situation at great personal cost and it will change her profoundly in the future, making her a formidable leader and an even more powerful agent for change. Steve Job's failure acted as a similar catalyst and it has been the making of him. He doesn't mince words about how it felt and the power of its consequences.

'It was awful-tasting medicine, but I guess the patient needed it. Sometimes life hits you in the head with a brick. Don't lose faith. I'm convinced that the only thing that kept me going was that I loved what I did. You've got to find what you love ... the only way to do great work is to love what you do. If you haven't found it yet, keep looking. Don't settle. As with all matters of the heart, you'll know when you find it.' [161]

---

[160] Steve Jobs: quotes extracted from the Commencement Address at Stanford University, June 2005 (as above)

[161] Steve Jobs, Commencement Address at Stanford University, June 2005 (as above)

The heart of success

'One person with belief is equal to a force of 99 who have only interests.'

John Stuart Mill

The capacity to dream is a key element of strategic thinking because it takes us beyond the normal self imposed limitations that we place upon ourselves. Instead of asking 'why' we begin to ask 'why not'. The country star, Garth Brooks, was rejected by all the major music labels in the US before he finally got a contract with Capitol Records, part of the EMI group. He has gone on to sell nearly 130 million albums, becoming one of the most successful US solo artists of all time.[162] In 1992 he single-handedly accounted for 9% of EMI Music's $5 billion global sales. There are undoubtedly many reasons for Garth Brooks's success but his sense of self-belief and the sheer passion and commitment that he had to make his dream a reality are a vital part of it. When we have a dream we begin to challenge the assumptions and beliefs that would otherwise make our dream 'impossible' to achieve. We explore the possibility of doing things differently. We consider adopting alternative strategies and we look for answers in different places. Most of all, we challenge ourselves. Dreamers are demanding of other people but they are hardest on themselves. Yes, dreams are powerful and energising and they have the capability to elevate us beyond ourselves. But they can also be frightening because they present us with the challenge of arriving!

When Rob Parsons, leading author and Executive Director of Care for the Family, wrote *'The Heart of Success'* he quite rightly included believing in the power of dreams as one of his seven key 'laws' of success. He also identified the importance of what he calls 'dream catchers', those of us who can support the dreamer, rather than bring them down to earth with a bump! So often, full of well-meaning intentions, we concentrate on why something can't be done rather than help somebody achieve it! As Canadian singer/songwriter Bruce Cockburn acutely observes, 'it's more blessed to give than to receive, except for free advice I believe.'[163] Most importantly, however, Rob Parsons recognises that dreamers are *dangerous* people. As he says in the book, 'they break the rules, they

---

[162] For further information on Garth Brooks visit his web site at www.garthbrooks.com

[163] Bruce Cockburn, 'Tie Me at the Crossroads When I Die', available on the album 'Dart to the Heart' on True North, 1994. For further information on Bruce Cockburn visit his web site at www.brucecockburn.com or visit http://cockburnproject.net, which documents his work.

frustrate you with their sheer doggedness ... [but we] would do well to have a little humility in their presence, because although they will sometimes fail, they will fail reaching, stretching and, once in a while, they will bring that dream in'.[164] Dreams *are* dangerous, not at all soft and cuddly as we might expect. I work with quite a number of entrepreneurs and, quite frankly, they can be very tough people to work with. They are demanding and don't suffer fools gladly. They are highly energetic, obsessive and not at all good at observing the finer boundaries of life (such as normal working hours!). They can be restless, constantly changing and moving as they steer towards their dreams. They are difficult to keep up with and also demand extraordinary commitment and loyalty. It's not always easy working for a company that has a dreamer at the top. We had better share that dream, to 'get it', or begin to look for somewhere else to work. But here's the rub. They achieve the extraordinary. They regularly do the 'impossible'. They change the world.

Ideas in action

It is always tempting to illustrate the power of dreams with big 'blockbusting' examples of dramatic change but this would be a mistake. Dreams are not 'big' or 'small' and they cannot be understood in terms of success, immediate or otherwise. Some dreams 'fail' but inspire others on the way. Successful entrepreneurs often attract highly talented like-minded individuals at the beginning of a venture only to lose them along the way. Many go on to do their own thing, some becoming more successful than their mentors. Many dreams are small-scale but have a profound impact on the community around them. Some dreams appear to fail miserably because they are ahead of their time but are picked up much later by someone else who, inspired by that vision, now sees a fruitful place to express it and bring it into reality. As Ralph Waldo Emerson put it, 'a weed is a plant whose virtues have not yet been discovered.' Henry David Thoreau's obsessive passion for the natural world was never fully understood or appreciated by his peers; ironically, not even by Ralph Waldo Emerson who was his mentor! However, many years later, he profoundly influenced Martin Luther King and Mahatma Gandhi and his ideas about living in harmony with nature are highly relevant to us today. We tend to think about dreams in linear terms but, in reality, it is a dance

---

[164] Rob Parsons, 'The Heart of Success', published by Hodder & Stoughton, 2002. For further information visit the web site of Care for the Family at www.careforthefamily.org.uk

between the dream and the dreamer. Dreams have their own sense of timing and destiny.

All dreams have one critical element in common. They are built one step at a time. A couple of weeks ago my family attended a Lenten lunch at our village church, which was organised alongside a collection of used bikes to be sent to Africa. We only intended to stop by for five minutes to drop off my youngest son's old bike, but the charity that was organising the collection was making a small presentation on its work so we decided to stay and listen. I am very glad that we did. Jole rider (pronounced 'jolly rider') is a UK charity that was started in 2005 and it is best known for its *'Bikes4Africa'* programme, which refurbishes used donated bikes and sends them to secondary schools in Gambia. The bikes become assets of the school and teachers allocate them to students who have the longest walks to school. When the student finishes their education their bike remains at the school, ready to be used by a younger student. For African students, who often face a walk of ten miles or more in searing heat, a bike makes an enormous difference. Moreover, by increasing the number of children who are able to go to school the entire community can benefit because increased education plays a vital role in the process of moving away from poverty. Jole rider also supports their bike donations with skills training and maintenance workshops so that students and teachers alike can learn to maintain their bikes. This also gives students a valuable education in basic engineering, equipping them to start their own businesses in metalworking or mechanical repair.

To date, over 1,000 bikes have been shipped to 10 schools in Gambia, building 'positive change in Africa ... one bike at a time.'[165] Jole Rider's strategy is firmly practical and incremental, focused on small scale, community oriented projects. It recognises the importance of building up infrastructure in England and the Gambia, including the significant community benefits that accrue in both as a result. The current three-year strategy emphasises expanding gradually to cover more schools in Gambia and, if possible, adding two further African countries each year to the programme. The charity's philosophy is also grounded, stressing the two way benefits from the exchange, as much what Africans can teach those in the UK as the English can do for Africa. Already, children from schools in the UK have visited the Gambia to see for themselves how the bikes are being used and learn about life in Gambia. In a country where children are so keen to learn and with such a deep well of cultural wisdom this offers a

---

[165] Source: Jole Rider web site (www.jole1000.org) at www.jole1000.org/bikes4africa.html

tremendous amount to those on both sides of the exchange. It is both a simple idea and a visionary one, a dream that is being built 'one bike at a time' from a very practical day-to-day perspective.

In my own local area, living close to Marlborough in Wiltshire, many of the community ventures that bring me most pleasure are the result of dreams. We have a thriving local concert scene run by Marlborough Folk Roots that attracts acoustic artists from all over the country. It was set up by Andrew Bumphrey in 1999 to provide an opportunity for local people to hear great acoustic music live and was born of his own love of live music. It started out with one 'simple' act. Having been 'bowled over' by several concerts by the highly talented acoustic folk duo, Show of Hands, he invited them to Marlborough to perform. Since then, as he puts it, 'what began as a hobby is rapidly becoming a way of life.'[166] One of the best venues for these concerts is St Peter's Church, situated at the Western end of Marlborough High Street. The church was made redundant in the 1970's (and nearly turned into a parking lot!) but was rescued by a group of dedicated people, who have not only kept it open but have completely renovated and revitalised it in the process. It now sells local trade products, houses an excellent coffee shop and the Church Tower is open during the summer for some of the best views of the town.[167] It is a very special experience to be at a concert in these beautiful surroundings and it is also a great place to meet local people, fostering a real sense of community. St Peter's Church was also home for a while to Mustard Seed, a Christian bookseller and coffee shop. This has gone on to establish itself in a larger independent location by the side of the River Kennet, providing a lovely place to have afternoon tea. In turn, Mustard Seed has also built a significant presence in the local community, for example, by organising speakers at regular intervals.[168] And there are many more linkages. As a keen supporter of independent artists, I know of at least two who have gone on to collaborate together as a result of both playing gigs in Marlborough. Dreams are contagious!

It is very easy to look at any of these ventures in hindsight and

---

[166] This section on Marlborough Folk Roots is drawn from a conversation with Andrew Bumphrey in early 2007. The concerts continue to thrive! For further information visit its web site at www.marlboroughfolk-roots.co.uk.

[167] Several reference points exist for St Peter's Church in Marlborough but one of the best is www.enjoyengland.com/Attraction/Marlborough/Church-or-Chapel/134095/St-Peter's-Church,-Marlborough.htm

[168] Mustard Seed has a comprehensive web site at www.mustardseedbooks.com which contains more detailed information on its activities.

minimise the courage and commitment that was needed to make them a reality. When Andrew Bumphrey invited Show of Hands to perform in Marlborough he took a risk, not only that the event might not be a success, but also that he would appear foolish. I believe that it is often the second thing that stops us from achieving our dreams; we don't want to look foolish. We fear our well-intentioned friends saying to us, 'Bob, *whatever* were you thinking, that could *never* have worked! Get a grip!' And, of course, things are always obvious in hindsight! The point about dreams is that we will sometimes be flying blind, guided only by our vision and that can be a very scary place. There will be days that are as 'dark as a crow flying through a pitch black night', to steal a phrase from the novelist, Lemony Snicket, author of 'A Series of Unfortunate Events'.[169] That is when it is helpful to remind ourselves of Steve Jobs' advice to the graduates at Stanford University: 'Don't lose faith.'[170] It is also why it is so important for us to encourage those around us who have dreams, to be supporters rather than detractors; to affirm what they are doing without being too judgemental. It can make a very big difference. I once emailed a singer/songwriter to say that my elder son (only about eight at the time) was still talking about the concert we went to the year before. I ended my email with 'Keep the faith.' His reply knocked me back. 'Thanks for that,' he said, 'I've had a really tough time of late … it really helps to keep me going.' I learned a lot from that. What we say matters and we should use our words wisely. Let's help to build dreams not to destroy them.

Moving our dreams into reality

'Don't' ask what the world needs. Rather ask what makes you come alive; then go and do it! Because what the world needs is people who have come alive.'

Howard Thurmon [171]

Some dreams are with us from the very beginning and others come through our experiences, often crystallising at the most difficult times of

---

[169] Lemony Snicket, 'A Series of Unfortunate Events: Book the Twelfth, The Penultimate Peril', published by Egmont, 2005. This is a wonderful series and highly recommended with more information at www.lemonysnicket.com

[170] Steve Jobs, Commencement Address at Stanford University, June 2005 (as above)

[171] Howard Thurmon was a preacher and a poet who was a contemporary of Martin Luther King. For further information refer to Wikipedia at http://en.wikipedia.org/wiki/Howard_Thurman.

our lives. Dreams emerge and evolve, sometimes coming to the fore, while at other times receding into the background of our lives, masked by the cacophony of urgent matters clamouring for our attention. There are times in our lives when we are so fully engaged in day-to-day activities that we put on our dreams 'on hold'. If we have three young children under five, just looking after them does not allow much free time for dream contemplation! Most often it is a combination of life experiences that precipitates the time for action. Dreams may be born of disappointment, anger and even tragedy, igniting the will for us to act, but circumstances also play an important role in shaping those actions too.

Welsh singer/songwriter, Martyn Joseph, began to write songs in early adolescence but he was torn between music and golf. He was a very good golfer, winning many championships and even becoming the youngest club champion at one of Wales' oldest golf courses. But he feared that he wasn't quite good enough to make it as a professional golfer. It was a combination of this disappointment and his anger at the injustices of the world that have led him to become one of the most passionate and inspirational acoustic artists today. In reality, it has taken years for Martyn's dream to take shape and evolve. He initially began playing in the 'Christian' market but later broadened his song-writing to fully express his humanity for the suffering that we inflict on the world and on each other. Most of all, although he jokes that he only writes 'depressing songs' there is always a deep message of hope and compassion in his work that uplifts and carries his audience through times of suffering and disappointment. He is capable of writing a passionate, fiery tirade against injustice one moment and a deeply personal and achingly beautiful ballad the next. There is no doubt that Martyn is very gifted as a songwriter and has an exceptional amount of 'raw talent' but it also takes a lifetime of experience to learn how to truly craft and express this talent.[172] In reality, even for the most gifted of us, dreams rarely pop up 'fully formed'. They may take years to fulfil and sometimes it is, quite literally, a lifetime's work.

There are times when the most important thing we can do is simply to listen to our promptings and to acknowledge them, knowing that they will blossom when the time is right. As Langston Hughes reminds us, 'hold on to your dreams for if dreams die life is a broken winged bird that cannot

---

[172] Martyn Joseph is an extraordinary artist to see live if you have the chance. For more information on Martyn visit his web site at www.martynjoseph.co.uk.

fly.'[173] By acknowledging our dreams we keep them alive. I have a broken winged crow who visits my garden regularly to feed beneath the bird table on the seed droppings left by other birds. His wing is permanently broken and we worry about his chances of survival, probably with good cause. He can flutter for a moment in mid-air, leaping from branch to branch but more than that seems to be beyond him. We call him 'Broken-Wing'. Broken-Wing may not be able to fly like the other birds but my wife, Tracy, called me the other day to witness something remarkable. I had thought that he must always be confined to hopping for seeds on the ground but I was wrong. By a process of leaps and bounds, and the occasional mid-air flutter, he proceeded to scale the farm fence and then the branches of the very tallest of the trees that surround the bird feeders. Having reached the top he was able to come down the tree to the bird feeder just like any other self-respecting bird. Call me anthropomorphic if you like but I thought there was a look of triumph and self satisfaction on his face.

---

[173] Langston Hughes was an American poet, novelist, short story writer and columnist; best known for his work during the Harlem Renaissance. For further information refer to Wikipedia at http://en.wikipedia.org/wiki/Langston_Hughes

PART 3

THE LEADERSHIP JOURNEY

9

A FRAMEWORK FOR STRATEGIC THINKING

'If you want your child to be brilliant read them fairy stories. If you want your child to be a genius, read them more fairy stories.'

Albert Einstein

Seeing the whole

In *'The House at Pooh Corner'* by A. A. Milne,[174] one of the many adventures that the animals have is searching for 'Small', one of Rabbits many friends-and-relations. One morning, as Winnie the Pooh is happily counting his honey pots, Rabbit rushes in to give him the exciting news that Small is lost and a search has already begun. Before he can get in a word edgeways, Pooh finds himself 'organized'. He is to search the area by the Six Pine Trees and work his way towards Owl's house before meeting up with Rabbit and the others an hour later. 'Do you see?' asks Rabbit. 'No,' says Pooh, but it is too late as Rabbit, filled with the importance of his task, is already half way out of the door. Immediately he is gone Pooh realises that he does not know who or what Small is, whether he is the sort of 'friend-and-relation who settled on one's nose, or the sort that got trodden on by mistake.' The only solution is to visit Piglet to find out whether he knows. But that is easier said than done because Piglet has also been 'organized' to search his own 'special place' in the forest. As Pooh is a 'bear of little brain' he decides to set it all out in his head so he won't be confused. This is how he summarises his tasks:

---

[174] A.A. Milne, 'The House at Pooh Corner', published by Methuen & Co Ltd, 1928 (Chapter 3). This section refers to the story of the search for Small.

ORDER OF LOOKING FOR THINGS

1. Special Place (*To find Piglet*)
2. Piglet *(To find who Small is)*
3. Small *(To find Small)*
4. Rabbit *(To tell him I've found Small)*
5. Small Again (To tell him I've found Rabbit)

Now that his plan of action is set out logically Pooh can clearly see that it is going to be a 'bothering sort of day' and he stumps off to begin his tasks. Of course, all this activity and organisation comes to nothing. It is Piglet who eventually finds Small, but only after both he and Pooh have accidentally stumbled into the same deep pit where Small had the misfortune to fall into earlier on. 'Pooh!' cries Piglet. 'There's something crawling up your back.' 'I thought there was,' says Pooh. 'It's Small!' cries Piglet. 'Oh, *that's* who it is, is it? replies Pooh. The search for Small can be called off and the animals can get back to normal life. All, that is, except Eeyore, the donkey, who is forgotten about in all this excitement and patiently continues his search until he happens to bump into Rabbit two days later. 'What are *you* looking for?' asks Rabbit. 'Small of course,' replies Eeyore. 'Haven't you any brain?' 'Oh, but didn't I tell you? says Rabbit. 'Small was found two days ago.' At this point there is a moment's silence. 'Ha-ha,' says Eeyore bitterly. 'Merriment and what-not. Don't apologize. It's just *what* would happen.'

This is one of my favourite stories of Winnie the Pooh and I think it says a great deal about how we set about doing things in our world. We don't take the time to try to see the whole picture when we engage in so much of our activity. As a result, our hard work and efforts are often wasted and sometimes, sadly, prove counter-productive. We are so keen on action and activity that we forget to think more deeply about what we are trying to do in the first place. We often compound this blinkered approach by a lack of attention to what is happening around us and thus fail to see the signals that would alert us to the need to amend our course of action. Dogged determination is a useful quality in getting things done but not at the expense of compromising or simplifying our understanding of reality! If Rabbit had explained who Small was in the first instance, Pooh would have had a much less bothering day (although arguably a much less interesting one too!). That is because Small was actually found through a process of synchronicity (the chance happening of events) and serendipity (the faculty of making fortunate discoveries by accident) rather than as a result of all Rabbit's organisation. There is a natural flow to life that will bring us to our destination if we can only learn to emulate Pooh Bear and quieten our mind so that we can be more receptive to the bigger picture. How many of us have found ourselves in the position of Eeyore in this story, still beavering away, unaware that everyone else has moved on long ago!

The seven disciplines

'I'm still defeated by the conundrum of God. But, I have the devil clear.'
'And what's he?'
'Not seeing whole.'

John Fowles, Daniel Martin [175]

At its core, strategic thinking is the capability to see the whole. During this book we have explored seven key disciplines, which, if used consciously together, build up an integrated capacity to do so. As we have seen, the disciplines are 'know your own story', 'think small', 'go slowly', 'serve others', 'reflect', 'be simple' and 'dream'. They are all simple principles, even if some of them are somewhat counter-intuitive at first. We have also seen how these disciplines are reflected in some of the most successful organisations today. These enterprises are all strategic leaders in their fields, defining the territories in which they operate. Some are obvious global leaders, such as Apple, Honda, Toyota and Virgin, which operate on a world stage and have immediately recognisable brand names. Others may be less well known outside the national or local area in which they are based. Nevertheless, they make a very significant contribution to the communities around them and often influence policy-making well beyond their boundaries. Organisations like the National Trust, The Prince's Trust, Care for the Family and Kennet Valley School make a big difference, regardless of scale or size. It is the quality of the thinking process within an endeavour that is most critical to its success and it is *this* that marks out these organisations as strategic leaders.

---

[175] Source: John Fowles, from his novel 'Daniel Martin', published by Vintage, current edition, 2004. John Fowles died in 2005 and a brief summary of his life can be found at www.independent.co.uk/news/obituaries/john-fowles-514345.html

Being a strategic leader is not easy. The economist, Joseph Schumpeter, observed that leaders are confronted by all sorts of obstacles and that successful business people stand on ground that is 'crumbling beneath their feet'. This is one reason why so many of our leading organisations have powerful, even driven, leaders, such as Steve Jobs at Apple and Sir Richard Branson at Virgin, who combine the characteristics of being both remarkably receptive to opportunity and being very capable of acting quickly and decisively. Indeed, the word 'entrepreneur', literally meaning 'one who undertakes', has a distinctive bias on action. Again, we come back to that combination of vision and action that defines strategic leadership, which Schumpeter described as 'the dream and the will to found a private kingdom'. Schumpeter was the first person to highlight the critical importance of entrepreneurs as the agents of innovation and to recognise that it is innovation that is the main driving force of economic progress in general. In short, strategic leaders translate new thinking into effective action and this underpins the wellbeing of society as a whole.[176]

Up to this point we have looked at examples of organisations that exemplify strategic thinking by concentrating on one discipline at a time. Now we need to redress this balance and recognise that successful enterprises tend to be skilled in many of the key disciplines simultaneously. Individual organisations may excel in specific areas but there are striking similarities between them in terms of their strategic approach overall. Strategic leaders tend to be visionaries, who build their organisations around a strong sense of purpose and a set of core values based on a dream of making some aspect of our world a better place. This is sometimes on a grand scale, as in the case of BP, which under the leadership of John Browne began to tackle environmental and climatic change. In other cases, it is focused on a specific aspect of improving our quality of life, such as the role of Pret A Manger and Innocent fruit drinks in enabling their customers to eat healthily despite the hectic lifestyles associated with contemporary culture.

The leaders of these organisations understand the importance of developing their businesses one step at a time ('go slowly'), often accompanied by an obsession for maintaining consistently high standards and a keen eye for detail ('think small'). Honda, Toyota, Starbucks and Amazon are all good examples of these core principles. Without exception,

---

[176] Source: The Economist, 'Joseph Schumpeter: In Praise of Entrepreneurs', April 28th 2007. This article is a review of the book, 'Prophet of Innovation: Joseph Schumpeter and Creative Destruction', by Thomas K. McCraw, published by Belknap Press, 2007.

these organisations have a clear sense of who they ('know your own story') and the boundaries of their operations ('be simple'). Many are overtly in the service business ('serve others') but all have a broader sense of service, of acting on behalf of a broad body of stakeholders and society at large. Indeed, some, like eBay, place the highest strategic priority on serving their communities, which they rightly regard as the lifeblood of the enterprise. Finally, these strategic leaders often simplify organisational structures and processes to allow time for deeper reflection in decision-making. A remarkable number have flat structures with minimal levels of hierarchy. In fact, as we saw in the case of BP, the more complex the business becomes the more important it is to keep things simple. It is now time to join up the dots and look at how one organisation, Whole Foods Market, uses all the key disciplines of strategic thinking to adopt a more holistic approach to running its business; one that explicitly acknowledges the importance of its relationships with the complex communities that it serves, with society as a whole and with the planet at large.

Whole Foods Market

'Our motto – Whole Foods, Whole People, Whole Planet – emphasises that our vision reaches far beyond just being a food retailer … We believe that we have a responsibility toward all people involved in our business – shoppers, shareholders, Team Members, suppliers … and … social responsibility to producer communities in developing countries, where we source some of our products.'

Whole Foods Market, an extract from the Declaration of Interdependence and Whole Trade Guarantee [177]

Whole Foods Market is the world's largest retailer of natural and organic foods in the world with over 270 locations in the United States, Canada and the United Kingdom. The stores feature a wide array of natural products including produce, seafood, meat and poultry, beer, wine, cheese and a bakery. The emphasis is on freshness, taste and experience as well as healthy eating. Stores include sampling stations, cooking demonstrations,

---

[177] Source: Whole Foods Market web site (www.wholefoodsmarket.com). The 'Declaration of Interdependence' is available at www.wholefoodsmarket.com/company/declaration.html and the 'Whole Trade Guarantee' is available in full at www.wholefoodsmarket.com/products/wholetrade/index.html

café tables and specialist facilities such as an in-house meat smoker, and the business is supported by bake houses, commissary kitchens, a coffee roasting operation and even a seafood processing facility. Visiting Whole Foods Market reminds me of the colourful experience of going to a traditional market where there is the excitement and hum of specialist vendors selling a huge variety of tempting products. Certainly something has gelled with customers. Whole Foods Market has expanded rapidly since it went public in 1992 with annual growth rates of over 20%. By 2007 it was a Fortune 1000 company and had revenues of $6.6 billion. It now employs over 41,500 people and has been included in Fortune magazine's annual list of the '100 best companies to work for' every year since the list's inception in 1998, one of only 14 companies to achieve this. In 2008 it ranked 16th, its second best placing. Yet this success very nearly didn't happen at all.

In 1981 on Memorial Day the worst flood in 70 years devastated the city of Austin, Texas, the home of the first Whole Foods Market store. Floodwaters wiped out the store's inventory of natural food and damaged most of the equipment. Losses amounted to $400,000 and the company had no insurance. It was saved by its community. Customers and neighbours joined with staff to clean up the mess and repair the equipment. Instead of putting the business under, suppliers and investors provided critical breathing space for the store to get back on its feet and it reopened just 28 days after the flood. Serving the broader community continues to be central to the core philosophy of Whole Foods Market to this day. In 1985 it became enshrined in the 'Declaration of Interdependence' that summarises the core philosophy of the company. As Walter Robb, Co-President of the company, puts it, 'our mission in simple terms [is], No. 1, to change the way the world eats, and No. 2, to create a workplace based on love and respect. We believe business should meet the needs of all the stakeholders, as opposed to operating it for shareholders.'[178]

Whole Foods Market began its journey in 1978 as the dream of a 25 year old college drop-out, John Mackey, when he and his girlfriend borrowed $45,000 from family and friends to open a small natural food store in Austin called SaferWay (a spoof of Safeway, which operated stores

---

[178] Source: Boardmember.com, 'Whole Foods: Second Banana on Being Green', January/ February 2007. Full text is available (on registration) at www.boardmember.com/issues/archive.pl?article_id=12688. Original source: Wikipedia at http://en.wikipedia.org/wiki/Whole_Foods

in Austin at the time). From the beginning it had a deep commitment to customers and a unique corporate philosophy that emphasised its responsibility to its wider community and the environment, which John Mackey sees as a key stakeholder in the business. The company's retailing success is based on a fanatical attention to operational detail (always the hallmark of good retail) and an obsessive focus on customers. Customers clearly drive the business and they are the foundation of the Whole Foods Market community. 'The deepest core of Whole Foods, the heartbeat if you will, is customers first,' says Walter Robb, 'then team members, balanced with what's good for other stakeholders, such as shareholders, vendors, the community, and the environment.' [179] The unique thing about Whole Foods Market is that the company lives and breathes this mission in everything it does. This makes it not only very successful in commercial terms but also a strategic leader in the *way* it runs its business. Not bad for a business concept that CEO, John Mackey, thought would remain relatively small scale. 'In all my profound wisdom I decreed a maximum of 100 stores,' he recalls 'and thought that would saturate the United States.'[180] Not only is there considerable potential for further expansion in the company's homeland but it is also considering moving overseas. With a new store in London, Whole Foods Market has its sights set firmly on the European market.

Living the seven disciplines

If we use the seven key disciplines of strategic thinking as a framework to look at Whole Foods Market we quickly see that it embodies all the key principles as a way of life. There is no doubt that it is a business that 'knows its own story', expressed in its unique stakeholder philosophy, a passion for the natural foods business and the high level of dedication and commitment to the customer experience. It has been widely recognised for its advocacy of social responsibility and for its treatment of team members. Whole Foods Market placed 12th overall in the Harris Interactive/Wall Street Journal ranking of the world's best corporate reputations and it achieved a top 5 ranking in the Environmental Protection Agency's 'Green Power Partner' survey (which measures green

---

[179] Source: Boardmember.com, 'Whole Foods: Second Banana on Being Green', January/February 2007 and Wikipedia as above.
[180] Source: The Economist, 'Face Value: A Wal-Mart for the Granola Crowd', July 30th 2005. John Mackey made this comment in 1992 when Whole Foods Market went public.

power purchases) each year between 2006 and 2008 (having won the Green Power Leadership award in both 2004 and 2005). At the same time, John Mackey has held firm to his belief that organised unions represent an adversarial relationship between management and employees despite the fact that many have criticised his stance. In short, rightly or wrongly, Whole Foods Market has a very clear sense of what it is all about, making sure that its operational policies and standards clearly reflect these core values. It is not afraid to voice what it believes in and act upon it, even if (as in the case with union recognition) its position is not popular with all parties. It is prepared to walk the talk and to live its story in all aspects of its business. It does not compromise its core values. Although a great many people have helped contribute to the success of the company (it is now just outside the top 50 retailers in the US) the story began as the *dream* of a young man, determined to change the way the world eats.

Like all exceptional retailers Whole Foods Market has a keen eye for operational detail *('think small')*. In fact, when we walk around a store we quickly realise that getting the detail right and consistently delighting the customer is an obsession with Whole Foods Market. As a premium food proposition every element of its store operation has to be executed at the same consistently high standards. Although the company has grown rapidly this has never been at the expense of these impeccable standards or its core focus. Its identity and integrity have remained intact *('go slowly')*. Employees, called 'team members', are not only exceptionally well trained but are also highly enthusiastic and knowledgeable about produce and company policies alike. As the company takes its 'green mission' very seriously indeed, team members need to be able to address customer queries on a whole range of environmental and ethical issues (for example, sustainable fishing, the treatment of animals raised for sale in stores and the purchasing of local products) in addition to normal day-to-day matters, such as the clarification of ingredients contained within its natural foods. This helps give the company very clear boundaries and a sharp focus on its marketplace *('be simple')*. There is an alignment within the organisation that stretches directly from its corporate philosophy and purpose to store management policies. When Whole Foods Market was criticised for some of its practices in relation to animals sold in the stores it responded by creating the Animal Compassion Foundation, a separate non-profit organisation, which helps producers adhere to standard policies designed to raise animals naturally and humanely. In doing so, the company was not only being receptive to the needs and opinions of its customers but it was acting in a way that is entirely consistent with its deeper philosophy and values. As we have seen, this philosophy emphasises service to the wider community (*'serve others'*) and the relationship between all the parties that make up this community (*'reflection'*). John Mackey expresses it as follows:

'Long term profits are maximised by not making them the primary goal ... Management's role is to optimise the health and value of the entire complex, evolving and self adaptive system. All of the various constituencies connect together and affect one another. If we optimize the health and value of the entire interdependent system and the well-being of all the major constituencies, the end result will also be the highest long-term profits for the investors as well'[181]

Whole Foods Market is an exceptional example of holistic thinking and the ability to act from a wider perspective *and* be successful commercially. This does not make it a perfect organisation. It suffers from the same crises and failures that are familiar to all endeavours. Indeed, both its share price and profits fell in the first quarter of 2008 as a result of the economic downturn in the US and costs associated with the integration of the Wild Oats Markets acquisition in 2007. What distinguishes it, however, is its ability to learn from the circumstances that cause things to go awry. In the late 1990's, for example, it was criticised for not supporting a campaign by the United Farm Workers to improve conditions of agricultural workers labouring on strawberry farms. Given John Mackey's ambivalence to trade unions, Whole Foods Market responded by holding a 'National 5% Day', where five per cent of that day's sales, $125,000, was donated to organisations that provide social services to farm workers. When the company recognised that many consumers regarded its prices as too high (earning it the nickname 'whole Paycheck') it added its '365 Everyday Value' product line, giving better value for money without compromising high product quality standards. Its responses are measured (it often takes its time thinking through the implications of problems and issues) but often proactive in a wider sense, drawing on insight about the bigger picture. Its response to worries about toxic chemicals in products such as

---

[181] John Mackey, 'Conscious Capitalism: Creating a New Paradigm for Business', extracted from his blog on November 2006, contained in the section, 'The Paradox of Profits'. The full blog is available on Whole Food Market's web site at wholefoodsmarket.com/socialmedia/jmackey/2006/11/09/conscious-capitalism-creating-a-new-paradigm-for-business/

baby bottles and children's cups, for example, was to stop selling the offending products even though manufacturers have largely dismissed claims that there is any health risk. There is a consistent pattern here. Whole Foods Market lives its core values and philosophy but it also seeks genuine 'win-win' solutions and it is prepared to adapt its business practice accordingly. This is organisational learning that involves compromise of the healthy sort, improving operational processes but maintaining core integrity and identity.

All the key disciplines of strategic thinking are embedded in Whole Foods Market's culture. It is for this reason, as well as the sheer passion with which the business is run, that both the company and John Mackey continue to win plenty of awards for company's holistic business and social practices. John Mackey appears on Barron's list of the world's best CEO's, an award that specifically recognises both corporate performance and leadership strength and industry stature. However, the awards are only icing on the cake. It is within each store that we see the company expressing its active community philosophy and really making a difference through its vision of playing a 'unique role as a community meeting place where friends can gather, interact, and learn, while at the same time discover the many joys of eating and sharing food ... like the pubic markets of years past.'[182]

Recognising our relationship to the whole

Underlying all the key disciplines of strategic thinking is one critical factor; the importance of opening up a space for reflection. It is from within this space that all creativity, inspiration and insight ultimately come. 'If you want to understand the nature of water you had better not ask a fish' as the old saying goes.[183] When we are too close to something, too immersed in it, we cannot see the bigger picture. Instead of developing a capacity to see the whole, we tend to focus on the fragment that we *can* see and then extrapolate what works at this level into the wider world. Not only is this likely to be ineffective (we find ourselves continuously reinventing the

---

[182] Source: Whole Foods Market, publicity materials. The concept of a 'store as community' is one of the key strengths of Whole Food Markets, although frustratingly, I have mislaid the document from which this quote was sourced.

[183] My thanks to my colleague, John Middleton, for bringing this saying to my attention. Originally, he believed that it originated from China but according to his students in Hong Kong this is not the case!

wheel) but it is also dangerous, since we tend not to consider fully the potential consequences of our actions on either ourselves or on others. Indeed, if there is no personal cost attached to the side effects of our decisions we may choose to ignore them, regardless of whether this results in a net reduction in the health and effectiveness of the wider community or society as a whole. This limited thinking also blinds us to alternative courses of action, which require a broader knowledge of the whole and a deeper understanding of how the parts within it fit together, including our own relationship with it. We are all deeply connected in the web of life and it is becoming increasingly important that we recognise this and act accordingly.

The consequences of fragmented and simplistic thinking are already evident in terms of the 'big issues' that we face such as climatic change, our inability to deal effectively with global poverty and disease and the rise in terrorist activity across the world. We notice it within the bloated public administration that is no longer connected effectively to the provision of social and community services. We see it also in the results of our neglect of community and by the subsequent erosion of the social fabric of our societies and the alarming rise in addiction and dependency. However, we suffer from unanticipated consequences at *every* level of our lives in ways that are very real and practical. Indeed, I am reminded of it each time I walk a country footpath and have to step over the debris of broken bottles, litter and other waste that results from our 'throw-away' society. For me, a humorous sign posted by an employee of London Underground on one of the station kiosk windows makes the point very nicely. 'This is a non-profit making institution. It wasn't intended to be, it's just the way it turned out.' Linear and simplistic thinking also has another hidden and potentially more devastating cost. We remain blind to the very real opportunities that are right in front of us, hidden in the shadows. For Innocent and Pret A Manger our unhealthy 'fast food' culture has provided a very significant business opportunity for healthy eating. Starbucks has succeeded in establishing its coffee shops as the 'third hub' in its customers' lives partly because of the erosion of other community facilities. The National Trust has widened its appeal by fully embracing conservation of our landscape and environmental change as well as the care of historic buildings. The cultures of Toyota and Honda embody a deep respect for the individual that has transformed the soul-destroying nature of traditional mass production techniques. What has enabled these organisations to grasp these opportunities is their common capability to see the world around them from a wider, more holistic perspective.

Until now those of us in the wealthiest nations have been getting away with this disconnected way of thinking largely because the costs borne by others (and on our world as a whole) have not been sufficiently large to rebound on us. That time is rapidly running out. As we become more aware of the damage that our actions are having on others we no longer have any excuse to ignore the moral and ethical imperative to change our ways and begin to act responsibly. Ignorance is no longer an excuse. We need to begin to act decisively now before the consequences of our actions, and our way of life in general, become more devastating still. We need to act before it is too late. At the root of making a change is a shift to thinking more holistically. We begin by acknowledging our part in the whole and recognising the natural limits to our independence. We remember that 'the system is us' in the words of the renowned physicist, David Bohm.[184]

Ideas in action

'The story of water almost everywhere involves abuse, waste and even tragedy. Nor are things getting better: indeed much of the worst damage has been wrought in the past 100 years. Water resources have been exploited with no heed to either sustainability or to the environmental consequences. And water-policy has suffered from a near-total disregard for the discipline and tools of economics, especially pricing, trading and cost-benefit analysis ... modern engineering has made possible irrigation disasters on a massive scale.'

The Economist, Survey on Water [185]

Water is the very foundation of life and most of us take it completely for granted. We shouldn't do. It is a very precious thing indeed. The story of water demonstrates more vividly than anything else the importance of holistic thinking; the need to see ourselves as part of the whole and act accordingly. Darfur is a barren, mountainous land just below the Sahara desert in western Sudan. Over the last four years some 200,000 people have been killed in fighting and 2.5 million more have been made refugees

---

[184] David Joseph Bohm was an American-born quantum physicist who made significant contributions in the fields of theoretical physics, philosophy and neuropsychology. Further information is available on Wikipedia at http://en.wikipedia.org/wiki/David_Bohm
[185] The Economist, 'Priceless: A Survey on Water', July 19th 2003

in what has been called the world's worst human-made disaster. The roots of the conflict are often seen as an ethnic as Arabs and black Africans struggle over limited supplies of good land. What is overlooked is that the conflict may have more to do with ecology than ethnicity. The Sahara desert is advancing relentlessly southwards covering good soil with sand and the traditional compromises and accommodations made between peoples since time immemorial are no longer adequate. The devastation of Darfur owes its origins to declining rainfall over the last half century causing drought and conflict over available resources. Time Magazine neatly summed up the situation in May 2007.[186] 'There are too many people in a hot, poor, shrinking land and it's not hard to start a fight in a place like that.' The United Nations estimates that as many as 90 million Africans, many in the area in and around the Sahara, could be at risk on account of global warming. A report by CNA Corporation, a think tank, published in April 2007 warns that climate change is a 'threat multiplier' in volatile parts of the world leading to increased conflicts over water, food production and land use. [187]

Half a world away, in Australia, a region that accounts for 40% of the country's agriculture and 85% of its irrigation is on the verge of ruin. The Murray-Darling Basin is Australia's longest river system and it is suffering a devastating eight year drought. Australians are now facing water shortages unprecedented in the two centuries since Europeans settled there, with the Murray-Darling Basin flowing at its lowest levels in a century and the flow continuing to fall. The rivers drain a basin the size of France and Spain combined, flowing from Queensland in the North to Adelaide in the South. The trouble is that the river system no longer carries enough water for it to make its own journey to the sea. This is partly cyclical. The 'Federation drought' of the late 1890's and early 1900's was so severe that it prompted the six independent colonies in Australia at the time to form a united commonwealth. It is also partly due to human intervention. Water management systems have traditionally given little thought to the downstream effect of the dams, weirs and locks placed further upstream, a problem exacerbated by the fact that the basin flows through four states, each of which has its own interests to represent. Significant water

---

[186] Time Magazine, 'Africa: How to Prevent the Next Darfur: Step One: Get Serious About Climate Change', May 7th 2007
[187] The full findings are available on the Woodrow Wilson International Center for Scholars website (www.wilsoncenter.org) at www.wilsoncenter.org/index.cfm?topic_id=1413&fuseaction=topics.event_summary&event_id=236344. See also the CNA Corporation web site at http://securityandclimate.cna.org

management issues started to arise in the early 1990's when it was became apparent that too much water was being allowed for irrigation. By 1994 human activity was consuming 77% of the river's average annual flow, even though the actual flow falls far below the average in dry years. Those dry years have now come and there is a strong possibility that things are going to get much worse. Scientists warn that global warming may also be a significant factor causing the Murray-Darling Basin to heat up and dry out. The Commonwealth Scientific and Industrial Research Organisation ('CISRO') warns that climate change could reduce the river flow by as much as 5% in 20 years and 15% in 50 years or, in a worst case scenario, by an alarming 20% in 20 years and 50% in 50 years. It has taken this prolonged and severe drought for Australians to wake up and take water seriously. And what Australia is experiencing is being mirrored all over the world as water shortages become an increasingly prominent issue. [188]

The next 50 years are likely to see unprecedented conflict around access to water and we need to act quickly to reduce the potentially catastrophic impact of disputes. Philip E. Clapp, President of the Washington-based National Environmental Trust, warns that the problems seen in Darfur may be 'an advance warning' of climate related apocalypses to come. The impact of rising sea levels on Africa and Asia alone is frightening. Five of Africa's largest cities are coastal and 40% of Asia's population of 3.9 billion (some 1.5 billion people) live within 100 km of the sea. 'It may be the last warning,' he says 'before the consequences of climatic change become so enormous that they are beyond the capacity of industrialised nations to deal with.'[189] As the world warms up, hundreds of millions of people are likely to face the same ecological crisis that the residents of the Murray-Darling Basin are confronting today. The continued drought in Australia is significant enough to have reduced the national growth rate by one percentage point in 2006. As water levels dwindle, rows about how water should be used are erupting between farmers and city-dwellers and setting environmentalists against politicians. The government is trying to broker a federal solution but this is proving difficult. If a wealthy country like Australia is struggling to come to terms with this kind of crisis it is easy to imagine how drought will tear apart less prepared parts of the world.

If we look from a long term perspective we see that water problems are not new. Indeed, irrigation catastrophes have befallen civilisations since

---

[188] Full further details refer to the CSIRO Land and Water web site at www.clw.csiro.au
[189] Time Magazine, 'Africa: How to Prevent the Next Darfur', as above.

the dawn of time. Sandra Postel, the author of a book on irrigation called the 'Pillar of Sand', maintains that no civilisation based on irrigation has survived for long with the single exception of Egypt.[190] Sometimes the water has simply run out. Archaeological evidence suggests that much of the area that is now the Sahara desert was once green and fertile until the excessive depletion of ground water turned it into a desert. In other cases, there was a fatal build up of silt or salt. Too much irrigation causes the excess water to evaporate leaving the salt behind, a process of salination that will eventually render the soil infertile. This seems to be the fate of the Hohokam Indians, who developed a remarkably sophisticated irrigation system but died out suddenly in the early 15th century.

Modern engineering techniques have allowed us to increase the scale of mismanagement enormously and given us the potential to produce monumental disasters such as the fate of the Aral Sea, once the world's fourth largest inland sea. Since Soviet planners diverted much of the inflowing river water for irrigation in the 1950's (following Stalin's dictum in 1929 that 'water that is allowed to enter the sea is wasted'[191]), the Sea has been reduced to a quarter of its original size with devastating environmental consequences. Other countries, including the United States, are now learning hard lessons about the hidden costs of the huge engineering projects (including gigantic dams and water diversion projects) that have encouraged overexploitation of water resources in naturally dry areas such as the American west. In the United Kingdom periodic water shortages in the South East have been caused as much by overbuilding and poor water infrastructure as lack of rainfall, cyclical or otherwise.

There is something very symbolic about the water crisis. The stakes are high and we will need to learn to work together from a holistic perspective if we are to solve global water problems. Cyclical patterns and climate change are exacerbating problems of our own design, whether it is short term planning (failing to limit water extraction to long term sustainable levels or building on flood plains) or simplistic and linear thinking (failing to look at the environmental system as a whole and the unanticipated consequences of water management systems). Whilst it is true that some

---

[190] Sandra Postel, 'Pillar of Sand: Can the Irrigation Miracle Last?', published by W. W. Norton & Company, 1999

[191] This was apparently said by Stalin in 1929 and is often quoted in relation to the mismanagement of water supplies. It has even been called one of the three 'water myths' in relation to the Australian water crisis. Full details available at CSIRO Land and Water web site (www.clw.csiro.au) at http://www.clw.csiro.au/publications/clw-link/clwlink-apr03/page06.html

of the key issues can be resolved by adopting sensible market-based pricing systems, which recognise the real value of water, other solutions rely on our ability to work together from a holistic perspective in harmony with the environment rather than in opposition to it. Water flows across borders and climatic systems are often global. No single nation can act alone. The horror of the suffering in the sub-Sahara should be a wake-up call for all of us. The words of Palouma Ponlibae, an agriculture and natural-resources officer for the relief agency CARE in Darfur, are chilling. 'The water is going. The firewood is gone. The land has lost its ability to regenerate. The refugees are going to have to move. There's going to be nothing here to sustain life.'[192] More than anything else we will be required to work together and recognise our interdependence, our relationships to each other, to the environment and to the planet as a whole.

Tools and techniques

'A mind that lives in the known is always in prison.'

Krishnamurti [193]

We have looked at many ways to open up the space to think more holistically and creatively during this book. Walking, exercise, hobbies, creative work and movement will all do the trick as will more 'formal' exercises such as meditation and reflection practices. There is nothing particularly mysterious about the process, it is as natural as breathing. Indeed, being conscious of our breathing is a very simple and time-effective method in itself. After all, the word 'inspiration' is derived from the Latin word, 'spirare', to breathe. All these methods aim to lengthen the gap between each thought to allow insight and creativity to flow through us. Just taking the time out of our busy schedule may allow us to come away with a different perspective on our issues and, quite possibly, a more balanced and creative approach to resolving them. We can achieve the same thing by going deeply into something outside our normal environment, especially in the context of active service to others. Visiting an elderly neighbour for morning coffee is not an act of charity but an

---

[192] Time Magazine, 'Africa: How to Prevent the Next Darfur: Step One: Get Serious About Climate Change' as above.

[193] Jiddu Krishnamurti was a popular writer and speaker on philosophical and spiritual subjects. Interestingly he became a good friend of David Bohm (see above) sharing a deep mutual interest in philosophy and the state of humanity.

exchange that gives much to both parties. In our world we largely ignore the knowledge and wisdom of our elders and we are all the poorer for it. Listening to the stories of those who have accumulated a lifetime of experiences is a profound learning experience, one that has always been deeply embedded in tribal cultures. Sometimes, we only need to be open to what is immediately before us. It can be that simple.

There is nothing as powerful as a story and we can use story-telling techniques to broaden and deepen our perspective on issues and problems that arise in our working and personal lives. We looked earlier at how the use of scenario analysis and 'corporate' story-telling enables us to deal overtly and consciously with all sorts of things that are buried in the 'shadow side' of organisational life. It gives us permission to talk about things that are not easily discussed within the organisational culture, to challenge core assumptions and beliefs, to acknowledge our weaknesses and to come up with a range of lateral and creative solutions that are unlikely to arise through conventional business processes. Ironically, story-telling is one of the best ways to encourage an honest appraisal of reality, our relative strengths and weaknesses in relation to the decision at hand. We live in a culture where it is frowned upon to be 'negative', to be a 'naysayer'. But whilst a 'can-do' attitude is admirable it can also be dangerous when it is over optimistic and not founded on a robust understanding of the way things actually are. Stories are a particularly powerful way of looking at the feasibility of a project or endeavour and examining potential obstacles without labelling the exploration as 'positive' or 'negative'. Usefully, it also de-personalises the discussion and takes away some of the blaming culture that is endemic in our society.

Developing greater capacity for thinking strategically takes time. I was once on a course that incorporated kata (Japanese movement exercises similar to yoga) as one of its key elements. As I struggled to bend and stretch my body in accordance with the instructions of the facilitator, mostly getting hopelessly into a muddle, I couldn't help but notice how much more agile the ladies on the course were. How effortless it appeared to be for them! At the break I foolishly asked one of them, 'How do you bend your body like that?' Her answer was both simple and instructive. '20 years of practice!' In essence, this is equally true for all the strategic thinking tools and techniques. It all comes down to practice. Simple things done over long periods of time are transformative. Something that all of us who have learned a musical instrument know only too well!

Simple rules

Over the years I have formed some very basic 'rules' around my strategic thinking work, which I find helpful. In essence, the quality of strategic thinking depends on three things; the degree of commitment (our intention), the quality of the environment and our personal wellbeing. Firstly, commitment to the process is the foundation stone because insight depends on openness and this in turn depends on intention. Like any creative endeavour we have to acknowledge that we are essentially acting as 'receivers'. As a writer, it is my job to be sufficiently open and non judgemental to capture those things that come to me, to 'write down' rather than to 'think up'. When we think something up it is often heavily filtered by our beliefs, assumptions, judgements and prior experiences of what is possible. On the other hand, when something is 'received' and our role is simply to record it, the content is far less likely to be distorted. We may need to work on it, mould and adapt it, but the form is much purer. When I am writing I am aware that I am in a dance with the spirit of the book, a muse that guides me with the inner knowledge of what the book is truly about and what should go in it. When we are committed our intention allows this process to unfold naturally without it seeming in the slightest bit strange. We are able to put our doubts to one side and accept that we cannot control the process. Trust is built on the foundation of intention. Whether we talk in terms of the artist's muse, gut feel or intuition, the process is the essentially the same. We become listeners.

The second rule, the quality of the environment in which we chose to do our thinking, is also critical. It is hard to do good thinking in the basement of an inner city hotel next a major road artery. Nature is not only a good healer when we are overstressed but it does wonders for creative and strategic thinking. As part of my mentoring work I regularly walk with clients in natural surroundings and we achieve far more than we ever could by meeting in a conventional business context. It is healthy and much more fun. This way of working feeds body, heart and soul as well as the mind and I regularly witness my clients having breakthroughs in their thinking. There is also the opportunity to have a good lunch! Thirdly, the importance of personal wellbeing in strategic thinking is something that I have only recognized recently. I must confess that I am not always very good at it. Like so many of us, I have a tendency to work too hard, run too fast, sleep too little and 'wire' myself up with too much caffeine to help me make it through the day. I seem to be constantly fighting deadlines, rushing from one place to another and multi-tasking on all fronts. This is no state to be in if we are trying to think more deeply. The first order of priority in any strategic work is to slow down, relax and put ourselves into some kind of preparedness. In the longer term, the key disciplines of strategic thinking are founded on a healthy lifestyle based on simple principles of sound sleep, good exercise and a balanced diet. If we arrive late to an early morning meeting after just five hours sleep, and with the rest of the day's activities and demands whirling around in our head, we are off to a rocky start. It is very unlikely that we will be able to separate the wood from the trees, let alone think of creative solutions to the issues at hand.

If we look carefully we will see that the hyper-active life that many of us lead is not delivering and that it is coming at a very great cost, to us personally, to our organisations and within society as a whole. And, of course, a healthy lifestyle has other significant advantages too; we live longer, feel better and experience richer lives. It also helps us to profit from growing older by acknowledging and using our experiences, insights and the other benefits that aging can bring. Dr Andrew Weil, the American author and physician, describes these as 'wisdom, depth of character, the smoothing out of what is rough and harsh, the evaporation of what is inconsequential and the concentration of true worth.'[194] This is a heady list and bears a remarkable similarity to some of the characteristics that we have observed in the strategic leaders that we have studied throughout this book!

The personal challenge

'The fact that an opinion has been widely held is no evidence whatever that it is not utterly absurd; indeed, in view of the silliness of the majority of mankind, a wide-spread belief is more likely to be foolish than sensible.'

Bertrand Russell

Strategic leaders act decisively to change the world for the better, sometimes through an explicit sense of mission but often guided by their passion for their chosen area of endeavour. In many cases it is both. This strong sense of purpose and altruism allows them to create a compelling vision of the future, drawing others to them and enabling them to make a significant impact on the world. This matching of what is most important to

---

[194] Time Magazine, 'Living Better Longer: Aging Naturally: An Interview with Dr. Andrew Weil', September 24th 2005. See also Dr Weil's related book, 'Healthy Aging: A Lifelong Guide to Your Physical and Spiritual Well-Being', published by Knopf in October 2005 and his comprehensive web site on www.drweil.com

us and what the world needs is a very powerful thing. American author, Frederick Buechner, defines that place as our calling, 'where our deepest gladness and the world's hunger meet'.[195] Strategic leaders are distinguished by their ability to integrate this calling within the practical context of daily life. By laying the pathways for us, scouting ahead and marking out the route, these leaders are showing us the way forward and they are usually doing it from the most practical of perspectives. It is time that we place our feet firmly on the ground and follow them, for there is much work to be done.

We do need, however, to do something before we place our first foot forward. The foundation for our journey rests on an acknowledgement of our whole selves. This means owning and integrating those elements of ourselves that have been repressed for millennia; the Body, the Shadow and the Feminine, which dance therapist and Jungian analyst, Joan Chodorow, refers to as the 'unholy trinity'.[196] Carl Jung considered the integration of this trinity to be the most important challenge of our times. Bringing together the 'masculine' aspects of our humanity (the will to act, structure and order) with the 'feminine' aspects (feeling and intuitive understanding) is essential to being whole and therefore to developing holistic thinking. Moreover, reintegrating the repressed parts of our psyche also allows us to recognise and act upon the unseen opportunities that lie in the shadows. This is another way of acknowledging our humanity as the integration of body, mind, heart and spirit. For centuries masculine energy has been allowed to run unchecked and it has created havoc in our world. Now, it is time to redress this balance. Nowhere is the integration of the feminine more elegantly summed up than by Christopher Booker in his excellent book, 'The Seven Basic Plots, Why We Tell Stories':

'It is this which alone can bring masculine strength fully to life by giving it the vital ingredient of connection, of joining up; through feeling, which gives a link to others and to the world outside the ego; through that intuitive insight which gives proper understanding, by allowing [us] to perceive the wholeness of things and their mysterious, hidden connections.'[197]

---

[195] Frederick Buechner is a Presbyterian minister and an American author.
[196] Source: Caduceus Magazine, Issue 70, Winter 2006, Tina Stromsted, 'Re-inhabiting the Body: Authentic Movement as a Pathway to Transformation'. For further details and references see www.caduceus.info
[197] Christopher Booker ,'The Seven Basic Plots, Why We Tell Stories', published by Continuum, 2004

10

THE WAY FORWARD

> 'This is the way the world ends
> Not with a bang but a whimper.'
>
> T S Elliot [198]

The choices we face

I am lucky enough to live next to one of the most beautiful bluebell woods in the country, West Woods in Wiltshire. Each year in May the bluebells thrust through the forest floor and cover the woods with deep carpets of purple-blue. The sight is beyond description. We moved here in the month of May and I remember the previous owners of our home recommending that we visit the woods to see this wonderful sight. I recall nodding my head politely, thinking it was a rather clever ruse designed to increase the desirability of the house. I was quite wrong. When we did visit the woods we were astounded at the sight that met our eyes. The vibrancy of the flowers, contrasted against the emerging green canopy of the beach tree leaves, was simply stunning. It literally took my breath away. Now, much humbled, I make the same recommendations to my visitors, often with the same slightly sceptical response! Throughout the year the wood changes but it is always beautiful, from the first early spring flowers to the magnificent autumnal display in the fall. Even in the depths of winter it has its own character, particularly after a snowfall, when the branches hang low, laden with snow. [199]

It seems churlish to suggest that anything is amiss in such a beautiful

---

[198] T. S. Eliot, "The Hollow Men', 1925, published by Faber and Faber in a number of different selections of Eliot's poetry.

[199] A search on the web will reveal a number of information sites on West Woods. A good starting point is Kennet Tourism available at http://documents.kennet.gov.uk/Tourism/features/bluebells/index.html

environment. Yet, there are some disturbing signs. West Woods is actually a working plantation and sustainable logging takes place on a regular basis. A series of dry years combined with the removal of larger trees (which draw water down into the water table and contribute to the health of the wood as a whole) has resulted in the unmistakable orange-brownish hue that appears on the surface of trees that are lacking enough water. The wood is primarily a single-species plantation of beach, which makes it more vulnerable to disease and drought as it lacks the bio-diversity of a natural forest. None of this means that it is in imminent danger. Sensible and sustainable logging practices combined with a small variety of coniferous and other deciduous tree varieties should keep it healthy in future. However, the future of the wood depends on recognizing that it is a delicate and vulnerable ecosystem. Taking too many trees out for commercial purposes, in combination with other climatic and social changes could damage it permanently. Increased population in the area, for example, has meant that the woods are now being used more for recreation, including the disturbing trend for motorbikes to enter illegally and use it for scrambling practice along the pathways. No one issue is likely to prove decisive but a combination of events and activities is beginning to take its toll on this uniquely beautiful area. Since much of this change is occurring below the surface (quite literally in this case) the effects are largely unseen at the moment. We have a clear choice. We can change our way of thinking and become conscious of the way in which we co-exist with this natural environment as a complex ecosystem and modify our behaviour and policies accordingly. Alternatively, we can continue as we are and watch the long-term health of the woods suffer. The choice is ours.

The crossroads

'It's only when the tide goes out that you discover who's been swimming naked.'

Warren Buffet

We are at a unique crossroads in human history. The world as we understand it is dying. *That* world is one that is separate from us, where we act from an illusion of independence and ignore the consequences of our actions on others and on our planet as a whole. We are rapidly reaching a 'tipping point' beyond which there will be no turning back. Ervin Laszlo, scientist and founder of the Club of Budapest, warns that we have five to six years to head off the unsustainable economic, social and ecological trends before these systems will begin to break down. This will not only happen at the global level through issues which we are now all too familiar with; the results of climate change, increased political and social unrest, escalating maverick and organized warfare, the effects of continued destruction of bio-diversity and so on. It will also happen in our back yards, in our own 'West Woods'. As we are all part of the whole we will no longer be isolated from the consequences of our collective actions. In common with many other scientists, leaders, thinkers and artists who are sensitive to the changes taking place, Ervin Laszlo calls for new thinking that is holistic and encompasses *all* the relevant factors.[200] This is the kind of thinking that we have been looking at in this book, one that sees the forest and not just the trees, one that is 'an evolution of our ideas, feelings, values and perceptions: an evolution of our consciousness.' Laszlo goes even further and suggests that a new more evolved consciousness is now a precondition for our collective survival. What we do today will critically decide the shape of tomorrow. Artists often act as the sentinels of our society. They tend to be more sensitive and receptive to those changes that are happening below the collective consciousness. Today, across the whole creative spectrum, many echo the urgency of the situation that we face. Singer-songwriter, Joni Mitchell, is particularly blunt about the choices we face: 'I'm not interested in escapist entertainment when the planet is on red alert,' she says, 'the spaceship we are all riding is dying. Will somebody tell the captain to stop punching holes in the wall.'[201]

From denial to despair

It may seem strange to admit that I only discovered the core purpose of this book when it was two-thirds completed. After all, it has its origins in more than twenty years of experience in strategic consultancy, teaching and facilitation. Indeed, I developed the seven core disciplines of strategic thinking some time ago and I have been working with them with my clients

---

[200] Ervin Laszlo, 'The Chaos Point: The World at the Crossroads', published by Piatkus, 2006 and 'A Holistic World View for a Planetary Civilization', an interview with Ervin Laszlo published in Caduceus Magazine, Issue 68, Spring 2006. For more information on Ervin Laszlo see the web site of the club of Budapest at www.clubofbudapest.org and Wikipedia at http://en.wikipedia.org/wiki/Ervin_Laszlo.
[201] Joni Mitchell in an interview with Word Magazine in April 2007, reported by CTV.ca, 'Joni Mitchell Returns With New Music and Art', on August 31st 2007, available at http://www.ctv.ca/servlet/ArticleNews/story/CTVNews/20070831/joni_mitchell_070831?s_n ame=&no_ads=

and students for several years before I commenced the book. Moreover, the concept, outline, structure and core case studies were in place long before I set pen to paper. However, as a writer, I know that it is not uncommon for the spirit of the book to emerge as it is written, and that it is my job to recognize it when it happens. In this case, it happened quite late in the process.

In March 2007 I met with my colleague and good friend, John Tucker, founder of the International Centre for Families in Business, to talk about his work with family business, one of the key case studies in the book.[202] We had arranged to meet in Marlborough in Mustard Seed, a coffee shop by the River Kennet, which enjoys fine views and offers a nice relaxed ambience. Before we started our conversation in earnest we relaxed and chatted about life as we watched the river flow by and the ducks chase each other up and down stream. I found myself talking about the seriousness of the issues that confront our world, particularly the destruction of the environment and our imbalance with the natural world. 'Is talking about this cathartic for you?' John asked. I responded in the affirmative and he continued expectantly, 'so will you be talking about it in the book?' The question caused me to pause because the answer, I knew, was 'no', or more truthfully, no more than was necessary as a backdrop to discussing how important it is for us to think strategically in our world today. 'There are plenty of other books that already do that,' I replied, 'and they do it far better than I am able to.' This, of course, begged the question as to *what* the book was actually about and *why* I was writing it. I have known John for far too many years to make the mistake of thinking that he would let me get away with an evasive response on that one. 'It's about what we can *do* about it.' I finally replied.

As it happens, the following day I had the opportunity to see 'An Inconvenient Truth', for the second time. This time I was struck by Al Gore's comment that he was increasingly meeting people who were moving from denial to despair. The place of positive action was missing. Recognition did not necessarily bring the will to act but a kind of resigned hopelessness. Something immediately clicked. The purpose had revealed itself to me; to support those of us who are living in that place between denial and despair. This, in no way, minimizes the challenging nature of many of the problems and issues that we face. It simply puts the emphasis of the book on how we can begin to make a difference in resolving these

---

[202] John Tucker can be contacted through the web site for the International Centre for Families in Business at www.icfib.com

problems. A Chinese proverb warns, 'if we do not change direction, we are likely to end up exactly where we are headed.'[203] At present, it is not too late yet to change direction and the case studies and stories in this book give plenty of practical advice on how this process of change can begin. However, time is running out. Developing the capacity to thinking strategically has never been more important.

Strategic leadership

'[He] had through his power over words, but still more through his power over the hearts of men, that rare ability to call out from those who had heard him the sense that they were a necessary part of something greater than themselves; the ability to make each one feel just that much greater than he had been.'[204]
Harold Wilson writing on Winston Churchill

'A leader,' said Napoleon, 'is a dealer in hope.' The strategic leaders in this book certainly do that but they also do more, they deliver on their promises. They regularly achieve the 'impossible', whether it is the 'indestructible' hat pioneered by Alex Tilley of Tilley Endurables, or one of Sir Richard Branson's ventures, 'creating a business that others thought impossible', as Mark Cuban, owner of the Dallas Mavericks, so succinctly puts it.[205] Despite very different personalities and temperaments these strategic leaders have many key characteristics in common. All combine vision with the capacity to act and all are able to 'think outside the box'. In spite of achieving great personal success they tend to remain remarkably open and eager to learn. During his time at the helm of Toyota, Katsuaki Watanabe has been extraordinarily successful by any standards. Yet, as Brian France, CEO of the National Association of Stock Car Auto Racing ('NASCAR'), observes, 'he remains humble and willing to learn ... he

---

[203] I believe the source of this proverb is Lao Tze, the reputed author of the 'Tao Te Ching' and the founder of the Taoist religion in China. His name means 'Old Master' and 'Tao' means the 'Way'.
[204] Harold Wilson, 'A Prime Minister on Prime Ministers', published by Weidenfeld & Nicolson and Michael Joseph, 1977.
[205] Source: 'The Time 100, 2007'; 82 of 100; Richard Branson by Mark Cuban, Chairman of HDNet and owner of the NBA's Dallas Mavericks. The full text is available at www.time.com/time/specials/2007/time100/article/0,28804,1595326_1615737,00.html

understands that acceptance precedes commercial success.'[206] This is important because NASCAR is an emphatically American institution and Toyota is the first automotive maker from outside the US to compete. It shows a level of sensitivity on the part of Watanabe as well as an acknowledgement of the need to learn from others. As Apple goes from strength to strength Steve Jobs loses none of his reflective ability and philosophical outlook. Indeed, his recent brush with cancer has made him, if anything, even more introspective, without losing any of his entrepreneurial instinct. Although he makes regular appearances in Time's annual list of the 100 most influential people, the magazine argues that 'prosperity hasn't robbed him of his disrespect for conventional wisdom, his spooky ability to see round corners, and his feral determination to make perfect products at all costs.'[207] He remains, in fact, quintessentially Steve Jobs.

Strategic leaders also share a determination to contribute to their communities and to make some aspect of the world a better place. Part of the core philosophies of both Toyota and Honda is recognizing the importance of investing in their communities, understanding how all the elements fit together and contribute to the whole, including the critical nature of relationships and interdependencies in defining commercial success. Leading retailers go well beyond good practice and customer focus. As we have seen from looking at Starbucks, Whole Foods Market, Pret A Manger and Waitrose, they obsess over detail, constantly improving the quality of the customer experience and are extraordinarily responsive when things do not go quite right. Indeed, they take a deep, almost excessive, interest in the welfare of their customer communities from both the product angle and the service side. As a result they don't simply inhabit their market segment they define it and own it.

Membership-based organisations such as the National Trust and Care for the Family have a very special relationship with their membership communities, involving a shared sense of purpose and identity. They recognize that trust is paramount in this relationship and they operate accordingly. The other day I ordered a work-book from Care for the Family for my wife, Tracy, to use for a series of seminars. I was promptly emailed

---

[206] Source: 'The Time 100, 2007'; 87 of 100; Katsuaki Watanabe by Brian France, CEO of NASCAR. The full text is available at
www.time.com/time/specials/2007/time100/article/0,28804,1595326_1615737_1615688,00.html
[207] Source: 'The Time 100, 2007'; 95 of 100; Steve Jobs by Lev Grossman. The full text is available at www.time.com/time/specials/2007/time100/article/0,28804,1595326_1615737_1615876,00.html

confirmation of my order with details of the payment to be charged to my credit card. This morning the book arrived with a 10% discount applied. I suspect that it is a small 'thank you' for being a 'partner' of the organisation but I cannot be sure. It has simply been done with no fuss or fanfare. Like Care for the Family, leading organisations value their communities and acknowledge them in all areas of their relationship because, contrary to what we might think, it is the small things that matter most. Commercial companies like eBay and Amazon are no less diligent in protecting their communities, which they see as the lifeblood of their businesses. In short, community matters to strategic leaders because their vision tends to be all encompassing. They have a unique ability to see the whole and their part within it and act accordingly. It is through this combination of self-knowledge, capability in action and strength in relationships that they develop the ability to bring others along with them on their journey.

Strategic leaders excel in both the 'masculine' aspects of leadership (power and control) and the 'feminine' aspects (relationships and an intuitive ability to see the whole). To lead others we need both these aspects. When I run a leadership seminar I often begin by asking groups to prepare a list of their 'top 10' leaders and use this to explore the characteristics that we associate with leadership. Even today, in the first lists there are inevitably a disproportionate number of male political and military leaders. These normally include figures such as Winston Churchill, Alexander the Great, John F Kennedy, Genghis Khan, Mahatma Gandhi, Martin Luther King, Nelson Mandela and others who epitomize the 'masculine' leadership energies, the will to act. They tend to be overwhelmingly male, although the inclusion of Mahatma Gandhi, Martin Luther King and Nelson Mandela already point to a broader definition of leadership. Female political leaders and business executives appear in much smaller numbers, even though some, one clear example being Margaret Thatcher, embody far more masculine leadership qualities than most men! Many of the women who do make the list are personal mentors and leaders from within the working context of the group members (most often 'my boss'). This is normally a good point to move towards an exploration of what makes these individuals different. The answer invariably distils down to the fact that they exhibit some measure of both the masculine and feminine characteristics of leadership. This provides an opportunity for us to re-examine our original leadership lists and see the same combination of qualities underlying the dramatic stories of Nelson Mandela, Mahatma Gandhi and others who have significantly changed our world for the better. A very good example is Winston Churchill, the quintessential war leader. Former Prime Minister, Harold Wilson, talks about Churchill's great humanity and ability to empathize with those who were suffering. This was a key element in his ability to carry the people with him through desperate times when the country was almost on its knees:

'There was his great quality of humanity. The man who could move armies and navies and embrace the world in one strategic sweep could himself be moved to uncontrollable and unashamed tears at the sight of an old soul's cheerfulness in a shelter, or of a street of devastated houses, at the thought of the human realities which lay behind the war communiqués.'[208]

Finally, in our group discussion, we are able open up the topic of leadership completely, defining it as the capacity to influence people over the long term. Then something interesting normally occurs. Out of the shadows come the great spiritual teachers and leaders of the ages who have played such as key role in defining our civilization and our humanity. At the same time, from the very opposite side of the spectrum, come the unsung heroes and heroines. These are the people who have deeply influenced us on a personal level, very often through their own example; significant friends, mentors, business colleagues, artists, teachers, writers and all sorts of 'ordinary' folk that we cross paths with in everyday life. They are, in fact, all those who have helped us to define our pathway ahead and supported us on our way. This is strategic leadership seen as the capacity to influence others in day to day life and it is something we can all do in our own ways. I find the leadership sessions very humbling because at the end we inevitably come full circle and begin to consider the importance of our own families in defining us and enabling us find our own way in the world. We acknowledge the importance of our own background, heritage and family history. When the Dalai Lama addressed Columbia University in the early 1990's he spoke of how the great teachers of the world were not the professors, gurus or lamas but the mothers. For it is from our mother that we get the first feeling of being wanted, of affection and love, which provides the foundation for us to go out into the world. This is true leadership expressed through *all* that we do, no matter whether the outside world attaches importance to our activities or not.

---

[208] Harold Wilson, 'A Prime Minister on Prime Ministers', published by Weidenfeld & Nicolson and Michael Joseph, 1977.

Strategic leadership, like strategic thinking is ultimately a state of mind. When we are in that state we do not need others to tell us that what we are doing is important, we know it is and we simply do it.

Embracing ambiguity

Let's be honest. There is also a negative side to becoming a strategic leader. If we are successful in the eyes of the world, we become public property. We may even achieve that ultimate accolade in our society, becoming a 'celebrity'. It sounds nice but for most of us it isn't! I cannot think of one strategic leader that I know who is not deeply ambivalent about the price of public recognition. In fact, most actively dislike this aspect of their work. Sometimes, there can be a very heavy price attached to public notoriety. As we have seen, John Browne was forced to resign in May 2007 as a result of allegations about his private life despite his very significant leadership role within BP and his legacy on climate and environmental change. In my experience there is always some price attached to being a leader, even in the smallest or humblest of contexts. We may decide that it is a price worth paying but it is as well to acknowledge it. As leaders we are expected to live by exemplary standards when we are, of course, normal human beings. This is exacerbated by our tendency to unconsciously project aspects of ourselves, both positive and negative, onto our leaders, resulting in the familiar 'hero' and 'villain' mythology. The 'middle path' quickly disappears. We treat our leaders as either visionary heroes who can do no wrong or quite the reverse. We forget their common humanity, that they are normal people with strengths and failings just like us. For those leaders who are in the media spotlight the attention can be merciless and unforgiving. It is hard to convey the complex reality of a situation in a sound bite. Issues can be easily distorted and facts take on a selective interpretation, curiously detached from the messy nature of the real world.

Above all, strategic leaders carry the torch (or the burden on bad days) of making things happen. Simon Burke, a transformational leader with much experience of turning around organisations, often describes this process as 'rolling a snowball uphill'.[209] This not only requires considerable tenacity on his part but the whole process is inclined to go into reverse as soon as he

---

[209] Simon Burke is currently Executive Chairman of Superquinn, a premium Irish supermarket chain. He is also currently a Trustee of the National Gallery in London and acts as Chairman of Majestic Wine plc. A short biography is available at www.retailweekconference.com/page.cfm/link=37

takes his eye off the ball. Being a leader is to tackle inertia, at all levels from individuals to organisations, not as a theoretical concept but as a practical day to day reality. It means repeating the core messages (purpose, vision, values, practices, standards) endlessly and acting them out on a personal level in everything we do; really walking the talk. There is no other way and it can be utterly exhausting. I have come to realize that there is an unacknowledged secret in our world; a rather important one in fact. Almost inevitably, behind all endeavours, small or great, there will be a tiny group of individuals (often just one or two), who *carry* the process, who make things happen. This should be of immense comfort to us for it means that, as individuals, we can make an enormous difference at every level.

Learning to think strategically will inevitably push us into a leadership position, whether the endeavour is 'great' or 'small', and whether the context is highly visible or not. In this case size and overt recognition are not important. Indeed, some of the most influential people that I know do what they do very quietly and well away from the public eye. Whether we like it or not, however, the mantle of leadership comes, to a greater or lesser extent, with taking on the projections of others, sometimes being both lionized and demonized in almost the same sentence. June Burrough, founder of the Pierian Centre in Bristol recalls one such instance. She was listening to some very positive feedback from a client who had used the Centre for the first time, when the lady introduced a friend who had a very different opinion into the conversation. 'I'm so pleased that I didn't listen to Mary,' the lady said in confidential tone, 'she thinks this place is dreadful and she has no time for you either.' Taken a little by surprise June tried to remember the critical person to whom Mary was referring but found that she couldn't recall her. 'I'm sorry but I'm not sure I remember Mary,' she confessed, eager to find out what had upset the lady so. 'Oh, you wouldn't,' came the reply, 'she's never been here, she certainly wouldn't set foot in the place!' At this point, it might have been tempting for June to make all sorts of observations! Instead, she concluded, 'Well, I've certainly rattled *her* cage. That proves I must be doing *something* right!' Strategic leaders have a habit of rattling peoples' cages. It is part of the job even, and perhaps *especially*, when they have never met. [210]

---

[210] For more information on June Burrough and the Pierian Centre refer to the web site at www.pierian-centre.com.

The shadow side

There was one thing that took me by surprise when I reviewed the case studies and leadership stories after I had finished this book. It is not simply the positive qualities of these organisations and individuals, their ability to think strategically and take a leadership position in their industries and environments, which draws them together. They also attract a significant number of detractors. It is interesting to explore why leading organisations elicit this kind of response. Naturally, all leaders (and all organisations) make mistakes but the views expressed sometimes go well beyond this. Starbucks is accused of driving local competition out of business. The National Trust is seen as too elitist and divorced from the needs of 'normal' folk. The Prince of Wales is criticized for being too idealistic in his thinking, for not being 'realistic' enough. Sir Richard Branson is perceived as a cynical opportunist to be distrusted except by those who are naïve and gullible. BP's re-branding as 'Beyond Petroleum' is seen as self-serving marketing hype. Clearly something is going on. In many ways, the role of a being a strategic leader will inevitably attract some negative projections. Leaders shake things up; they present us with uncomfortable truths and complex realities. Likewise, when we begin to think more holistically we had better prepare ourselves for some opposition as well as affirmation. Taking a holistic perspective on issues and problems is critically important in today's world but it is not guaranteed to make us popular. We will inevitably attract our own fair share of detractors.

This is not just the result of the natural antipathy between those who are perceived to be making the decisions and those who are affected by them. It is also something to do with the way that strategic leaders embrace paradox. Generally, most of us do not cope well with self contradictory propositions. We prefer a world that is either black or white, but not both simultaneously. Even living with shades of grey can make some of us uncomfortable and disoriented. 'It is true on the one hand but on the other hand …' is never a good way to reassure somebody. Yet, leadership is a deeply paradoxical affair. We find it hard to accept that Starbucks can be exceptionally community oriented yet still be commercially astute. Similarly, the National Trust may have evolved from a focus on managing stately homes but the experience that the organisation gained in that role is now proving vital in understanding how climate change affects the broader environmental and ecological systems in which we live. We all too easily overlook the importance of Sir Richard Branson's dyslexia in forging *both* a unique opportunistic sensibility and a genuine desire to make the world a better place. Similarly, BP is both one of the most commercially successful organisations in the world today and one that is absolutely committed to its green business model. We are inclined to look at the Prince of Wales' ideas in a superficial context, ignoring the fact that they are based on a holistic worldview that acknowledges a deeper level of reality:

> 'It seems to becoming harder and harder in this age to stick to what we believe – or feel. We are told constantly that we have to live in 'the real world' – but the 'real world' is within us. The reality is that 'Truth, Goodness and Beauty' in the outer manifested world are only made possible through the inner, invisible pattern – the unmanifested archetype.'[211]
>
> The Prince of Wales

Strategic leaders are comfortable with ambiguity and harness it to their own needs because their overriding vision is broad enough to encompass a complex world where seemingly contradictory things can exist simultaneously. If they can't achieve their aims one way, they will find another way to do it. It is this combination of idealism and a pragmatic action orientation that is one of the hallmarks of leadership. As dealing with paradox makes most of us uncomfortable we tend to simplify situations into 'either-or' responses and judge leaders according to the same criteria. Naturally, there are aspects of strategic leaders that are less positive. As we have seen, they can be compulsive, demanding and obsessive. They can also be confrontational, egocentric and unwilling to compromise. At times, it can be very tough working for somebody like that. But that is precisely why they get things done!

The key elements of success

'If you believe you can or if you believe you can't … you're right.'
Henry Ford

Having a good theoretical framework for making a difference is quite different from actually doing something! We can certainly improve our skills in strategic thinking by using the seven key disciplines explored in this book. To become a leader, however, we need to integrate this framework

---

[211] The Prince of Wales, quoted by David Lorimer in 'Radical Prince: The Practical Vision of the Prince of Wales', published by Floris Books, 2003

into our actions. The extent to which we are successful will depend largely on three things; firstly, our level of our commitment; secondly, the degree to which we focus on our task; and, thirdly, our 'stick-to-it-ness'. In other words, success depends on intention, attention and persistence. Commitment is vital. The word 'vital' is derived from the Latin word, 'vitalis', meaning belonging to life and it gives us a clue to what is needed from the very beginning of an endeavour. Commitment is founded on our *intention* to make a difference, to sustain or make some aspect of life better. It provides purpose, vision and the ability to bring others along with us on our journey. It helps keep us going when things get tough, which inevitably happens from time to time. Secondly, we need to be focused, to give our full *attention* to the matter in hand. We have observed this demonstrated consistently by strategic leaders throughout this book, often through an apparently obsessive attention to detail. Finally we need to be *persistent*, to recognize that failure is simply 'the opportunity to being again more intelligently,' in the words of Henry Ford. As we have seen, this is one of the most important characteristics of entrepreneurs, although not always acknowledged as such. These three things, intention, attention and persistence, underlie our capability to bring our dreams into reality. Together they provide a simple template for making a difference.

The importance of personal commitment as the foundation for making our dreams come true is often underestimated. A wish becomes a dream when we commit to making it happen and a dream begins to manifest in reality when we act upon it. It is a point made famously by William Hutchinson Murray, a Scottish mountain climber, who climbed extensively in Scotland and also took part in several international expeditions. Murray spent much of the second world war in prisoner of war camps and while imprisoned he wrote his first book, '*Mountaineering in Scotland*'. For the first draft he used the only paper that was available to him, rough toilet paper. When this was discovered by the Gestapo and destroyed he simply started all over again. This resolve amazed his colleagues. There was the continuing risk of confiscation and the near starvation conditions that the prisoners endured cast considerable doubt on whether he would survive the war, let alone recommence his climbing career. In fact, he did both. The book was finally published in 1947 and he went on to act as deputy leader on the Everest Reconnaissance Expedition in 1951. It was in his book on this expedition that he comments most memorably on the power of intention. It remains one of the most elegant quotes on the subject, even if the couplet ascribed to Johann Wolfgang von Goethe is, in fact, a rather loose translation!

'... but when I said that nothing had been done I erred in one important matter. We had definitely committed ourselves and were halfway out of our ruts. We had put down our passage money – booked a sailing to Bombay. This may sound too simple, but is great in consequence. Until one is committed, there is hesitancy, the chance to draw back, always ineffectiveness. Concerning all acts of initiative (and creation), there is one elementary truth the ignorance of which kills countless ideas and splendid plans: that the moment one definitely commits oneself, then providence moves too. A whole stream of events issues from the decision, raising in one's favor all manner of unforeseen incidents, meetings and material assistance, which no man could have dreamt would have come his way. I learned a deep respect for one of Goethe's couplets:

Whatever you can do or dream you can, begin it.
Boldness has genius, power and magic in it!*[212]

The Black Farmer

We have seen how the principles of intention, attention and persistence repeatedly reinforce each other in the case studies and stories throughout this book. Another excellent example is the story of Wilfred Emmanuel Jones, often simply known as 'The Black Farmer' and, quite possibly, the only Afro-Caribbean in British Farming. He was born in Jamaica and came to the United Kingdom when he was four, living in a part of Birmingham that was, at that time, one of the poorest areas in Europe. As one of nine brothers and sisters living in a small terraced house he sought solace in his father's allotment, where for the first time he experienced a sense of space. It was then that he decided that he would like to buy 'my part of rural England and enjoy the open space and connection with nature.' Thirty years later that dream came true when he purchased a farm deep in the rolling hills on the Devon and Cornwall border near Launceston. 'The power of dreams is amazing,' Wilfred says, 'I had this dream at age 11 and at the age of forty I managed to buy this place.' Using his experience of producing and directing his own food and drinks programmes at the BBC

---

[212] Source: W.H. Murray, an extract from 'The Scottish Himalayan Expedition', published by J.M. Dent & Sons Ltd in 1951. More information on W. H. Murray is available on Wikipedia at http://en.wikipedia.org/wiki/W._H._Murray

and then running his own food and drinks marketing company, he launched 'The Black Farmer' range of sausages and sauces in 2004. 'When I came here,' he comments, 'I was the only black person that many of these people had met. They called me 'the black farmer' and I thought 'that's a great brand name!' His range of sausages has helped to redefine customer expectations of quality, containing 85-90% pork, winning awards and supermarket shelf space alike. This doesn't happen without a great deal of passion for the product. 'I'm a self-confessed 'sausageaholic' – passionate about great tasting sausages,' Wilfred says. 'I was frustrated at not being able to find a really good meaty sausage, so I set about creating the ultimate sausage, an award winning sausage.' [213] The company is now successfully expanding its distribution across the United Kingdom with international expansion firmly in its sights. [214]

There is no doubt that Wilfred Emmanuel Jones is completely committed to his dream and that 'The Black Farmer' brand represents his vision of 'everything a sausage should be.' Having spent long periods of time travelling the world for the BBC he noticed that 'what I looked forward to most on my return was an English breakfast – then I knew I was home.' But Wilfred's vision extends far beyond one simple product. 'Most immigrants are from a rural background originally,' he says, and "The Black Farmer' brand and the 'Flavours Without Frontiers' strap line are statements that we live in a multicultural society where Black and Asian people are not confined to urban Britain.' Following up this strong belief he has set up The Black Farmer Rural Scholarship programme to give inner-city teenagers a taste of rural life under his personal mentoring. This is born out of the idea that Black and Asian people should be given the opportunity to experience living and working in the countryside so that they can decide for themselves whether it suits them or not. Wilfred sees many similarities between the ethnic and rural communities. 'Many people in the rural community feel disenfranchised,' he says, 'that they are not heard and that prejudice surrounds them, much like ethnic minorities in Britain's cities.' His vision is expansive with a strong commitment to encouraging young 'pioneers' to take their rightful place in the countryside

---

[213] Source: South West Investment Group, 'The Black Farmer Goes National'. Full text of the interview is available at www.southwestinvestmentgroup.co.uk/docs/newsArticle_blackfarmer.htm
[214] I have used a number of sources for this section (including South West Investment Group above) but the principle quotes are taken from an interview with Wilfred Emmanuel Jones by Sustainability South West (www.sustainabilitysouthwest.org.uk) in Sightings, Issue no 5, summer 2005, which is available in full at www.sustainabilitysouthwest.org.uk/assets/files/pdf/diversity_sightings_summer_2005_final.pdf

and a deep love of the land and the West Country, which he now calls his spiritual home.[215]

Wilfred Emmanuel Jones' undoubted entrepreneurial flair helps him tackle many of the thorny issues that arise from combining sustainability with commercial viability in his farming practices. At the same time, he is committed to living in harmony with the land, supporting the broader rural community and moving forward his ideal to encourage more Black and Asian people to live in the countryside. That is a very broad agenda and it is a testament to his considerable abilities and commitment just how much he has already achieved. There is no doubt that he is very much a strategic leader, breaking down existing barriers and opening up new possibilities. He has all three of the key elements of success in abundance. He is intensely committed, very focused on achieving his goals (guided by his underlying sense of purpose and values) and he doesn't give up easily. As a result, he is injecting much needed new thinking into some of the most topical rural and community issues of the day. And, not least, I am told that he is also very personable. In May 2007, The Black Farmer was the official sausage vendor at the Chippenham Folk Festival in Wiltshire. When Wilfred visited the organizer of the event, Bob Berry, to talk over details, Bob asked him how he liked his coffee. He replied simply, 'Just like me.'[216]

Grasping the nettle

We no longer live in a world where we can take for granted that difficult policy issues will be resolved within the public domain. Increasingly, the role of strategic leadership is being undertaken outside our political institutions and public infrastructure. Politicians, in particular, are often more comfortable supporting initiatives that have already gained a groundswell of support. That puts much of the initiative for real change on us, either as individuals or in our role with organisations and communities. Al Gore makes this point very bluntly, 'Be a part of the change. No one else is going to do it. The politicians are *paralyzed*. The people have to do it for

---

[215] The best starting point for further information on the Black Farmer is his web site at www.theblackfarmer.com

[216] My thanks to Bob Berry for relating this humorous incident to me just before the Chippenham Folk Festival in May 2007. More information on the Festival is available at www.chippfolk.co.uk and Bob Berry can be contacted at Wiltshire Folk Arts at www.wiltshirefolkarts.org.uk

themselves.'[217] The economist, Jeffrey Sachs, talks about the very significant contribution that social entrepreneurs are now making, partly in response to this policy making vacuum. The philanthropic principle embodied by John D. Rockefeller, when he set up the Rockefeller Foundation in 1913, is alive and well. It is being carried forward by a very broad cross section of individuals and organisations which see the imperative for change. Corporations are playing an increasingly important role as engines of social change, sometimes under the guise of 'social corporate responsibility' but more often as a result of the ideas and values of those in key positions. We have seen that this overriding sense of mission plays a key role in many of the organisations that we have looked at in this book but there are many other examples from enterprises right across the spectrum. In the spring of 2007, for example, Google posted satellite imagery of Darfur in the Sudan in an effort to raise awareness of the devastation that was occurring in this region and to encourage technical solutions. This is very much part of the Google culture, the belief that information technologies can be powerful agent to change the world for the better.

Social enterprise, the combination of entrepreneurial business methods with overt social as well as commercial objectives, is growing rapidly. Social enterprises are dealing with many societal issues, such as drug and alcohol addiction, which would have traditionally been firmly within the public sector. Slowly, politicians are recognizing that this 'third way' offers many benefits, particularly when combined with the growing work of charitable concerns. Social enterprises and charities are also prepared to raise the profile of issues, such as policies towards refugees, which are politically sensitive. This is just one reason why the co-existence between social enterprises and the public sector can be a little bit difficult at times. There is nothing new about such tensions. When Rockefeller decided to use his fortune for public purposes he originally offered to endow a federal institution in the United States to fight disease, poverty and ignorance. Congress refused to support this act of generosity because many thought that Rockefeller was simply trying to buy a good name. As a result, he was forced to endow his own Foundation, setting a pathway for others to do so in the future. The foundation established by Bill Gates, for example, has funds of over $30 billion and is dedicated to supporting technology-led solutions to extreme poverty on a global basis.

---

[217] Source: Time Magazine, 'The Last Temptation of Al Gore, May 16th 2007. The full text is available at www.time.com/time/nation/article/0,8599,1622009-2,00.html

Jeffrey Sachs argues that the potential transformative effect of this wealth put to social causes could 'outflank the world's governments in ending poverty and pandemic disease'. He points to the work of the Rockefeller Foundation in furthering the cause of international development during the twentieth century as a case in point. It led the way in the eradication of hookworm in the American South, helped Brazil eliminate a malaria-transmitting strain of mosquito and funded the Asian Green Revolution, the transformation of agriculture through dramatically increased crop yields that enabled countries to 'escape endless cycles of famine and poverty'. Sachs concludes that the dynamism of social entrepreneurship 'makes a mockery ... of our political leadership,' and that the work of social entrepreneurs leaves 'Washington in the dust'.[218] The potential is dramatic. According to Forbes magazine there are 950 billionaires in the world, with an estimated combined wealth of $3.5 trillion dollars. Clearly philanthropic ventures could make a very big difference in the future. It is not, however, only a matter of the potential funding available for social causes that could prove important. It is the strategic leadership qualities that we have looked at in this book that will really make a difference. It is the combination of innovative visionary solutions and the capacity for action, which can be brought to the issues at hand.

Funding alone will never solve the major issues that we face unless we combine resources with new thinking. There is a danger attached to traditional thinking that equates 'big' with 'better' and this includes the availability of resources. In fact, too *much* funding can kill a project as certainly as too little. Having a big vision for change is important but recognizing that sustainable change takes place incrementally, step by step from small beginnings, is also absolutely critical. This can be seen clearly in the field of international aid. William Easterly, in his recent book on development aid, argues against 'top down' aid policies because they inevitably begin with the wrong question, 'what does the end of poverty require of foreign aid?' He insists that this puts the question backwards. The right question is 'What can foreign aid do for the poor?' He suggests that institutions should concentrate on what can actually be accomplished and see that it gets done. This is a piecemeal approach in the best sense of the word. He thinks that donors should do one thing at a time, using small

---

[218] Source: Jeffrey Sachs, Time Magazine, 'The Power of One: Sharing the Wealth', May 21st 2007. Jeffrey Sachs is the Director of The Earth Institute, Quetelet Professor of Sustainable Development and Professor of Health Policy and Management at Columbia University. For further information please refer to the web site of Earth Institute at Columbia University (www.earth.columbia.edu) at www.earth.columbia.edu/articles/view/1804

trials and thus making small errors. His book is a refreshing indictment of the damage that can be done by utopian social engineers who are fully equipped with a vision for change but lose sight of the reality check that keeps this vision grounded and effective.[219]

This scenario is, sadly, a disease in government today. A combination of 'wish driven' policies, control mania and the politicization of the public policy decision-making process produces a deadly cocktail for waste and ineffectiveness. More funding is never the solution. In fact it is often part of the problem. It can so easily produce the phenomenon known as 'winner's curse', the tendency to dispense largess on an unhealthy and unsustainable scale. Igor Kusyszyn, professor of psychology at York University in Toronto, argues that finding additional revenue sources will never solve government's financial problems because 'people haven't realized that government is a *compulsive* spender. And everybody knows that the worst thing you can do is give a compulsive spender more money.'[220] It is not that public policy frameworks will be any less important in the road ahead, in fact, quite the opposite is true. Public policy frameworks are essential to ratify and codify change for the benefit of all. However, the *initiatives* for change will most often come from outside the public sector. Moreover, sustainable and radical change will start small scale and be built step by step, as it always has done.

The Starfish tale

A small boy lived by the ocean. He loved the creatures of the sea, especially the starfish, and spent much of his time exploring the seashore. One day he learned that there would be a minus tide that would leave the starfish stranded on the sand. The day of the tide he went down to the beach and began picking up the stranded starfish and tossing them back into the sea. An elderly man who lived next door came to the beach to see what he was doing.

'I'm saving the starfish,' the boy proudly declared. When the

---

[219] Source: The Economist, 'Development Aid: In Praise of a Small Thing', a review of 'The White Man's Burden: Why the West's Efforts to Aid the Rest Have Done So Much Ill and So Little Good', by William Easterly, published by Penguin Press, 2006.
[220] Source: YorkU, the alumni magazine of York University in Toronto, 'Profiles: Dice Squad' by Michael Todd. For further information on Igor Kusyszyn, professor of psychology at York University in Toronto, please refer to his home page at the University at www.psych.yorku.ca/igor

neighbour saw all of the stranded starfish, he shook his head and said, 'I'm sorry to disappoint you, young man, but if you look down the beach one way, there are stranded starfish as far as the eye can see. And if you look down the beach the other way, it's the same. One little boy like you isn't going to make much of a difference.'

The boy thought about this for a moment. Then he reached his small hand down to the sand, picked up the starfish, tossed it into the ocean and said, 'I sure made a difference to that one.' [221]

The way forward

'Somebody said that it couldn't be done.
He with a chuckle replied
Maybe it couldn't but he'd be the one
Who wouldn't say so till he tried.
So he lifted his chin with a slip of a grin
On his face, if he worried, he hid it.
And he started to sing as he tackled the thing
That couldn't be done and he did it.'

Edgar Guest [222]

I remember listening to a Head Teacher talk about the importance that every teacher has in defining the learning environment in the classroom. One thing that he said has stayed with me forever. 'Those who don't think they are making a difference are making a mistake. They are making a difference – a sad difference.' We all make a difference. We hope to make a good difference. We sometimes fail so we pick up the pieces and start again. It is not possible to talk about what makes an 'important' difference and what does not. The environment of classroom support, care and trust at Kennet Valley Primary School has made a huge difference to my two boys. This difference cannot be quantified or analyzed. It just is. In our

---

[221] Source: Anonymous. I have been unable to find a source for this wonderful tale, although it is frequently passed around on the web. I certainly cannot take any credit for it except to reproduce it for others to enjoy.

[222] Edgar Guest, 'It Couldn't Be Done'. Edgar Guest was a British-born American writer who was nicknamed the 'people's poet'. Some find his sentimental, optimistic poems rather cloying but I rather like this one. More information can be found on Edgar Guest on Wikipedia at http://en.wikipedia.org/wiki/Edgar_Guest. Singer-Songwriter, Vin Garbutt, has written a fine song to these lyrics, which appears on his 2005 album, Persona ... Grata', available on Home Roots Music Ltd at www.vingarbutt.com.

different roles and responsibilities we can all make that kind of dramatic difference. I hope that the seven disciplines of strategic thinking will help you to access greater personal creativity and develop the ability to see the bigger picture more consistently; that vital connection between us and the greater whole. This world desperately needs this kind of thinking at all levels and in all areas. By thinking outside the box new solutions and opportunities will automatically open up. Some will emerge from 'the shadows', those areas of our personal and collective lives that are hidden from our conscious awareness. Thinking strategically will help us to open up these areas and unleash the potential that lies within. This ability to think more holistically pushes us naturally into a strategic leadership position, one where we have greater influence, and thus greater responsibility, towards those around us. The process will not all be plain sailing. There will always be those who protect their position regardless of whether this impacts negatively on the whole. As Al Gore reminds us, 'it is difficult to get a man to understand something when his salary depends on him not understanding it.'[223] However, we will increasingly find ourselves in a position to influence positive change.

It is true that the journey to becoming a true leader, of making a real difference, can be downright exhausting and painful at times. But it is a journey worth taking. The reward is not only in the success that we have, in the visible progress that we make towards our goals. It is in knowing that none of us is ever privileged to see the whole story. Behind the visible lies the invisible. This includes all the innumerable consequences of our actions, all those people that we have influenced and the countless connections that emanate from our original intent. All this ripples out into the wider world. It is for this reason that I believe that the most enduring characteristic of a true strategic leader is humility. The more that we know, the more we understand how little we know. Questions outweigh answers. We become learners, listeners and seekers. This is the only true foundation for changing the world. And with it, nothing is impossible.

---

[223] Al Gore, 'An Inconvenient Truth', available on DVD from Paramount Home Entertainment, 2006

APPENDIX

INSIGHTS ON STRATEGIC LEADERSHIP

Apple

Apple is driven by a missionary zeal for product development, sleek empathetic design and an entrepreneurial flair for seeing opportunities in related markets. Much of Apple's corporate ethos comes from its CEO, Steve Jobs, who continues to have a healthy disregard for conventional wisdom combined with an almost uncanny ability to see round corners and a steely determination to make perfect products at all costs. Apple goes well beyond the widely accepted market definitions for functionality and design, leading consumers to new places by meeting desires that they cannot immediately articulate. This is deeply embedded in its culture and it has been relentlessly innovative as a result. We explore Apple in more detail in chapter eight on dreaming.

Google

Mathematics! The founders of Google, Sergey Brin and Larry Page, both come from mathematical family backgrounds. The critical factor that made the Google search engine so successful was the application of implicit mathematical order to the search process. We take a brief look at Google in Chapter two on the importance of knowing your own story.

Starbucks

It is more than a coffee shop! The principle of playing an active role in its communities (staff, suppliers and the local communities around it) is deeply engrained as a core value within Starbucks and is a key part of its culture. We look at Starbucks in chapter five when we consider the critical role that serving others plays in determining success.

Virgin

The glue that holds Virgin together is clearly Sir Richard Branson but how? Virgin is not product, customer or market focused in any conventional sense and its brand is notoriously elastic! To truly understand Virgin we need to understand its founder and that means digging below the surface level of the standard entrepreneurial qualities such as risk taking, creativity and vision. We will be doing this in chapter two on the critical importance of knowing your own story.

Toyota

There is no simple answer to this question because the statement is itself contentious! Toyota's core business philosophy is to eliminate waste combined with a commitment to sustainable technology. It is largely responsible for inventing the production system currently used within the automotive industry with its emphasis on continual improvement, responsiveness and just-in-time production. A long term planning horizon and a fearsome record of efficiency in all aspects of the business are also critical and we have as yet barely scratched the surface! We look at Toyota and Honda in more detail in chapter four on acting slowly.

Amazon

Its reviews, ratings and interactive feedback systems combined with its technology infrastructure make it a superb retailer allowing customers to choose between different suppliers and make those choices based on exemplary editorial and merchandising skills. As a result, it is able to 'profit from obscurity', in the words of the Economist [224], with about one third of its sales coming from outside its top 130,000 titles (the physical capacity of the world's largest bookstores). Amazon is explored in chapter three on thinking small.

Social entrepreneurs

Traditionally, an entrepreneur would be regarded as a commercial business manager or owner who, by risk or initiative, seeks to make profits.

---

224 The Economist, Economics focus, Profiting from obscurity, May 7th 2005

This has always been an over-simplistic definition since entrepreneurs have many other motives for running independent businesses. The last decade, however, has seen the rise of social entrepreneurs who are still further away from this definition since their primary objective is to change some aspect of the world for the better, with profit seen as simply a means to this end rather than an objective in its own right. In terms of behaviour, energy, commitment, attitude to risk and the capability to get things done, however, they have all the hallmarks of being an entrepreneur. We will be using examples of social entrepreneurs throughout this book.

Garth Brooks

The honest answer is that we don't know! It is possible to produce a coherent argument to explain the success of Garth Brooks from a retrospective perspective but this misses the point. At the time when Garth Brooks was actively seeking a record deal no one could have anticipated his future success. That is both humbling and should inform our thinking process! We look at the Garth Brooks phenomenon briefly in Chapter eight on the power of dreaming.

Index